GOD, KNOWLEDGE, AND MYSTERY

GOD
KNOWLEDGE
& MYSTERY

Essays
in Philosophical Theology

PETER VAN INWAGEN

CORNELL UNIVERSITY PRESS

ITHACA AND LONDON

First published 1995 by Cornell University Press.

Printed in the United States of America

Library of Congress Cataloging-in-Publication Data

Van Inwagen, Peter.
    God, knowledge, and mystery : essays in philosophical
theology /
    Peter van Inwagen.
        p.   cm.
    Includes bibliographical references and index.
    ISBN 0-8014-2994-3 (alk. paper). — ISBN 0-8014-8186-4 (pbk. :
alk. paper)
    1. Philosophical theology.   2. Knowledge, Theory of (Religion)
I. Title.
BT40.V34   1995
230'.01—dc20   95-1426

TO ALVIN PLANTINGA

A city that is set on a hill cannot be hid.
Neither do men light a candle, and put it under a bushel,
but on a candlestick;
and it giveth light unto all that are in the house.

—MATTHEW 5:14, 15

Contents

GOD, KNOWLEDGE, AND MYSTERY

General Introduction

THESE essays are records of the attempts of a philosopher to think about various theological questions.[1]

But why not leave theological questions to the theologians? This question can be met with a counterquestion: Who are the theologians? If the first question is taken to imply that only those who are members of faculties of theology or who possess a degree or diploma that somehow involves the word 'theology' are theologians, then, in my view, the implication is rather restrictive. It seems to me comparable to the suggestion that only those with degrees in politics or "political science" should discuss political questions.

It seems to me, moreover, that philosophers have certain advantages over most theologians (in the narrow sense of the word) when it comes to discussing theological questions. It is true that the philosopher, even the most learned historian of philosophy, will almost certainly lack the historical training—the training in the history of doctrine and in the methods of biblical studies—that is the central component of the educa-

---

1. All the essays in this book are previously published. I list here several of my essays and reviews on theological subjects that are not included in this collection: "The Possibility of Resurrection," *International Journal for the Philosophy of Religion* 9 (1978), 114–121. Reprinted in *Immortality*, ed. Paul Edwards (New York: Macmillan, 1992), and in *Philosophy of Religion: An Anthology*, ed. Louis P. Pojman (2d ed.) (Belmont, Calif.: Wadsworth, 1993). Review of O. K. Bouwsma, *Without Proof or Evidence*, in *Faith and Philosophy* 4 (1987), 103–108. Review of John Leslie, *Universes*, in *Faith and Philosophy* 10 (1993), 439–443. "Quam Dilecta," *God and the Philosophers*, ed. Thomas V. Morris, (New York: Oxford University Press, 1994), pp. 31–60. "Reflections on the Essays of Draper, Gale, and Russell," in *The Evidential Argument from Evil*, ed. Daniel Howard-Snyder, forthcoming from Indiana University Press. "Doubts about Darwinism," in *Darwinism: Science or Philosophy?* ed. Jon Buell and Virginia Hearne (Richardson, Texas: Foundation for Thought and Ethics, 1994), pp. 177–191.

tion of present-day academic theologians. But historical training, though important in theological studies, is not the only thing of importance. Large parts of theology are really philosophy, although philosophy carried on within the constraints of Christian or Jewish or Muslim faith. Or, if you insist that philosophy is, by definition, unfettered by theological presuppositions, it is at any rate true that the *method* of large parts of theology is indistinguishable from the method of philosophy. If someone says that theology is an essentially historical discipline, and that its methods are therefore essentially the methods of the historical studies, I will reply that that is a natural view for someone to take whose academic training has been almost entirely historical—I am willing to bet that anyone who says this will be the product of a course of study whose content has been almost entirely historical—but I do not believe it for a minute. (It should be noted that "theological historicism" will have to be regarded by its adherents as a thesis about the proper method of theology *at certain points in the history of theology*. One cannot coherently imagine a theological tradition in which theology has been regarded ab initio as a study of its own history.)

It must also be said that the present-day academic theologian, like the thirteenth-century theologian, is likely to have absorbed, in one way or another, a good deal of philosophy—and here I mean not the methods and techniques of philosophy but the ideas and conclusions of particular philosophers. A great deal of this philosophy will have come, directly or indirectly, from either Kant or Heidegger. Much of the philosophy that has been imported into theology seems to me to have been imperfectly understood, and, much more importantly, to have been accepted with no clear sense of how provisional and shaky all philosophical ideas and conclusions are. One advantage philosophers bring to theology is that they know too much about philosophy to be overly impressed by the fact that a particular philosopher has said this or that. Philosophers of the present day know what Thomas Aquinas and Professor Bultmann did not know: that no philosopher is an authority. Philosophers know that if you want to pronounce on, say, the project of natural theology, you cannot simply appeal to what Kant has established about natural theology. You cannot do this for the very good reason that Kant has established nothing about natural theology. Kant has only offered arguments, and the cogency of these arguments can be (and is daily) disputed.

There is a third advantage, harder to describe, that the philosopher brings to theology. It might be put this way: The philosopher is not likely to be impressed by a piece of text that looks like an argument but is only an assertion. What I have in mind is best explained by example. Consider the following notorious sentence of Bultmann's:

> It is impossible to use electric light and the wireless and to avail ourselves of modern medical and surgical discoveries, and at the same time to believe in the New Testament world of daemons and spirits.[2]

The philosopher (and, indeed, any moderately reflective reader of these words) is capable of recognizing that this cannot be a factual or socio-logical thesis, for, as Bultmann was perfectly well aware, vast numbers of people do just what is said in this sentence to be impossible. The philosopher, and, no doubt, a pretty good proportion of the moderately reflective readers, will see that, if the thesis Bultmann is putting forward is to be at all plausible, the sentence must be read in some such way as the following: If we avail ourselves of modern technology and yet believe in daemons and spirits, we adopt a philosophically incoherent position. But this is not an argument. This is not an ordered presenta-tion of the reasons for believing something. This is simply one of the "somethings" that are from time to time proposed for our belief: in other words, this is an assertion. It is an assertion that I myself happen not to accept, and I can't see why anyone would think that it was true—or even plausible. If Bultmann knew of some reason for believing this assertion, he did not share it with his readers. If I may venture a guess, Bultmann thought that the sentence I have quoted was something between an assertion and an argument: He thought the proper response to it would be something like, "Ah, now that you put it that way, I can see that what you are saying must be right." I have no idea why anyone would think this a proper response to the words I have quoted. So far as I can see, the proper response is a blank stare. I can only wonder what Bultmann—who could not have given an account of the workings of a "wireless" to save his life—would have said to a radio engineer who confessed to a belief in the New Testament world of demons and spirits (that is, to a belief in demons and spirits). Such people are not terribly uncommon, after all. I expect that Bultmann thought that a twentieth-century theologian and New Testament critic (and student of Kant and Heidegger) was more truly a citizen of the twentieth century than someone who merely possessed a vulgar under-standing of the actual workings of those devices the ubiquity of which

2. Rudolf Bultmann, "New Testament and Mythology," in *Kerygma and Myth*, ed. Hans W. Bartsch (New York: Harper & Row, 1961), p. 5.

determined what it was "possible" for one to believe in the twentieth century.

However this may be, the philosopher is merely going to be puzzled by Bultmann's assertion. The philosopher who is an atheist will be as puzzled as the philosopher who is a theist. A particularly long-winded philosophical atheist might very well make a speech along the lines of the following:

> People believe in demons and spirits because they are credulous, not because they don't have radios and electric lights. If I believed that people got raised from the dead and walked on water, I'd also believe in demons and spirits, and there is no reason to think that electrical devices couldn't operate in a world in which there were demons and spirits. Knowledge of the laws of nature—the kind of knowledge that is exploited in the construction of radio sets—is simply detailed knowledge of how the natural world works when no demons or spirits are meddling with it in their supernatural way. If you were sufficiently credulous, you could have a much better knowledge of the workings of the natural world than any scientist has today and still believe in demons and spirits. Knowledge of the laws of nature alone simply tells you which of the stories you hear would imply supernatural agency *if they were true.* Suppose you and I are in perfect agreement about the laws of nature. In particular, we agree about the principles of biochemistry and the second law of thermodynamics. We hear a story about a man being raised from the dead on the third day. You believe it and I don't. We shall agree that *if* the story is true, a supernatural agency must have been involved, for, if the natural world is left to itself—if its inhabitants are left at the mercy of the principles of biochemistry and thermodynamics—such an event cannot happen. You believe the story because you are credulous. I reject it because I am skeptic. I am right and you are wrong. We are both citizens of the twentieth century (unusual only in that we both actually know something about biochemistry and thermodynamics, a rare accomplishment). I am one of the skeptical citizens and you are one of the credulous ones. It's too bad that there are credulous citizens of the twentieth century, but then it was too bad that there were credulous citizens of the first century. (It would have saved the world a lot of trouble if everyone had responded to Paul's preaching of the risen Christ like Festus: "Paul, you are raving!") What is certain is that knowledge of how a radio works—much less simply using a radio as if it were a magic box, which is what most people, including Professor Bultmann in his time, do—has no tendency to train anyone to a healthy skepticism about stories that, if true, would have to be reports of the operations of supernatural agencies. Knowing that there are laws of nature, even knowing what the laws of nature *are,* does not make people skeptics about whether the laws of

nature have been set aside on a particular occasion by agencies outside the scope of those laws. Although Festus didn't know the thousandth part of what even Professor Bultmann knew about the workings of nature, he knew that certain stories weren't to be believed. A twentieth-century scientist or engineer who is a traditional Christian (a Christian of the kind that Professor Bultmann called superstitious) doesn't know what Festus knew, and this despite the fact that Festus didn't know the thousandth part of what he or she knows about the workings of nature. Professor Bultmann was certainly right to suppose that certain stories shouldn't be believed. He was wrong to think that the ubiquity in his environment of devices that depended on a sophisticated understanding of the workings of nature had anything to do with the legitimacy of this conviction. And it's hard to see why someone who had given a moment's careful thought to the matter *would* think that.

So speaks my imaginary philosophical atheist, and one does see his point. I have quoted his imaginary lecture at some length to try to explain why the philosopher, even the philosopher who shares Bultmann's skepticism about the reality of the supernatural, will simply be exasperated by the cast of mind illustrated by Bultmann's sentence. And this completes my discussion of the advantages that, in my view, philosophers bring to theology, advantages that may do something to compensate for their lack of training in biblical studies and the history of doctrine.

I do not contend that all, or most, theologians are unable to tell the difference between an assertion and an argument; and I do not contend that all, or most, theologians uncritically defer to the authority of Kant or Heidegger or any philosopher. I do, however, believe that these two intellectual vices (so I would describe them) are not as uncommon among academic theologians as one might wish, and are no barrier to a successful academic career. No doubt there are intellectual vices characteristic of philosophers that are no barrier to successful academic careers, and I must confess that the virtues I have ascribed to "philosophers" cannot with perfect honesty be said to be universal among philosophers in the narrow or departmental sense. They are, to be frank, the virtues of the philosophers I am closest to professionally and most admire, and whom I like to think of as the real representatives of philosophy.

Philosophers—I mean those I think of as the real representatives of philosophy—are almost without exception either irreligious like my imaginary philosophical atheist (perhaps about nine-tenths of them, about the same proportion that prevails elsewhere in the academy) or religious in a very old-fashioned way. Any sort of "liberal" or "secular-ized" or "modernist" religion (religion of Bultmann's sort) tends to be regarded with disdain by philosophers, who view modernist versions of Christianity or Judaism as irreligion wearing a disguise that they are professionally incapable of not seeing through.

I am one of the old-fashioned ones. I believe many of the stories that Bultmann and my atheist agree shouldn't be believed. I believe that a man was raised from the dead on the third day, and a good deal more besides. None of the essays in this book is what might be called a defense of the "general propriety" of believing these stories.[3] In a more restricted sense, however, the essays are defenses of orthodox Christian belief. (The essays in Part I are defenses in this restricted sense of beliefs that Christians share with Jews and Muslims.) I have said that they represent attempts to think about various theological questions, and this is perfectly true as far as it goes. I must admit, however, that they all have their roots in apologetics. I began thinking about these questions in the context of various intellectual attacks on theism in general and Christianity in particular. I think to think that some of these essays have merits that go beyond the needs of apologet-ics, but, in my case at least, the desire to answer various critics of Christian belief has been the beginning of theology.

The essays in Part I deal primarily with the problem of evil. "The Problem of Evil, the Problem of Air, and the Problem of Silence" and "The Magnitude, Duration, and Distribution of Evil: A Theodicy" are specifically directed at this problem. The former is abstract and "philo-sophical" and takes as its topic all the suffering that occurs in the natural world. The latter draws heavily on the specific teachings of Christianity and will probably be of interest mainly to those who accept those teachings. It is directed entirely at those evils that involve human beings. (The former, moreover, is in no sense an attempt at a theodicy. Its goal is negative and narrowly circumscribed: the refutation of a particular argument for the conclusion that certain facts about the distribution of pain render belief in God unreasonable.) The other two essays in Part I deal with preliminary matters. "The Place of Chance in a World Sustained by God" is an attempt to explain how much of what occurs in the world can be due to chance, despite the fact that the world has been created and is ontologically sustained and providen-tially governed by an omnipotent and omniscient God. "Ontological Arguments" has been placed in this section because it presents system-

3. For such a defense, see "Quam Dilecta," cited in note 1.

atically a thesis that I use extensively in the essays on the problem of evil, the thesis I call "modal skepticism." (This is the only essay in this collection that I wrote before I became a Christian. I still accept all the substantive points that are made in it; some of the incidental remarks that occur here and there in the essay no longer represent my views.)

The essays of Part II are attempts to reply to attacks on traditional Christian belief that are based on "recent" discoveries—or alleged discoveries. (Some of the "modern knowledge" whose consequences are explored in these essays is, in my opinion, knowledge and some isn't.) It is certainly a popular opinion that traditional Christianity, the doctrinal basis of which was codified centuries before the advent of modern natural science and historical scholarship, has been "caught out" by the developments in science and scholarship that have been such a striking feature of the last several centuries. The Christian who becomes aware of these developments must (according to this popular opinion) cease to be a Christian, retreat into voluntary ignorance of or ludicrously inept attacks on the findings of modern science and scholarship, or accept some sort of modernist "Christianity" that violates the historically determined essence of Christianity. In Part II, I consider the claim made on behalf of evolutionary biology, the claim made on behalf of biblical scholarship, and the claim made on behalf of the comparative study of religions, to have confronted the Christian with these alternatives. These claims seem to me to have no merit whatever. Those who make them, in my view, either ascribe to modern science and scholarship discoveries and proofs that do not in fact exist, or else have simply not thought very well about the capacity of traditional Christian belief to come to terms with new knowledge.

In Part III, I consider the contention that there are two essential Christian doctrines that are straightforwardly logically self-contradictory: the doctrine of the Trinity (which, it is sometimes held, either asserts of three things that there is only one of them, or asserts of one thing that there are three of it) and the doctrine of the Incarnation (which, it is sometimes held, asserts of something that it is both a human being who came into existence in Palestine at a definite date and a divine being who is eternal, omnipresent, and the creator of the world). Christian theology has always held that both these doctrines are "mysteries" in the sense that human reason cannot possibly reach an understanding of how either could be true. I do not attempt to explain how either could be true. Rather, I attempt to show how each can be stated in a way that is free from formal contradiction: I attempt to show that the doctrine of the Trinity does not involve the casual identification of two distinct integers, and that the doctrine of the Incarnation does not imply that anything has each of two mutually contradictory properties. The two essays, moreover, represent the doctrines of the Trinity and the Incarnation as intimately related.

I have written an introduction to each of the three sections of the book. Each of the introductions shows how the essays in a section are related to one another. The introductions have, moreover, afforded me the opportunity to say some things that, after their publication, I came to wish I had said somewhere in the essays.

Some of the essays make use of the techniques of analytical philosophy and some do not. The two essays in Part III will be very hard going for anyone who has not been formally trained in analytical philosophy. Essay 1, "Ontological Arguments," is also highly technical, and Essay 3, "The Problem of Evil, the Problem of Air, and the Problem of Silence," only a little less so. The remaining five essays do not presuppose any acquaintance with the techniques or vocabulary of analytical philosophy.

PART I

Chance, Evil, and Modal Skepticism

Introduction

MANY writers on the problem of evil stress one aspect or another of the undoubted fact that there are more things in heaven and earth than are dreamt of in our philosophy. Two of the essays in the present section (Essays 3 and 4) directly address the problem of evil, and they stress one aspect of human ignorance: our *modal* ignorance, our inability to know what is possible and necessary except in matters closely related to our everyday concerns.

In the first essay in this section, "Ontological Arguments," I discuss systematically the topic of "modal skepticism"—the thesis that we are largely ignorant of modal matters that are remote from the concerns of everyday life.[1] (I have also discussed this topic in a review of Richard Swinburne's *The Coherence of Theism*. An anonymous reader has suggested that the review be included in this collection. Rather than go so far as to do that, I quote a part of it later in this Introduction.)[2]

One way to get a good grasp of what I mean when I speak of "modal

1. Ignorant, that is, insofar as we have to rely on our native human powers. If there is such a thing as divine revelation, we might know all sorts of things we could not have found out for ourselves. And we should thereby quite often acquire modal knowledge, since, if one does not know whether something is possible, then to find out that it is true is to find out that it is possible. I claim to know that *creatio ex nihilo* is possible and that it is possible for there to be a being that is both concrete and necessary. But I do not claim to know these things through the exercise of my own, unaided cognitive powers. Rather, I claim to know that *creatio ex nihilo* has occurred and that God is a necessary being (and hence to know that these things are possible) as the result of the interplay of several factors, of which divine revelation is one. There is, incidentally, at least one *false* proposition of theological significance that I believe is possibly true and whose modal status I do not believe anyone could discover without some sort of divine assistance: That God did not create anything.

2. See also the important essay by George Seddon cited in "Ontological Arguments."

skepticism" is to consider the analogy of distance. In my view, modal judgments are analogous to judgments of distance made by eye. That is, they are analogous to judgments of the sort that we make when—just on the basis of how things look to us—we say things like, "That mountain is about thirty miles away" or "It's about three hundred yards from that tall pine to the foot of the cliff." Such judgments are not, of course, infallible, but in a wide range of circumstances they can be pretty accurate. There are, however, circumstances—circumstances remote from the practical business of everyday life—in which they are not accurate at all. People had no idea about how far away the sun and the moon and the stars were till they gave up trying to judge the distance of these objects by eye and began to reason. ("You can see a significant portion of the shadow of the whole earth on the moon when the moon is entering or leaving the earth's shadow, so the moon must be a lot farther away than anyone would have guessed. . . .") Analogously, I should say, we have some sort of capacity to know modal truths about familiar matters. I know that it is possible that—that there is no intrinsic impossibility in its being the case that—the table that was in a certain position at noon have then been two feet to the left of where it in fact was. I know that it is possible (in this sense) that John F. Kennedy have died of natural causes, that it is impossible for there to be liquid wine bottles, and that it is necessary that there be a valley between any two mountains that touch at their bases. And, no doubt, reason—operating on a combination of basic modal intuitions like those displayed in the previous sentence and facts about the way the world is put together—can expand the range of our modal knowledge considerably. But I should say that we have no sort of capacity that would enable us to know whether it is possible for there to be a being that is both concrete and necessarily existent, whether it is impossible for there to be a three-inch-thick sheet of solid iron that is transparent to visible light, or whether it is necessary that the laws of physics have the same structure as the actual laws. To my mind, philosophers who think that they can hold such concepts or states of affairs as these before their minds and determine by some sort of intellectual insight whether they are possible are fooling themselves. (They could be compared to an inhabitant of the ancient world who thought that he could just *see* that the moon was about thirty miles away.) The illusory character of the conviction of some philosophers that they have such a power is sometimes disguised by talk of "logical possibility," for it is often supposed that there is a species of possibility that goes by this name and that one can determine a priori whether a concept or state of affairs is logically possible. But there is no such thing as logical possibility—not, at least, if it is really supposed to be a species of possibility. I don't deny that there is such a thing as logical *impossibility*. This is an epistemological category: the logically impossible is that which can be known to be impossible on the basis of logical considerations alone—or, to be liberal, logical and semantical considerations alone.[3] A round square is logically impossible because a square must, by definition, have vertices or corners and a round thing must, by definition, have no corners, and a round square would therefore both have and not have corners. I do not want to dispute the cogency of arguments like this one. What I dispute is the contention that if a concept or state of affairs is not logically impossible, then it is "logically possible." It hardly follows that, because a certain thing cannot be proved to be impossible by a certain method, it is therefore possible in any sense of 'possible' whatever. Suppose that the infallible Standard Atlas marks many islands as uninhabitable, none as inhabitable, and makes no claim to completeness in this matter. We could, if we liked, say that the islands marked 'uninhabitable' in the Standard Atlas were "cartographically uninhabitable." In doing this, we should be calling attention to the fact that our knowledge that these islands were uninhabitable had a certain source. But would there then be any sense in saying that an island was "cartographically inhabitable" just in the case that it was *not* cartographically *un*inhabitable? Very little, I should think. We *could* use words this way, but if we did we should have to recognize that "cartographical inhabitability" was not a species of inhabitability.

The epistemology of modal statements is a subject about which little is known. In my view, at least, I know a good deal about the epistemology of certain classes of nonmodal statements. For example, I would say that I know many statements to be true on the basis of observation (and memory). This may not be a very interesting thesis, but it is true. What *is* interesting is the fact that there is no such truism that one can cite in the case of even the simplest and most obviously true modal judgments. The table could have been a few feet to the left. Of course it could have. We *know* that. There is an intrinsic impossibility in the notion of a round square; there is *probably* an intrinsic impossibility in the notion of faster-than-light travel; there *may* be an intrinsic im-

---

3. If there is logical impossibility, there is also logical necessity, for a state of affairs is logically necessary if and only if its negation is logically impossible. The logically necessary is that which can be seen to be necessary on the basis of logical (or semantical) considerations alone.

possibility in the notion of transparent iron. But we *know*—despite the best efforts of Spinoza to convince us of the contrary—that there is no intrinsic impossibility in the table's having been a few feet to the left. We know—but *how* do we know? We could, of course, do what we often do when a question about the possibility of something arises in everyday circumstances. To wit, we could construct and examine intellectually a counterfactual scenario according to which the table was a few feet to the left of its actual position. (This morning it occurred to my wife that the room would look nicer if the table were a few feet to the left, so she moved it.) But the observation that we could construct such a scenario does not enable us to move from ignorance of how we know that the table could have been elsewhere to knowledge of how we know this. Constructing a (possible) counterfactual scenario will not show us how we know that something involved in that scenario is possible unless we know how we know that that scenario is possible. And if we knew how we knew that it was possible for my wife to have certain thoughts that she did not in fact have (we no doubt *do* know that this is possible), we should certainly have known how we knew that it was possible for the table to have been a few feet to the left.

Fortunately, we do not have to have an adequate account of how we know statements of a certain type in order to know some statements of that type or to know that we know some statements of that type or to know that we know a given statement of that type. But I am convinced that, however it is that I know the modal status of certain statements about everyday matters, this method or mechanism or technique or device or system of intuitions or whatever it should be called is of no value at all when it comes to judging the modal status of propositions remote from the concerns of everyday life.

A second theme that is of importance in the present section is chance. I argue that even if there is an omniscient, loving, and providential God who creates and sustains all things besides Himself, a God who is the source of all being, a God without whose sustaining action nothing can exist or retain its causal powers for even an instant, there are nevertheless states of affairs that have no explanation whatever.

Even the hairs on your head are numbered. Yes indeed. Perhaps—right at this instant—they number 87,256. If they do, God knows this. Some would say that he always knew that that would be their number at the present moment. But no doubt He does not *care* whether there are 87,256—as opposed to 87,198 or 87,911—hairs on your head. Why should He? And if He does not care, is there any reason to suppose that He will have so arranged matters, in the course of creating and sustaining the world, that your hairs number 87,256? If He has not so arranged matters, is there any reason to suppose that there is any explanation whatever for the fact that a possible world in which the hairs on your head number 87,256 is the actual world? And perhaps there are more impressive states of affairs than the number of hairs on your head that have no explanation—perhaps even, as I suggest in Essay 2, the existence of the planet Mars, the Local Group, and the human species are states of affairs that have no explanation, despite the fact that they occur in a world that is the creation of an omniscient, all-sustaining, loving, and providential Creator. On the other hand, there are states of affairs that—if the beliefs of traditional theists are anything like correct—certainly do have explanations: that there is a physical universe, for example, or that there is organic life, or that there are rational animals like ourselves. The explanations of these things lie in the will and power of God.

I argue that—from the point of view of traditional theism—among the states of affairs that have no explanation is the existence of evil: sin and death and disease and oppression and physical suffering of all the kinds that exist. I argue also that many particular evils—the existence of the rabies virus, for example—have no explanation. (That is: the existence of these things is not a matter of metaphysical necessity; neither God nor any other rational being decreed or willed or brought about their existence; they are not the productions of some impersonal "force" like the Dialectic of History or the Labor of the Concept.) I most emphatically have *not* offered this conclusion as a "solution" to the problem of evil, for the fact that God did not decree the existence of some evil does not entail that He did not foresee its existence throughout all the ages of ages or that He could not have prevented it. (I would in fact suppose that God foresees all evils before they occur, and that He could prevent the occurrence of each by a simple act of will. He could, in fact, have prevented the existence of any evil whatever—if in no other way, by the simple expedient of not creating anything.) But, although this fact does not provide, and is not intended to provide, a solution to the problem of evil, any adequate solution to the problem must incorporate it: No proposed solution to the problem of evil according to which the rabies virus or the Thirty Years' War or the Gulags are a part of God's plan for the world has any hope of being even faintly plausible.

A fourth factor that is present in the essays of Part I is this: there are some goods that are vague. This is pretty obvious when you think about it: consider a country's being fertile or a widow's having enough money to live comfortably. To say that a good is "vague" is to say two things: first, that there is some item or complex of items that can be present in varying amounts and on which the existence of the good depends, and, secondly, that there is no least amount in which it can be present that would secure the good. In the case of the good of fertile land, rainfall is an important component in the "complex of items"; in the case of having enough money to live comfortably, the variable item is, of course, money.[4] This point about goods also applies to evils. An unduly severe punishment is an evil. If, for example, someone who had parked illegally were punished for that dereliction by a fine of ten thousand dollars, that would be a bad thing. But if one were to reduce the imaginary fine *in intellectu* by small successive decrements (of, say, one dollar), one would not discover any dollar amount at which there was an abrupt transition between "punishment that is unduly severe" and "punishment that is not unduly severe."

Goods must sometimes be bought at a price. This can be true even if the buyer is an omnipotent being—or so most theists believe. (For example, according to the free-will defense, the good of creaturely freedom is, in a significant proportion of the possible worlds in which it exists, bought at the price of a certain amount of suffering caused by the creaturely abuse of free will.) The price at which a good must be purchased, if it is a price one would be reluctant to pay, may be said to be measured in evils—at least if we are willing to use the word 'evil' in a sufficiently abstract sense that we shall regard anything whose existence we are reluctant to allow as an "evil." But if goods and evils are sometimes vague, then it may happen that there is no least price at which some good may be purchased. This can easily happen if the "price" is to be measured in evils that can be more precisely measured than the variable factor associated with the good whose price they are. Amounts of money, for example, can be very precisely measured, but the good of being a punishment that is not unduly severe is pretty vague. As a consequence, there is no least amount of money such that a fine in any greater amount would be an unduly severe punishment for illegal parking. (And this is so despite the fact that there are fines that would definitely be unduly severe punishments for illegal parking.) Similarly, pain—although its measurement raises both practical and conceptual problems—can be measured much more precisely than the

4. No doubt the fact that some goods are vague—I should think that just about all of them are—is a consequence of the fact that just about all the concepts we employ outside formal logic and pure mathematics are vague.

good of "significant and widespread creaturely freedom." As a consequence, or so it seems plausible to me to suppose, there is no least amount of pain such that any greater amount of pain would be too high a price to pay for widespread and significant creaturely freedom. (Here I assume for the sake of the illustration that, just as the practice of levying fines in *certain* amounts is a morally permissible price to pay for the good of regulated parking, so there is *some* amount of pain such that it is morally permissible to allow that much pain if it is indeed necessary for widespread and significant creaturely freedom. And I grant, for the sake of the illustration, that some amounts of pain would *definitely* constitute too high a price to pay for this good.)

If this contention is correct, it has an important consequence for certain arguments from evil. (By "arguments from evil" I mean arguments that proceed from some fact or facts about the actual evils of the world to the conclusion that there is no all-powerful and perfectly good being.) I have in mind those arguments that proceed from the premise that some given evil—the death of a particular fawn in a forest fire, the Lisbon earthquake—could have been miraculously "deleted" from the world without any good being thereby lost. (My point will also apply to arguments that employ the weaker premise that it would be *unreasonable for us to believe* that the deletion of the particular evil would have resulted in the loss of any good.) For suppose that there is some good that is achieved by there being evil of the kinds and in *more or less* the amounts that actually exist. It may be that the same good could be achieved if any particular evil were "deleted." And it may be that there is no least amount of evil that would be necessary to achieve this good. If this is true, a world created and governed by an all-powerful and perfectly good being might contain particular evils that have, individually, no point whatever. At any rate, it is far from evident that this is false. To argue that it was obviously false would be like arguing that it was obvious that every day and every hour a convict spends in prison must have a point if the convict's sentence is not to be condemned as unduly severe. But it is really quite plausible to suppose that if the prison term prescribed for, say, felonious assault were reduced by a day (imagine, to simplify the illustration, that there is one perfectly definite prison term that is legally mandated for everyone convicted of felonious assault), no good would thereby be lost. And it would seem to follow that the last day someone convicted of felonious assault spends in prison has no point. A day spent in prison may plausibly be regarded as a bad thing: if you caused the sentence of a convicted felon to be extended by a day, the felon would no doubt regard this as an injury. Nevertheless, if the mandated prison term for felonious assault is ten years, there is no injustice in its being fixed at ten years rather than at ten years less a day, even if the shorter term would produce the same goods as the longer. If there were a minimum prison term that would serve whatever end a prison term prescribed as a punishment for felonious assault is supposed to serve (and if this minimum term were known), then it is certainly arguable that the legislature should write that term explicitly into the law, that the legislature should frame the relevant law in words like these: "Anyone convicted of felonious assault shall be imprisoned for a term of three thousand three hundred and forty-nine days, six hours, and twenty-seven minutes. . . ." But there is no such period of time. Still, some periods of time are "reasonable" ones to set as a term of imprisonment for those convicted of felonious assault, some are too short, some are too long, and some—owing to the vagueness inherent in such concepts as "just punishment" and "effective deterrent"—fall within the vague frontiers of these categories. We may argue by analogy that if there is no least amount of evil that would serve whatever purposes an all-powerful and perfectly good being might have in allowing the existence of evil of the kinds and in *more or less* the amounts that actually exist, then such a being might very well allow particular evils that are individually pointless. Those who wish to argue for the nonexistence of God on the basis of the observed evils of the world would therefore—so I maintain—do better to take as the basis of their argument the "general" fact that there exists evil of the kinds and in *more or less* the amounts we observe, rather than to argue from the (alleged) pointlessness of this or that evil.

There is some interplay between the two themes "chance" and "vagueness." If some evil is needed to secure a certain good and if, because this good is vague, there is no definite amount of evil that is the least amount that will suffice to secure the good, God may properly leave the exact amount of evil that is "used" to secure the good to chance—although he will be constrained by His own goodness to ensure that the amount is not *definitely* more than is required. Suppose, for example, that there is a certain good that will exist if—and can exist only if—He allows Satan to visit certain evils upon Job (and that the nature of this good is such that it would be morally permissible for one to secure that good at the price of those evils if there were no other way to get it); but suppose that, owing to the vagueness of the good that would be so produced, there is no least amount of evil that is necessary for its existence. It seems to me that if we may suppose all this, then we introduce no further difficulties if we continue the story by supposing that God provides Satan with certain rather vague guidelines concerning what he may do to Job, guidelines that ensure only that the evils Job suffers at Satan's hands shall not be *definitely* in excess of what is required to secure the intended good. If Satan has free will and a free imagination—and if, as is no doubt the case with all creatures if God leaves *anything* to chance, his desires and the range of his imagination are to a significant degree the products of chance—the sequence of evils that Job experiences will have many features that have no explanation beyond "That's what happened to occur to Satan to do to him." In short, if Satan is not an automaton, a being every detail of whose behavior is a part of God's design—and let us suppose that he is not—then the evils Job suffers will be to some degree a matter of chance. And, as I have said, I do not see how we can object to this if we have granted the presuppositions of the example.

All these matters have been developed at length in the essays. Here I have called to the reader's attention the themes in the essays that I believe to be significantly different from anything that occurs in the work of other writers on the same topics, and I have supplied a few illustrations of various points related to those themes that do not occur in the essays.

Here, finally, are the relevant passages from my review of Richard Swinburne's *The Coherence of Theism:*[5]

> Questions about whether something is possible, even in the very broadest sense of "possible," are not to be answered by telling stories. . . . Let me give an example to show why I find Swinburne's epistemology of modal statements unsatisfactory. Swinburne's argument for the coherence of the notion of an *omnipresent spirit* (obviously an important part of his proof of the coherence of theism) takes the form of an invitation to the reader to imagine that he, the reader, turns into one:
>
> > Imagine yourself . . . gradually ceasing to be affected by alcohol or drugs, your thinking being equally coherent however men mess about with your brain. Imagine too that you cease to feel any pains, aches, and thrills, although you remain aware of what is going on in what has been called your body. You gradually find yourself aware of what is going on in bodies other than your own and other material objects at any place in space—at any rate to

5. From *Philosophical Review* 88 (1979), 668–672. Copyright 1979 Cornell University. Reprinted by permission of the publisher. The passage quoted from *The Coherence of Theism* (Oxford: Clarendon Press, 1977) occurs on p. 105.

the extent of being able to give invariably true answers to questions about these things, an ability which proves unaffected by men interfering with lines of communication, e.g. turning off lights so that agents which rely on sight cannot see, shutting things in rooms so that agents which rely on hands to feel things cannot do so. You also come to see things from any point of view which you choose, possibly simultaneously, possibly not. You remain able to talk and wave your hands about, but find yourself able to move directly anything which you choose, including the hands of other people. . . . You also find yourself able to utter words which can be heard anywhere, without moving any material objects. However, although you find yourself gaining these strange powers, you remain otherwise the same—capable of thinking, reasoning, and wanting, hoping and fearing. . . . Surely anyone can thus conceive of himself becoming an omnipresent spirit.

Well, *I* can't. I can't imagine any of this. *I* can't even imagine myself ceasing to be affected by alcohol, in any sense that will help Swinburne. I can, of course, imagine my never again drinking any alcohol and thus "ceasing to be affected" by it; but clearly that isn't what Swinburne has in mind. Or I can (perhaps) imagine myself drinking alcohol that is removed from my system by Martians before it reaches my brain; but this gets us no forwarder. Can I imagine alcohol permeating my brain but having no effect on it, say because the structure of my brain is different or because the laws of nature have been altered? Can I imagine alcohol having its usual effects on my brain but no effect on my sobriety? I can't and I am sure that anyone who thinks he *can* "imagine" these things has just not thought the matter through. (Seddon's paper is very good on this [see note 2]). Now I don't wish to be dogmatic. Perhaps there is *some* sense of *imagine* in which I *can* "imagine" them. If so, in that same sense of "imagine," I can imagine that, say, Goldbach's Conjecture is false. (I imagine an enormous computer printing something out; I imagine respected mathematicians crying, "It's a counterexample to Goldbach's Conjecture!") But such a feat of imagination would not even be relevant to the question whether it is coherent to suppose that Goldbach's Conjecture is false. Or not in any sense of "coherent" that would be of interest in natural theology.

Obviously, if I can't imagine myself ceasing to be affected by alcohol, then I can't imagine *any* of the things Swinburne wants me to imagine in the quoted passage. Am I somehow deficient in my powers of imagination? I don't think so: I think that I can't follow Swinburne's stories because my imagination is too active. For example, Swinburne claims (p. 3) that it is coherent to suppose that the moon is made of green cheese. I think that anyone who thinks he can imagine that the moon is made of cheese has a very sluggish imagination: the active imagination demands a pasture for the antecedently necessary thousands of thousands of millions of cows, demands a way to preserve a piece of cheese in broiling heat, freezing cold, and vacuum for thousands of millions of years, demands some off-stage *machina* to protect a piece of cheese thousands of miles across from gravitational compression into noncheese, demands . . . But any *serious* attempt to imagine the moon being made of green cheese—and what besides a serious attempt could prove "coherence"?—must, like the unimaginable object itself, soon collapse under its own weight. Only a philosopher of very little imagination would think he could imagine the moon being made of green cheese; only a philosopher of very little imagination would think he could imagine turning into an omnipresent spirit. *Many* of Swinburne's stories could be accepted only by philosophers whose imaginations were very nearly quiescent. Therefore, his arguments do not prove that theism is in any sense *possible*; and therefore they do not prove that theism is in any interesting sense "coherent."

These words—they are an application of themes first developed in "Ontological Arguments"—were written before I had come (for the most part) to share Professor Swinburne's religious convictions. (And, I note with some embarrassment, they were written by a younger and more impatient man than I.) Nevertheless, I endorse their substance if not their tone. I believe that they constitute a cogent argument for the conclusion that Swinburne's attempt to demonstrate the coherence of theism fails—although, of course, I think that theism *is* coherent (And, in my view, the similar considerations advanced in "Ontological Arguments" constitute a cogent argument for the conclusion that Plantinga's attempt in *The Nature of Necessity* to demonstrate the reasonableness of belief in God fails—although, of course, I think that belief in God *is* reasonable.) The date of their composition is perhaps worth attending to, for it has been suggested[6] that my allegiance to modal skepticism is motivated by a desire to be in a position to raise doubts about the force of the evidential argument from evil.

6. By Richard Gale, in "Some Difficulties in Theistic Treatments of Evil," in *The Evidential Argument from Evil*, ed. Daniel Howard-Snyder, forthcoming from Indiana University Press.

I

Ontological Arguments

In this essay I shall delimit an infinite class of valid arguments I shall call *ontic* arguments. These arguments proceed from a premise that asserts of a set of properties that it satisfies certain conditions, to the conclusion that there exists something that exemplifies that set of properties. If the conclusion of an ontic argument can be read as asserting the existence of a Deity, then I call that argument an *ontological* argument. In the present sense of this term, there are infinitely many ontological arguments, all of them valid. I shall devote special attention to one particular ontological argument, the most modest, since many of its features are shared by all other ontological arguments. I shall argue that anyone who wants to claim either that this argument is sound or that it is unsound is faced with grave difficulties.

I shall take it for granted that the connection between what I call ontological arguments and traditional presentations of "the" ontological argument (there is of course, no one argument that can be called *the* ontological argument) is plain. I make the following historical claim without arguing for it: Every well-known "version of the ontological argument" is either (i) essentially the same as one of the arguments called ontological herein, or (ii) invalid or outrageously question-begging, or (iii) stated in language so confusing that it is not possible to say with any confidence just what its premises are or what their relation to its conclusion is supposed to be. I should myself be inclined to place all historical "versions of the ontological argument" in category (iii), but this is a function of the way I read them: I would place many of the arguments certain contemporary philosophers claim to see in the original sources in one of the first two categories. I shall examine

First published in *Noûs* (1977), 375–395.

one contemporary argument, that presented by Alvin Plantinga in *The Nature of Necessity*[1] and *God, Freedom, and Evil.*[2] Plantinga's argument falls into category (i). I shall dispute Plantinga's contention that his argument can be used to show that belief in God is not contrary to reason.

I

We shall require several preliminary notions. I shall assume the reader is familiar with the notion of a *possible world*[3] and understands locutions of the following forms:

(The proposition) *p* is true at (the world) w[4]

(The object) *o* exists at (the world) w[5]

(The object) *o* has (the property) *r* at (the world) w.[6]

1. Oxford: Clarendon Press, 1974, chap. X.
2. New York: Harper & Row, 1974, pp. 85–112.
3. For an extended discussion of "possible worlds" I would accept, see *The Nature of Necessity,* chaps. IV–VIII. "Possibility," as I use the word, is what might be called "absolute" possibility. Absolute possibility corresponds roughly to what is traditionally called "logical possibility," but I dislike this term, since there are absolute possibilities and impossibilities whose status as such has no obvious connection with logic. See, e.g., Saul A. Kripke, *Naming and Necessity* (Cambridge: Harvard University Press, 1980), and Hilary Putnam, "Meaning and Reference," *Journal of Philosophy* 70 (1973), 699–711. I take it to be obvious that every absolutely possible world is absolutely possible with respect to any absolutely possible world. Thus, the modal logic that "captures" absolute modality is S5.
4. A *proposition* is a nonlinguistic bearer of truth-value. A proposition is *necessary* if true at all worlds, *possible* if true at some, *contingent* if true at some and false (not true) at others, and *impossible* if true at none. It follows from the fact that every world is possible relative to any world that the modal status (necessity, possibility, etc.) of a proposition is the same at every world.
5. I am using 'object' as the most general count-noun: in the present vocabulary, everything is an object. Moreover, as I use the term 'object', it has no Meinongian overtones; 'Pegasus' and 'the golden mountain' do not denote objects, since they do not denote anything. I shall sometimes use 'thing' and 'entity' and 'being' as stylistic variants on 'object'.
6. Among objects, there are abstract objects. Among abstract objects, there are properties. As I use the term 'property', such properties as are expressible in a given language are defined by the "well-behaved" extensional one-place open sentences of that language. For example, associated with the sentence '*x* is red' there is a property, a nonlinguistic entity, that we might call "the property of being an *x* such that *x* is red," or, for short, "being red" or "redness." Certain sentences, such as '*x* does not exemplify *x*', must be regarded as "ill-behaved" and thus as failing to define properties. I shall not discuss the problem of how to separate well-behaved from ill-behaved sentences. Two or more properties will be said to be *compatible* with one another just in the case that there exists a possible world at which some single object has all of them. A *set* of mutually compatible properties will be said to be *consistent*. I shall use certain familiar terms

If an object has a certain property at every world at which that object exists, then we say it has that property *essentially*. If an object has a property but fails to have it essentially, we say it has that property *accidentally*.

Now consider the property an object has just in the case that it exists at every possible world, or (what is the same thing) would have existed no matter *what* had been the case. I shall call this property 'necessary existence', 'N' for short. In giving this property this name, I am giving the words 'necessary existence' what might be called their *Leibnizian* sense. I distinguish Leibnizian from *Thomistic* necessary existence—I am thinking of the Third Way—which an object has just in the case that there is no world at which it is generated or corrupted. Note that N is not the same property as that of having existence essentially (cf. the familiar phrase 'a being whose essence involves existence'), for everything has existence (the property associated with such open sentences as '*x* exists' or 'There is something identical with *x*' or '*x* is identical with *x*') essentially.

Some philosophers have held that N is an *impossible* property, one that, like the property of being both round and square, could not possibly be exemplified by anything. But I have never seen a plausible argument for this view.[7] Moreover, I have seen plausible arguments for the conclusion that N *is* exemplified. Arguments for the existence of abstract objects are well known,[8] and many abstract objects seem to have N. I shall take an orthodox realist view of certain abstract objects, to wit, *mathematical* objects, such as numbers. I generally use mathematical objects rather than some other sort of necessary object in illustrating the application of a definition or concept involving necessary existence because the question whether a given mathematical object has or fails to have a given property is often uncontroversial.

II

An ontological argument may be looked upon as an argument for the conclusion that a certain concept is such that, necessarily, something

---

drawn from the traditional language of properties (e.g., 'exemplified', 'coextensive') without explanation. *A* is the same property as *B* if and only *A* and *B* are coextensive at all possible worlds.

7. For a typical implausible argument, see J. J. C. Smart, "The Existence of God," in *New Essays in Philosophical Theology*, ed. Antony Flew and Alasdair MacIntyre (New York: Macmillan, 1955), pp. 28–46. See pp. 38–39 in particular.

8. For an extended argument for the existence of abstract objects, see Hilary Putnam, *Philosophy of Logic* (New York: Harper & Row, 1971).

falls under it. But since it is not altogether clear what "concepts" are, let us replace talk of concepts with talk of sets of properties. Is there any set of properties such that, necessarily, there exists at least one object that has every member of that set? Or, as we shall say, is there any set of properties that is necessarily *instantiated*?[9] Well, yes; {being prime} for example. But let us attempt a more general answer to this question. Consider the following two conditions on a set of properties:

(a) It contains N

(b) It is possible that there be something that has all its members essentially.

(Let us call a set *ontic* if it satisfies these conditions.) The set {N, the property of being the square of three} is ontic, since there is in fact, and therefore could be, an object that has both its members essentially. But the set {N, the property of numbering the planets} is not ontic, since whatever number has the property of numbering the planets has this property only accidentally. Moreover, it is obviously impossible for anything to have this property essentially.

It can be shown that any ontic set is instantiated. Consider an ontic set whose members are N and P. (The generalization of the following argument to the case of an ontic set containing any finite number of properties is trivial; we shall not consider infinite ontic sets, which play no part in the argument of this essay.) Since this set is ontic, there exists a world W at which

Something has N and P essentially

is true. Therefore, the following argument, which is manifestly valid, is sound at W:

At least one thing has N and P essentially. Let O be any of these, and let W' be any world. Since O has N, O exists at W'. And since O has N and P essentially, O has N and P at W'. Therefore, at W',

(∃) Something has N and P

is true. But since W' was chosen arbitrarily, (∃) is true at just any arbitrarily chosen world. Hence, we have:

---

9. Kant's famous dictum that "existence adds nothing to the concept of a thing" may be (I think) expressed in this terminology as: 'Every set of properties is such that, necessarily, it is instantiated if and only if its union with {existence} is instantiated'. This is true but is irrelevant to the task of judging the validity or soundness of the arguments called "ontological" herein. Cf. Alvin Plantinga, *God and Other Minds* (Ithaca: Cornell University Press, 1967), pp. 32–37.

Necessarily, something has N and *P*.

Now since this argument is, at *W*, a sound argument, it follows that its conclusion

Necessarily, something has N and *P*

is true at *W*. But since the modal status of a proposition does not change from world to world (see note 3), it follows that

Something has N and *P*

is necessary (and hence true) at every world, including the actual world. Therefore, something has N and *P*. Therefore, since we have derived this conclusion from a single premise, that the set of properties {N,*P*} is ontic, it follows that any two-membered ontic set is instantiated.

Let us call any argument having as its single premise ⌜*s* is an ontic set⌝, and as its conclusion ⌜*s* is instantiated⌝, where *s* is a term, an *ontic argument*. It is evident from the foregoing that all ontic arguments are valid. The referent of the term that occurs initially in the premise and in the conclusion of an ontic argument, we call the *set of* that argument. To save space, we shall, instead of writing out in full an ontic argument, write only the initial term of its premise and conclusion. Thus, for example, "'{N, omnipotence}'" names the ontic argument whose set is {N, omnipotence}.

Before we turn to the consideration of ontological arguments, we shall briefly consider *mathematical* ontic arguments. Mathematical ontic arguments are both interesting in their own right and similar in an interesting respect to the modest ontological argument we shall examine in Section III: in the case of mathematical ontic arguments and in the case of the modest ontological argument, a question of existence is reduced to a question of consistency.

Let us call any property *essential* that is possible (is exemplified at some possible world) and cannot be had accidentally.[10] For example, N is essential. (I think we may take it as intuitively obvious that no object can have at some world the property of existing at all worlds, and lack that property at another world, given our assumption that every world is possible relative to every other world.)

---

10. There are properties that are had essentially by some things and accidentally by others. For example, it seems to me that I am essentially male, at least on the cellular level, and I think I essentially have parents. It follows that I have essentially the property of having parents who have a son; but my sister has this property only accidentally. Thus, this property is not essential, though I have it essentially. Cf. *The Nature of Necessity*, p. 61.

Let us call an object *mathematical* if it is the sort of object whose existence might be proved or assumed in a piece of pure mathematics. For example, integers, real numbers, operations on complex numbers, and the like, are mathematical objects. Sets containing nothing other than mathematical objects are themselves mathematical objects, but not just any set is a mathematical object. For example, {Napoleon} is not. Now let us say of property A and property B that A *entails* B if, necessarily, whatever has the former has the latter. Let us call a property *mathematical* if it is an essential property that entails the property of being a mathematical object. For example, being prime, being a set of reals, and being everywhere continuous and nowhere differentiable are mathematical properties; numbering the planets is not. It seems a reasonable conjecture that, among possibly exemplified properties, all properties that would be of interest to the pure mathematician are "mathematical" in this sense. Moreover, it seems a reasonable conjecture that the property of being a mathematical object entails N (though it is not the case that being an abstract object entails N; for example, {Napoleon} fails to have N). And if this is the case, then all mathematical properties entail N.

Now let S be any consistent set of mathematical properties. Since every mathematical property entails N, it follows that $S \cup \{N\}$ is consistent. Moreover, if S' is a set of essential properties, then (since N is an essential property) if $S' \cup \{N\}$ is consistent, it is ontic. Therefore, if S'' is a consistent set of mathematical properties, then (since all mathematical properties are essential) $S'' \cup \{N\}$ is ontic. And, therefore, if S'' is a consistent set of mathematical properties, S'' is instantiated.

Hence, if we call an ontic argument *mathematical* if its set contains (besides N) only mathematical properties, a mathematical ontic argument whose set is S is sound if and only if $S - \{N\}$ is consistent. (Cf. Poincaré's remark that existence in mathematics is freedom from contradiction.)[11]

III

Let us now turn to *ontological* arguments. We said that these were ontic arguments that could be regarded as arguments for the existence of a Deity. But this is vague, since it is not clear in the case of every set of properties whether it could be instantiated only by a Deity. For

11. This remark is attributed to Poincaré in Mark Kac and Stanislaw M. Ulam, *Mathematics and Logic: Retrospect and Prospects* (New York: Praeger, 1968), p. ix. I do not mean to imply that Poincaré would accept the realist view of mathematical objects presupposed herein.

example, could something that is not a Deity instantiate the set {N, being the maker of the world}? It seems (epistemically) possible that, if there were a necessary being who was the maker of the world, this being might also be rather limited in power and knowledge, indifferent to the sufferings of its creatures, and perhaps even have made the world out of some inchoate stuff that existed independently of its will. Should we be willing to apply the term 'Deity' to such a being? Perhaps some would and some wouldn't, and this indicates that the concept of a Deity (and hence our concept of an ontological argument) is vague.

Let us therefore replace this vague idea of an ontological argument with a more precise one. It is clear that, whatever 'Deity' might reasonably be supposed to mean, any Deity must be a nonabstract object. (I shall call nonabstract objects *concrete* without regard for the etymology or philosophical history of this word.)

I am not sure how to go about analyzing the notion of an abstract object, but I think it is an important and intelligible notion. There are things we can see, hear, be cut or burned by, love, hate, worship, make, mend, trust in, fear, and covet. These are the sort of thing I mean by "concrete object." And there are things we could not possibly stand in any of these relations to—for example, numbers, properties, propositions, sentence-types, sets, and systems of natural deduction—and these I call "abstract objects."[12]

Let us suppose that the distinction between abstract and concrete objects is clear enough to go on with if we exercise reasonable caution, and let us use 'C' to stand for 'the property of being a concrete object'. Now consider the ontic argument '{N,C}'. Perhaps the conclusion of this argument is sufficiently weak that some people would be unwilling to regard it as an argument for the existence of a Deity. (It is certainly much weaker than the argument whose set we considered at the beginning of this section.) And yet '{N,C} is instantiated' does entail 'There

---

12. It may be objected that we can say that Tom loves poetry, hates mathematics, worships beauty, trusts in the law, fears the truth, and covets admiration. But it is not at all clear that in the preceding phrases the abstract nouns in the direct-object position are functioning as names of abstract objects. If they were, it seems to me, then we could express the same facts by saying, e.g., "Tom covets the abstract object admiration." But this, I think, is nonsense: a person who covets admiration does not want to become the owner of a certain abstract object called 'admiration' (whatever that might mean); rather, he wants people to admire him.

Alvin Plantinga has reminded me that the Pythagoreans are said to have worshiped numbers. I am afraid my response to this is what Antony Flew has called a "conventionalist sulk": the Pythagoreans could not have done anything properly called 'worshiping numbers' because nothing is properly so called.

exists a (Thomistically) necessary concrete thing whose necessity is not caused by another', which is the conclusion of the Third Way.[13] And the Third Way is generally regarded as an argument for the existence of a Deity. Therefore, we shall be doing nothing radically contrary to tradition if we regard '{N,C} as a *theistic* ontic argument, and hence as an ontological argument.

But if '{N,C}' can properly be called an ontological argument, it would be hard to think of a weaker or more modest ontological argument. Any ontic set must contain N, and every interesting property anyone might want to ascribe essentially to a Deity (other than N itself) entails C.[14] We may therefore plausibly define an ontological argument as an ontic argument such that whatever instantiates its set is concrete.[15] Thus,

{N, omniscience, perfect goodness}

and

{N, not being a number, being worthy of worship}

13. At least assuming Leibnizian necessity entails Thomistic necessity. There does exist the formal possibility that there is a being which exists at all possible worlds but which is, at some worlds, generated or corrupted. But I do not find this idea coherent. If a being is subject to corruption (might "come apart"), or was at one time generated, then, it should seem, there is a world at which it is never generated and hence does not exist, since its parts never, at that world, come together.

14. There are, of course, *uninteresting* properties which any Deity has essentially and which do not entail C. For example, not being a number, and being either necessary or contingent.

15. By this definition, '{N, not having N}', '{N, being the greatest prime}', '{N, being nonexistent}', and '{N, being a chair}' are ontological arguments. This consequence will do no harm that I can see, however, since no argument with an impossible premise is sound. It would not do simply to stipulate that no argument with an impossible premise is an ontological argument, since, for all anyone knows (divine revelation aside), *no* valid argument for the conclusion that a Deity exists lacks an impossible premise-set. This would be the case if various properties that are indispensable components of the idea of a Deity were (in some way we don't see) incompatible. Nor would it do to say that an argument fails to be an ontological argument if its premise is *known* to be impossible: "ontological argument" is not supposed to be an epistemological category. At any rate, the premise of each of these "odd" arguments does entail that God exists, and it seems simplest to leave them in the category of ontological arguments.

A more interesting case of an ontological argument that it seems odd to call "ontological" is this: '{N,C, not being the greatest being possible}'. Traditional "versions of the ontological argument" are attempts at proving the existence of a greatest possible being; but this seems to me to be logically adventitious. Suppose there is both a greatest possible being and a lesser but nonetheless necessary being. Then, I should say, the lesser being as much as the greater has the single ontological feature—an absolute incapacity to fail to exist—that is the ground for a thing's being liable to have its existence proved by an argument a priori.

are distinct (and, of course, valid) ontological arguments.

If we wish to answer the question, Which ontological arguments are sound? the best strategy would seem to be to examine the most modest of them first. The most modest ontological argument is by definition '{N,C}', which we shall call 'M' for short.

Is M sound? that is, is {N,C} ontic? This question can be reduced to a simpler question, since the property C seems to be *essential* in the sense defined in Section II: it does not seem to be a coherent supposition that there is or could be an object that is concrete at some world and abstract at another. In our discussion of mathematical ontic arguments, we saw that if S' is a set of essential properties, then $S' \cup \{N\}$ is ontic if it is consistent. It follows that {N,C} is ontic if it is consistent. Thus the question whether there exists a necessary concrete being is in one respect like a mathematical existence question, such as the question whether there exists an even number greater than two that is not the sum of two primes. If the property of being an even number greater than two and the property of not being the sum of two primes are compatible, there exists an even number greater than two that is not the sum of two primes; if necessity and concreteness are compatible, there exists a necessary concrete being.

How shall we discover whether N and C are compatible? Well, how, in general, do we go about trying to find out whether two properties are compatible? Sometimes we may settle such a question decisively by exhibiting an object that has both properties. But this method will not help us in our present inquiry. Clearly we shall have to find an argument for the compatibility of N and C that does not have 'Something has both N and C' among it premises, or else we shall have to find an argument for the incompatibility of N and C. Finding a plausible argument of either sort may be no easy task. Leibniz thought he had a way of showing that any two perfections are compatible,[16] and perhaps it is arguable that N and C are perfections, albeit C is a less impressive perfection than N or omnipotence. Or, if C is *not* a perfection, many perfections (e.g., omnipotence) *entail* C. Therefore, if N is a perfection, which we may grant, and if any two perfections are compatible, then N and C are compatible. But Leibniz's argument makes essential use of the notion of a simple, positive property. And this notion makes no sense, or, better, there is no such notion: there are only the *words*

16. See G. W. Leibniz, *Sämtliche Schriften und Briefe*, Prussian Academy Edition, II, i: 271–272. Russell's translation of this important passage, which Leibniz wrote to show to Spinoza, can be found in *A Critical Exposition of the Philosophy of Leibniz*, 2d ed. (London: Allen & Unwin, 1937), pp. 287–288.

'simple, positive property' (or *'qualitas simplex quae positiva est'*), words that make no sense because they have never been given a sense. At any rate, I have never seen a definition of 'simple, positive property' that is both intelligible and avoids the consequence that *every* property is simple and positive. (Definitions of 'simple, positive property' usually involve some confusion between what a thing is and how it is referred to: properties may have *names* that are simple and positive or *names* that are conjunctive or negative, but, of course, one and the same property may have names, even customary and idiomatic names, of both sorts.) Leibniz's "demonstration," therefore, is simply incoherent.[17]

Is there any good reason for thinking that N and C are compatible or that they are incompatible? I shall make a rather bold statement: we *cannot* find out whether N and C are compatible. (Or, at least, not without prior knowledge of God. For all I know, God may exist and may have revealed His existence and something of His nature to certain people. Perhaps such people could demonstrate to one another that God has N—and, a fortiori, that N and C are compatible—using as premises in their arguments propositions known on the basis of divine revelation. When I argue in this essay that various questions can't be answered, I don't mean to rule out cases of this sort.) I shall try to explain why I think this. N and C are compatible or they are incompatible. If they are incompatible, then to show they are incompatible we should have to do the following, or something equivalent to it. We should have to construct a formally valid argument having 'Something has both N and C' as one of its premises and an explicit contradiction as its conclusion; and we should have to show that the conjunction of the remaining premises of the argument is a necessary truth. On the other hand, if N and C are compatible, then to show they are compatible we should have to construct a formally valid argument having 'Something has both N and C' as its conclusion and show that the conjunction of the premises of the argument is possibly true.

I think we cannot show that N and C are compatible or that they are incompatible because I think the task of finding the required ancillary premises and of demonstrating that they have the required modal status is (in both cases) impossible. It is not, of course, hard to find *candidates* for such premises. For example, if 'Whatever has N does not have C' is conjoined with 'Something has both N and C', a contradiction fol-

---

17. For another argument for this conclusion, see Norman Malcolm, "Anselm's Ontological Arguments," *Philosophical Review* 69 (1960), 41–62, p. 59 in particular.

lows. But how should we go about showing that the former sentence expresses a necessary truth? One might argue that if this sentence expresses a truth at all, it expresses a necessary truth, and that it would be unreasonable to believe that anything concrete is necessary, since all the (relatively) uncontroversial examples of necessary objects are abstract. Alternatively, one might employ as premises, 'Whatever is concrete is material' and 'Whatever is material does not have N', arguing that the latter is a conceptual truth (since it is conceptually true that whatever is material is separable into parts, and any assemblage of parts is a contingent object since its parts might not have come together, in which case it would not have existed), and that it would be unreasonable to deny the former, owing to the fact that all the uncontroversial examples of concrete objects are material, or, at least, depend for their existence on material objects. But such quasi-inductive arguments are remarkably weak. Neither of these arguments seems to me to have any more power to compel rational assent than the following argument: All the infinite sets whose cardinality we know are either denumerable or have the power of the continuum or else have some higher cardinality; therefore, it is unreasonable not to believe that the continuum hypothesis is true.

Some philosophers might argue that the question whether N and C are compatible is, after all, a *conceptual* question, and that there *must* therefore be something that we philosophers, who are conceptual analysts, can say in response to it. But this reasoning is of doubtful validity. In whatever sense the question of the compatibility of N and C is a conceptual question, the question whether there occurs a run of four sevens in the decimal expansion of π is a conceptual question.[18] But, for all I know, there is no argument any human being could devise that would give us the least reason for thinking that there is or that there is not such a sequence of sevens. And, without venturing into the realm of abstract objects, we can find examples of "conceptual" questions that cannot be resolved through conceptual analysis. Consider Hume's story about an Indian potentate who refused to believe that under certain conditions water changes into a translucent solid. Suppose a philosopher, a conceptual analyst, who was a retainer in that prince's court, heard the stories about water "turning solid" and, while doubting the *truth* of these stories, began to wonder if they were *possi-*

---

18. I assume that either such a run occurs or no such run occurs. I have never been able to understand the arguments for the denial of this assumption. But anyone who denies it may concentrate on the other examples.

ble. What might he do to settle this question? He could, of course, visit colder climes to see whether the stories were true, but this would not count as a resolution of his question through conceptual analysis. Or perhaps he might try to see whether he could *imagine* water turning into a translucent solid: that is, he might try to form a mental image of, say, a goblet of water and then try to replace this image with an image of that same goblet filled with a translucent solid. If he had any power of imagination at all, he would succeed if he tried this. But what would his success prove? What would he say to the critic who said, "You didn't imagine water *turning into* a solid; you merely imagined water disappearing and being *replaced by* a solid"? I see no satisfactory reply to this. In fact, the "try-to-imagine-it" test for possibility is quite useless. I can *imagine* what it would be like to discover that '7777' occurs in the decimal expansion of π, but this feat of imagination would not support the hypothesis that such a discovery is possible.

If imagination fails our Indian philosopher as an instrument for investigating possibility, he might, to use a term favored by some philosophers, see whether he could *conceive* of water becoming a translucent solid. But what exactly does this mean? I do not know and I think no one else knows.

If our philosopher knew what we, or the scientists among us, know about water and heat (if he knew about the atomic constitution of matter, the electronic properties of the water molecule, hydrogen bonding, van der Waals' forces, the kinetic nature of heat, and a host of other things, and knew the correct mathematical descriptions of the relations that hold among them), then he might be able to determine by calculation that water has various solid phases. But of course the knowledge necessary for such calculation could not be got by analysis of the *concept* of water, but only by empirical investigation into the *nature* of water.

There are theories of necessary truth according to which, since the *meanings* of the words 'water' and 'solid' cannot, when taken together with the principles of formal logic, be used to show that 'Water sometimes turns solid' expresses a false proposition, it follows that the proposition it does express is *possibly* true, is true at some possible world. But I think that such "linguistic" or "conventionalistic" theories of modality have very little to recommend them, and that *how* little they have to recommend them has been adequately (in fact, brilliantly) revealed in various recent publications.[19] A related thesis is this: the

19. See Kripke, *Naming and Necessity*, and Putnam, "Meaning and Reference."

proposition that the water in a certain glass will someday turn into a translucent solid is an empirical proposition, and all empirical propositions are possibly true. I am not sure I fully understand the term 'empirical proposition', but I think I understand it well enough to see that this claim is very doubtful. Consider the proposition that some three-inch-thick sheets of iron are transparent to visible light. This, I suppose, is an empirical proposition; at least we know empirically that it is false. Is it possibly true? I don't know and neither does anyone else. Perhaps some people know (I don't) that the laws of nature (as we now conceive them) entail the denial of this proposition. But perhaps some possible sets of laws don't entail its denial. Perhaps if the charge on the electron were not 1.6×10^{-19} coulombs but, say, two-thirds that, the crystalline structure of iron would be altered in such a way that a beam of photons could pass through a sheet of iron without melting or vaporizing it. But, for all I know, there is *no* coherent set of laws of nature that would allow this: perhaps the electronic structure of the iron atom is such that, no matter what the charge on the electron was, iron atoms would have to fit together in such a way as to bar the passage of radiation in the visible frequencies. Or, for all *anyone* knows, perhaps the value the charge on the electron has in the actual world is the only value it *can* have. I think, therefore, that no one has any good reason to believe that the proposition

　　Some three-inch-thick sheets of iron are transparent to visible light

is possibly true. And thus there is no reason to think that just any "empirical proposition" is possibly true.

　　Let us return to our Indian philosopher. What can he do? Nothing, I think. The question he has set himself is unanswerable by means of conceptual analysis. And my suspicion is that the question of compatibility of N and C cannot be settled by conceptual analysis. Note that the question our Indian philosopher asks, the question whether '7777' occurs in the decimal expansion of π, and the question whether it is possible that there be a three-inch-thick sheet of iron that is transparent to visible light can all be rephrased as questions about the compatibility of properties. But while there are various methods of investigating these three questions, methods other than conceptual analysis, I see *no* way to approach the question whether N and C are compatible. It is, of course, inevitable that there be things we shall never know, though one can be mistaken about cases. But even if I *am* mistaken, and it is possible to find out whether N and C are compatible, no one *now* knows whether they are compatible, or even has any good reason for thinking that they are or that they are not, unless, perhaps, that person is the recipient (proximate or remote) of a divine revelation. Therefore, anyone who thinks he knows, or has good reason to believe, that there is *no* necessary concrete being is mistaken.

IV

I wish finally to examine an argument that is due to Alvin Plantinga. His argument (in its most modest form) is equivalent to the ontological argument

{N, omnipotence, omniscience, moral perfection},

which I shall call 'P'.[20] in the sequel, I shall attribute to Plantinga various assertions about P. These attributions are convenient fictions adopted for purposes of exposition. Plantinga's actual assertions, however, are logically equivalent to those I attribute to him.

Since the soundness of P entails the soundness of M, everything said above about the difficulty of showing M to be sound will apply a fortiori to the task of showing P to be sound. Of course, one reason it would be harder to show P sound than it would be to show M sound (assuming both arguments *are* sound) is that it would be harder to show P's set to be consistent. But there is a further difficulty. We have seen that M is sound if its set is consistent. There is, however, no reason to think that P has this property. Our demonstration that {N,C} is ontic if consistent depended on the premise that it contains only essential properties. But there seems to be no good reason to think that the set of P contains only essential properties. For example, couldn't there be a being that is morally perfect at some worlds and evil at others? To show that P's set is ontic, therefore, we must show not only that there is a possible world at which something has all its members, but that there is a possible world at which something has all its members *essentially*. A "consistency proof" alone would yield only the conclusion that there exists a necessary being who *might be* omnipotent,

20. See *The Nature of Necessity*, chap. X, or *God, Freedom, and Evil*, pp. 85–112. The central premise of Plantinga's argument is

There is a possible world in which maximal greatness is instantiated.

The property of maximal greatness is the property of having *maximal excellence* at every possible world. Maximal excellence is not fully explained, but it is held to entail omniscience, omnipotence, and moral perfection. If we identify maximal excellence with the conjunction of these three properties (thus obtaining the most modest possible interpretation of Plantinga's argument), then the above premise is easily seen to be equivalent to the premise of P.

omniscient, and morally perfect. (Note that there exists a contingent being who *might be* the man or woman who proves or disproves Goldbach's Conjecture, solves the problem of nuclear structure, and deciphers Linear A. I, for example, or you.)

Plantinga is well aware of the difficulty of showing that P is sound, and admits that this argument is "not a successful piece of natural theology" (*The Nature of Necessity*, p. 219). (I shall say very little about the difficulty of showing P to be *unsound*. The most promising line of attack would probably be to try to show that the set {omnipotence, omniscience, moral perfection} is not instantiated, which it would be if P were sound. And the only way I can see to show this would be to employ some variant or other on the argument from evil. The major difficulty facing anyone who decides to employ this strategy is chapter IX of *The Nature of Necessity*.) The argument P fails as a piece of natural theology, Plantinga says, because its premise is not "drawn from the stock of propositions accepted by nearly every sane man, or . . . nearly every rational man" (pp. 219–220). Nonetheless, Plantinga argues, while P does not constitute a demonstration of the existence of God, it can be used to show that belief in God is rational, that is, not contrary to reason. For, Plantinga argues, while it is true that one who rejected the premise of P would not thereby violate any canon of reason, neither would one who accepted the premise of P violate any canon of reason. He compares the premise of P to Leibniz's Law:

(LL) For any objects x and y and property P, if $x = y$, then x has P if and only if y has P

in the following passage:

> Some philosophers reject [(LL)]; various counterexamples have been alleged; various restrictions have been proposed. None of these 'counterexamples' are genuine in my view; but there seems to be no compelling argument for [(LL)] that does not at some point invoke that very principle. Must we conclude that it is improper to accept it, or to employ it as a premiss? No indeed. The same goes for any number of philosophical claims and ideas. Indeed, philosophy contains little else. Were we to believe only [that] for which there are incontestable arguments from uncontested premises, we should find ourselves with a pretty slim and pretty dull philosophy. . . .
>
> So if we carefully ponder Leibniz's Law and the alleged objections, if we consider its connections with other propositions we accept or reject and still find it compelling, we are within our rights in accepting it—and

this whether or not we can convince others. But then the same goes for [the proposition that {N, omniscience, omnipotence, moral perfection} is ontic]. Hence our verdict on these reformulated versions of St. Anselm's argument must be as follows. They cannot, perhaps, be said to *prove* or *establish* their conclusion. But since it is rational to accept their central premiss, they do show that it is rational to accept that conclusion. And perhaps that is all that can be expected of any such argument. (*The Nature of Necessity*, pp. 220–221)

This seems to me to be wrong. The more modest argument that can be got by substituting the premise of M (or the logically equivalent 'N and C are compatible') for '{N, omniscience, omnipotence, moral perfection} is ontic' in the above quotation also seems to me to be wrong. If the latter is wrong, obviously the former is too. Let us examine the latter, more modest, piece of reasoning, which (another convenient fiction) I shall attribute to Plantinga. Plantinga's argument, if I interpret it correctly, is that we are in just the epistemic position with respect to the proposition that N and C are compatible that we are in with respect to (LL). And (LL) is a proposition it is epistemically permissible for a philosopher to take a stand on, even though the question whether (LL) is true cannot be settled by any known philosophical argument. Thus, though a philosopher may have no argument for the proposition that N and C are compatible, he could reasonably assent to it. And if he were asked to defend his belief that N and C are compatible, there would be no epistemic impropriety in his saying only, "I've thought the matter over carefully, and it seems to me that N and C are compatible, though I have no argument for this."

I have several comments to make about this line of reasoning. First, Plantinga's choice of (LL) as an example of a proposition whose epistemic status is comparable to that of the premise of M is unfortunate. The sentence Plantinga uses to express (LL) is a free English translation of the symbolic formula

$$(x)\,(y)\,(z)\,(x = y \supset (Hxz \equiv Hyz)),$$

which is a theorem of the first-order predicate calculus with identity, on the basis of the scheme of abbreviation

Hab: b is a property and a has b.[21]

21. The notion of a (free) English translation of a symbolic formula on the basis of a given scheme of abbreviation is that of Donald Kalish and Richard Montague, *Logic: Techniques of Formal Reasoning* (New York: Harcourt, Brace & World, 1964). In order for the claim made in the text to be true, it must be the case that 'b is a property and a has b' be an extensional open sentence. But this certainly seems to be the case, at least

Thus, anyone who claims that (LL) is *false* is in the awkward position of denying the proposition expressed by an English translation of a theorem of standard logic. Of course, people who knew what they were doing have rejected various parts of standard logic. But since 'N and C are compatible' is not a translation of a theorem of standard logic, or, indeed, of any sort of logic—second-order, deviant, modal, or what have you—it hardly seems correct to say that (LL) and the proposition that N and C are compatible are on an epistemic par. That a principle is expressible by a translation of a theorem of standard logic is a *very* strong argument in its favor, an argument that can be overridden only by some extremely well worked-out, clear, and fundamental consideration. (Certainly we have no such strong argument in favor of the proposition that N and C are compatible.) In fact, I very much doubt whether there has ever been any dispute about the truth-value of (LL). Anything in the history of philosophy that looks like such a dispute is almost certainly, when properly understood, a metalinguistic dispute; a dispute, say, about the principle 'In a natural language, singular terms denoting the same object can replace each other in any context, *salva veritate*',[22] or a dispute about whether the word 'property', as it is used in the sentence displayed to the right of '(LL)' above, does or could mean anything, or (assuming it does or could mean something) what it does or should mean.[23] The regrettable tendency of philosophers to talk in the material mode when arguing about words may often produce the *appearance* of a dispute about the truth-value of (LL). But metalinguistic disputes don't seem to be what Plantinga has in mind: he seems to assert that there is a *proposition* properly called 'Leibniz's Law' (this much I think is true), and that some philosophers have asserted of that very proposition that it is false, in opposition to other philosophers who have asserted of it that it is true. And this latter claim is, at best, extremely doubtful.

---

if this sentence is meaningful at all. Suppose, e.g., that 'whiteness is a property and the Taj Mahl has whiteness' expresses a truth. And suppose that 'whiteness' and 'the color-property that Klan members like best' co-refer, as do 'the Taj Mahal' and 'the most famous building in Agra'. It certainly seems to follow that 'the color-property that Klan members like best is a property and the most famous building in Agra has the color-property that Klan members like best' expresses a truth. Moreover, I cannot see how any such inference could fail.

22. Cf. *The Nature of Necessity*, p. 15n.

23. Plantinga says little enough about *who* it is that rejects (LL). In a footnote to the passage quoted above he says, "Geach and Grice, for example" and leaves it at that. But the objections these two philosophers have to (LL) are metalinguistic. Geach, for example, thinks that the expression '$x = y$', which occurs in the sentence displayed to

But if this much is correct, I have convicted Plantinga only of having chosen a bad example. It does seem reasonable to suppose that if two philosophers who disagree on some issue but more or less agree on philosophic method were carefully and patiently to debate that issue to the bitter end, they might come upon some proposition that one of them thought was true and the other thought was false, and which was such that neither had any non-question-begging argument to support his position. Arguments, like explanations, come to an end somewhere. And perhaps each of these philosophers would be reasonable in taking the position he did. At any rate, I see no reason to think this *could not* happen, though uncontroversial examples of it would be hard to come by: there will generally be a third party in any such debate who insist that the apparent disagreement is a pseudodisagreement that has arisen because certain key terms in the debate have no clear sense. Still, perhaps in some cases the third party is wrong. Perhaps there is a philosophical proposition (that is, a proposition that many philosophers think is philosophically important—it needn't require for its statement any typically philosophical vocabulary) such that there are no cogent arguments for its truth or its falsity; and perhaps this proposition is such that any philosopher who considers it carefully, and thereupon forms an opinion about its truth-value, has an epistemic right to that opinion. Let us assume there are such propositions and let us pretend that 'φ' names one of them.

Plantinga's argument, then, could be replaced by an argument in which φ plays the role he assigns to (LL). But why should we think that the proposition that N and C are compatible is like φ? Certainly not just *any* proposition such that we have no cogent arguments for its truth or falsity has all the features ascribed to φ. For example, suppose we call a real number *septiquaternary* if '7777' occurs in its decimal expansion; and let us call a real number *perimetric* if it measures the circumference of a circle whose diameter measures 1. Then

Possibly, something is septiquaternary and perimetric

(or, alternatively,

Septiquaternity and perimetricity are compatible)

is obviously such that no philosopher has a "right to his opinion" about its truth-value.

---

the right of '(LL)' in the text, is incomplete, and thus that that sentence fails to express a proposition (or so I would describe his doctrine).

Now it is possible to imagine a case in which this proposition figures in an interesting argument for the existence of God. Suppose we should meet a puckish, rather Kierkegaardian archangel who is amused by our desire to *know* whether God exists. And suppose we have good grounds for believing that an archangel says only what is true. The archangel speaks: "So you want to know whether God exists? Well, I know and I'm not telling. But I will tell you this much: *if* septiquaternity and perimetricity are compatible, then God exists." If this happened, then, possibly, we should find the following argument ("the angelological argument") for the existence of God to be of some interest:

(1) Whatever an archangel says is true

(2) An archangel says that if septiquaternity and perimetricity are compatible, then God exists

(3) Septiquaternity and perimetricity are compatible

hence,

(4) God exists.

Quite possibly, we never shall and never *can* know whether septiquaternity and perimetricity are compatible. If so, then this argument would not serve as an instrument by means of which we could pass from ignorance to knowledge. But suppose someone were to argue as follows: "Since (3) is not drawn from the stock of propositions that nearly every rational man accepts, the angelological argument fails as a piece of natural theology. Nonetheless, one may rationally accept (3), and this shows that belief in God is rational." But one may *not* rationally accept (3). Perhaps there are propositions such that it would be rational to accept them or to accept their denials in the absence of any evidence or argument; if so, (3) is not one of them. And, it seems to me, 'Necessity and concreteness are compatible' is no different in this respect from 'Septiquaternity and perimetricity are compatible'. Therefore, argument M, the modest ontological argument, can no more be used to show that belief in a necessary concrete being is rational than the angelological argument could (if its first two premises were known to be true) be used to show that belief in God was rational. But the angelological argument could not, even if (1) and (2) were known to be true, be used to show that belief in God was rational. Moreover, if the modest ontological argument cannot be used to show that belief in a necessary concrete being is rational, then, a fortiori, P cannot be used to show that belief in a necessary, omnipotent, omniscient, morally perfect being is rational.

Of course, I may be wrong about the epistemic status of the premises of arguments M and P. But since Plantinga has not pointed out any epistemically interesting feature which these premises share with (LL)—or with whatever φ may be—and which they do *not* share with (3), his argument for the rationality of belief in God is, as it stands, no better than the argument involving (3) considered in the preceding paragraph; that is to say, it fails.

I should not want the reader to infer from the fact that I have attempted to refute an argument for the rationality of theistic belief that I think theistic belief is irrational. No argument I know of for the conclusion that it is irrational to believe that God exists has any force whatever. Moreover, many eminently rational people (Plantinga, for example) believe that God exists, and this fact, to my mind, tends to support the conclusion that it is *not* irrational to believe that God exists. But, of course, Plantinga's argument may fail to establish its conclusion even if that conclusion is true.[24]

24. Though I have been critical of a particular conclusion of Plantinga's, this essay could not have been written without the aid of his insights in the general area that might be called "the metaphysics of quantified modal logic." A careful reading of *The Nature of Necessity* is a sine qua non for anyone interested in this subject. I should like to thank Professor Plantinga for his careful comments on a draft of this essay, which have led to changes, particularly in Section IV, that I hope he regards as improvements.

I should like to thank José Benardete, John Biro, Carl Ginet, C. L. Hardin, William Mann, and Margery Naylor for helpful suggestions, and I am particularly indebted to Thomas McKay, Edward Oldfield, and Richard Taylor for saving me from making serious errors.

2

The Place of Chance
in a World Sustained by God

In this essay, I want to examine a number of interrelated issues in what might be called the metaphysics of divine action: creation, sustenance, law, miracle, providence, and chance. Thus my title is rather narrow for the topics considered. But it is the topic *chance* that I shall be working toward. My discussion of these other topics is a prolegomenon to my discussion of chance. (My discussion of chance is, in its turn, a prolegomenon to a discussion of the problem of evil; but that is a topic for another time. In the present essay I shall lay out some implications of what I say about chance for the problem of evil, but I shall not directly discuss this problem, much less suggest a solution to it.)

I will begin with a discussion of God's relation to a certain object that might variously be called "the world," "the universe," "Creation," "the cosmos," or "nature." It is necessary for us to have a picture of this thing. I will provide a picture that is scientifically naive and philosophically tendentious: the world consists of a certain number of small, indivisible units of matter I shall call "elementary particles"; there is only one type of particle, and there are always just the same particles, and they are in constant motion in otherwise empty infinite three-dimensional space ("the void").

This picture could be called a Newtonian picture, although I don't insist on the absolute space or the "absolute, true, and mathematical time" of Newton. It is, as I have said, from a scientific point of view, a naive picture. But if it were replaced with the sort of physical world picture provided by quantum field theories like quantum electrodynamics and quantum chromodynamics, I do not think that this replacement would affect in any essential way the philosophical points I want to make. I therefore retain the naive picture—not that I am equipped to carry on the discussion in the terms provided by any other picture.

The picture is philosophically tendentious. It presupposes that the created world is entirely material. But that could easily enough be changed. Anyone who wants to suppose that the created world contains, for example, Cartesian egos, may simply reject my assumption that the elementary particles are all indivisible units of matter, and assume that some of them are nonspatial and are capable of thought.[1] (A similar device could accommodate angels conceived as St. Thomas Aquinas conceives angels.) The generalizations I shall make about "elementary particles" in the sequel do not in any *essential* way presuppose that elementary particles are spatial, nonthinking things. And the generalizations I shall make about created persons do not in any essential way presuppose that no created person is a Cartesian ego.

Having given this naive and tendentious picture of the world or nature, I relate it—in a burst of simplistic picture-thinking—to God in the following way.

God created the world by bringing certain elementary particles into existence at some particular moment—six thousand years ago or twenty billion years ago or some such figure. These particles were at the moment of their creation suspended in the void—which is sheer emptiness, and not a physical object like the modern space-time or the modern quantum vacuum—and possessed of certain initial velocities. Each, moreover, possessed certain causal powers; that is, each possessed a certain intrinsic capacity to affect the motions of other particles.

Now these particles were (and are) not capable of maintaining themselves in existence or of conserving their own causal powers. For one of them to continue to exist, it is necessary for God continuously to hold it in existence. For it to have the same set of causal powers—the same set of capacities to affect the motions of other particles—at a series of instants, it is necessary for God at each instant to supply it with that set of causal powers. For that matter, for a particle to have

---

1. Unless this philosopher accepts the Platonic doctrine of the preexistence of the soul (as well as its immortality), he will also want to reject my assumption that there are always the same elementary particles.

different sets of causal powers at two or more instants is for that particle to be supplied with different sets of powers at those instants. To
say that God once created, and now sustains, the *world* is to say no
more than this: that God once created and now sustains certain particles—for the world, or nature, or the cosmos, or the universe, is nothing
more than the sum of these particles. Moreover, every individual created thing is the sum of certain of these particles, and the point that
was made about the created universe as a whole can be made about
each individual created thing. If, for example, God sustains a bridge in
existence and preserves its causal powers—its capacity to bear a ten-
ton load, for example—this action is just the sum of all the actions He
performs in sustaining in existence and preserving the causal powers
of the elementary particles that are the ultimate constituents of the
bridge; the powers, that is, by which they so affect one another as to
continue to form a configuration that exhibits a certain degree of
stability.

And this is the entire extent of God's causal relations with the created world. He does not, for example, *move* particles—or not in any
very straightforward sense. Rather, the particles move one another,
albeit their capacity to do so is continuously supplied by God. Here is
an analogy. Suppose that two pieces of soft iron are wound round with
wires and a current passed through the wires. The two pieces of iron
then become electromagnets, and, if they are close to one another and
free to move, they begin to move in virtue of the forces they are exerting
upon each other. It would be odd to say that the generator that is
supplying the current to the wires was moving the two pieces of iron.
It is more natural to say that the generator is moving only electrons,
and that the pieces of iron are *moving each other,* this movement being
a function of their relative dispositions and the causal powers that are
(in a sense) being supplied to them by the generator.

This is everything I want to say about the way in which God acts
in and sustains the created world—with one omission. We have not yet
raised the question whether the causal powers of a given particle are
constant over time. Let us suppose that this is at least very nearly true:
Each particle always, or almost always, has the same causal powers.[2]

2. This note is addressed to those who believe that there are created rational immaterial beings. It was suggested in the text that anyone who believed in such creatures
could accept most of what I say if he rejected my assumption that all "particles" were
material, and assumed that some "particles" were immaterial and rational. If anyone
avails himself of this suggestion, he must take care to except thinking, immaterial "particles" from the generalizations about particles that are made in the following discussion
of the metaphysics of miracles, since it would seem obvious that, e.g., a Cartesian ego's

That is, God always, or almost always, supplies it with the same set of causal powers. Now we have assumed, for the sake of convenience, that there is only one type of elementary particle. It seems reasonable to suppose that causal powers are the only relevant factor in classifying elementary particles into "types." It would follow that the causal powers possessed by a given particle at a given time are almost certainly identical with the causal powers possessed by any other particle at any other time. (This picture of God's action in the world has an interesting consequence. Consider again the example of God's sustaining a bridge in existence and preserving its causal powers. The particles that compose the bridge would have existed even if the bridge had not, since there are always the same particles, and—almost certainly—they would have had the same causal powers. It follows that what God does in sustaining the bridge in existence and preserving its causal powers is something He would have done even if the bridge had never existed, although, in that case, this action would not have fallen under the description "sustaining the bridge in existence and preserving its causal powers.")

Now suppose that God occasionally (and only momentarily) supplied a few particles with causal powers different from their normal powers. Such an action would cause a certain part of the natural world to diverge from the course that part of the world would have taken if He had continued to supply the particles in that part of the world with the usual complement of causal powers. Such a divergence would, presumably, spread—with decreasing amplitude—till it encompassed the entire universe. The early stages of such a divergence we shall call a *miracle*. For example, imagine that God momentarily supplies unusual causal powers to the particles composing the water in a certain pot, in such a way that those particles (in virtue of their momentarily abnormal effects on one another) follow trajectories through the void that they would not normally have followed, and that, as a consequence, they rearrange themselves into the configuration we call "wine"—at

---

causal powers will hardly ever be constant over time. Such a being's causal powers will vary with time (if for no other reason) because its internal representations of its circumstances will vary. If I took Cartesianism seriously, I would try to elaborate the model of the created world presented herein to provide a more comfortable niche for immaterial human minds; but I don't and I won't. As for angels, while I take them seriously, I know nothing of their metaphysical nature and thus have no idea of what sort of elaboration of the model would be needed to provide a more comfortable niche for them.

which moment God reverts to His usual policy and continues to supply each of the particles with its normal causal powers.[3]

I like this account of miracles better than either of the two alternative accounts I know of. On one account, a miracle is an "intervention" into the course of nature by God. But the word 'intervention' seems to imply that nature has some sort of native power, independent of God's, and that in working a miracle, God has, as it were, to *overpower* some part of nature. No theist can accept such a picture of the relation of God to nature; this account of miracles provides a better description of what the deist says God *doesn't* do than of what the theist says God *does* do.[4]

3. This definition of *miracle* is tailored to fit our account of the created world and its relation to God, an account that is in many respects too simple to be satisfactory. If the account were elaborated, our definition of *miracle* might have to be modified. For example, we have assumed, for the sake of simplicity, that there are always just the same particles. If we were to assume instead that God sometimes—but very rarely—annihilated particles, or created particles ex nihilo subsequently to the first, great Creation, then we should want to count as miracles the initial stages of the divergences occasioned by such actions from what would have otherwise been the course of events.

If we were to assume that God sometimes moved particles otherwise than by supplying them and neighboring particles with abnormal causal powers—that He sometimes moved particles "directly"—such episodes, too, should be counted as miracles. (It is not entirely clear to me, however, that the alleged distinction between God's moving particles "directly" and "indirectly" is ultimately intelligible. To adapt a remark of Frege's, sometimes I seem to see a distinction, and then again I *don't* see it.)

4. When this essay was read to the Society of Christian Philosophers, the commentator charged the author with deism. (Talk about *odium theologicum*!) In this he claimed to be following the medieval Latin authority: The position I propound, that alterations in the created world are not directly caused by God, "is stigmatized as (in effect) a form of *deism* by almost every important medieval Christian philosopher." Well, it would have to be "in effect," since the words *deista* and *deismus* occur in no medieval manuscript—or if they do, this is not known to the editors of the Oxford English Dictionary, who derive the French *déiste* directly from *deus*. Since 'deist' (when used in a dyslogistic sense; it has sometimes been used to mean 'theist') has never meant anything but "person who believes in a Creator on the basis of reason alone, and who denies revelation, miracles, Providence, and immanence," "in effect" cashes out to this: Someone who denies that God directly causes alterations in the created world denies God's immanence. But a God who continuously sustains all things in existence and continuously conserves their causal powers is immanent enough for me. In such a God, "we live and move and have our being" (Acts 17:28); "in him all things hold together" (Col. 1:17). (I hold, moreover, that no created thing *could possibly* exist at a given moment unless it were at that moment held in existence by God; and no created thing *could possibly* have causal powers at a given moment unless it were at that moment supplied with those powers by God.)

The alternatives to this position are occasionalism and concurrentism. Occasionalism is one of those high-minded philosophical depreciations of God's works that come disguised as compliments to God's person. As, for example, Docetism devalues the Incarnation, occasionalism devalues the Creation. What God has made and now sustains is

According to the second alternative account, a miracle occurs when God causes an event that is a "violation of the laws of nature." I like this alternative better than the other, but I have a rather technical objection to it. Let us call a contingent proposition a *law of nature* if it would be true if God *always* supplied the elementary particles with their normal causal powers, and would, moreover, be true under any conditions whatever that were consistent with this stipulation. For those who are familiar with the philosophical use of the concept of "possible worlds," here is a more precise definition: A proposition is a law of nature in a possible world *w* if it is a contingent proposition that is true in all possible worlds in which elementary particles *always* have the causal powers they *always or almost always* have in *w*. Now if the proposition L is a law of nature, then we can say that an event *violates* the law L if the particles whose joint activity constitutes that event follow, while the event is going on, trajectories that are inconsistent with the truth of L. Roughly: An event violates a law if the law

---

substance, not shadow. Concurrentism is the doctrine that God must cooperate with a created thing in order for that thing to act on another thing. I find this doctrine hard to understand. Does it credit created things with the power to produce effects or does it not? In the former case, why is God's cooperation needed to produce the effect? In the latter case, Creation is devalued.

The commentator also endorsed a curious medieval argument that is supposed to show that a certain sort of miracle requires either occasionalism or concurrentism. Consider the three young men in the fiery furnace. If fire and flesh really had intrinsic causal powers, powers that could be exercised without God's cooperation (the argument runs), then God could have preserved the three young men only by altering the powers, and hence the natures, of the fire or the flesh—in which case they would not have *been* fire or flesh. There seems to me to be little to this argument. The causal influence of the fire would have had to pass from one place to another to affect the flesh, and God could miraculously block this influence at some intermediate point in space without in any way altering the fire or the flesh. Interestingly enough, in the apocryphal "Song of Azariah in the Furnace" (which the Jerusalem Bible inserts between Daniel 3:23 and the Song of the Three Children), just this line is taken: "But the angel of the Lord came down into the furnace [and] drove the flames of the fire outward, and fanned in to them, in the heart of the furnace, a coolness such as wind or drew will bring, so that the fire did not even touch them or cause them any pain or distress." The commentator does consider this sort of possibility, but suggests that it represents God as engaging in an unseemly struggle with a creature; "resisting the power of the fire," as he puts it. Similarly, I suppose one might argue that God would not, whatever the Psalmist might say, send His angels to support one, lest one dash one's foot against a stone. That would be "resisting" the power of the stone or of gravity or something. Such mindedness is too wonderful for me; it is high, I cannot attain unto it. But if one must have a high-minded account of the preservation of the three young men, here is one consistent with what is said in the body of the essay (in a slightly modified version, which takes into account a little elementary physics): As the photons are on their way from the fire to the flesh, God ceases to sustain most of the more energetic ones in existence.

says that no events of that sort happen. A *miracle*, then, is an event that violates one or more laws. (It follows from this account of law and miracle that, if there are any miracles, then some laws of nature are false propositions. Some philosophers insist that, by definition, a law of nature, whatever else it may be, must be a true proposition. I can't think why.) I said that I had a rather technical objection to this account of the concept of miracle. The *objection* is simply that this account is not equivalent to the one I favor: Some events that my account labels 'miracles' this account does not. "Technical" comes in in explaining why. It comes down to this: The two accounts coincide only if the laws of nature are deterministic; that is, only if, given the present state of the world, the laws of nature are so strict that—miracles aside—they tie the world down to exactly one future, a future determined in every detail. For suppose that the laws are *indeterministic*. Suppose that they are sufficiently "loose" that they permit a certain event A to have either of two outcomes, B or C, and they don't determine which will happen. They allow history to fork, as it were, to go down either of two roads. Suppose that A has happened and suppose that God wants A to be followed by C and not by B. Suppose that, to achieve this end, God supplies certain particles with abnormal causal powers of such a nature that C *has* to happen. (Speaking very loosely, you might say that He locally and temporarily replaces the indeterministic laws with deterministic ones.) Then C will be a miracle by the account I have given, but not by the violation-of-laws-of-nature account. I prefer so to use the word 'miracle' that this event counts as a miracle. If you disagree, you may regard my use of the word as idiosyncratic.

It will be convenient in what follows to have a uniform way in which to describe God's actions with respect to the created world, a mode of description that comprehends both His ordinary sustaining of particles in existence and His miraculous departures from the ordinary. I shall suppose that whenever God brings about some state of affairs involving created beings, His doing this is the same action as His issuing a certain *decree*—a pronouncement of the form "Let such-and-such be" or "Let the following be so: . . ." For example, "Let there be light" is a decree, and God's issuing or pronouncing this decree is the same action as His creating light. For technical reasons, I shall want to suppose that God's decrees are, as philosophers say, "closed under entailment." This means that if God issues certain decrees—say a decree that p and a decree that q—and if, as a matter of absolute or metaphysical necessity, if p and q are true then r must also be true, then it follows that God, in decreeing that p and q, also decrees that r. For example, suppose that one of God's decrees is "Let the waters be divided from the waters"; suppose that, as many philosophers, myself included, believe, it is a matter of absolute or metaphysical necessity that if there is water, then there are protons. Then it follows that in issuing this decree, God also issues the decree "Let there be protons." (It will, however, be convenient to except necessary truths from the closure requirement: Let us say that if God decrees certain propositions, and these propositions jointly entail p, it follows that God decrees p, provided that p is a contingent proposition.)

In this "decree" language, we may represent the action of God with respect to each elementary particle at a given moment as follows. His action consists in His then issuing a decree of the form "Let *that* now exist and have such-and-such causal powers." If God wished to annihilate a certain particle, therefore, He would not do something *to* the particle, as I might hit a vase with a hammer if I wished to destroy it. He would simply stop issuing such decrees. (But in our rather simple model of the relations of God to the world, we tacitly assume He never ceases to hold any particle in existence, since we assume there are always the same particles. This feature of our model is not essential to any of the points made in this essay, and could be removed at the cost of putting up with a slightly more complex model.) And for God to work a miracle is for Him temporarily to decree different causal powers for certain particles from the ones He normally decrees. God's actions with respect to the entire created world at any moment subsequent to the Creation are simply the sum of His actions at that moment with respect to all the particles composing the world.[5] Thus, God's action

5. We shall presently discuss God's action at the *first* moment, the moment of Creation. In what follows in the text and in subsequent notes, generalizations about what God does at particular instants should be understood as referring to instants subsequent to the first.

This way of talking raises the question: What, exactly, is the relation of God and His actions to *time* in our model of God's relation to the world? Let us say the following. First, we shall assume that the existence of time, of "before" and "after," is a function of the existence of the physical world: If there had been no world, there would have been no such thing as time, and one can make no sense of talk of temporal relations except in reference to the physical world. As both St. Augustine and Stephen Hawking have insisted, it makes no sense to ask what happened *before*—at least in the literal, temporal sense of the world—the world existed. (Hawking employs this analogy: You might as well ask what is happening north of the North Pole.) Secondly, we shall assume that some of God's decrees can be assigned dates (dates provided by the processes of the physical world, the only dates there are): We can ask with respect to a time t what decrees God *then* issues. (I shall not attempt to prove that these two assumptions are consistent.) Because of our closure condition, however, it is possible that there be decrees of God that are not issued at any particular time. (An example of such a decree can be

in the created world at any given moment consists, on this model, in
His issuing a vast number of decrees—as many as there are particles—
of the form, "Let *that* now exist and have such-and-such causal powers."[6] His issuing these decrees is identical with His sustaining the
world.

Let us now turn to the question, What is the place of chance in a
world sustained by God? Can chance exist at all in such a world? Or,
if it does exist, must its realm not be restricted to trivial matters—say,
to such matters as where a particular sparrow falls—if its existence is
to be consistent with God's loving providence?

In order to approach these questions, let us ask what it would be
for there to be chance in the world. There are various things that can
be meant by the word 'chance.' What I shall mean by saying that an
event is a "chance" occurrence, or a state of affairs a "matter of
chance" or "due to chance," is this: The event or state of affairs is
without purpose or significance; it is not a part of anyone's plan; it
serves no one's end; and it might very well not have been. A chance

---

found in note 11.) I do not insist that the two assumptions I have made about God and
time represent the ultimate metaphysical truth. Those who hold that God is entirely
"outside time" are faced with certain authoritative documents—such as the Bible—
which, on the face of it, say that God does one thing at one time and another thing at
another time. Such philosophers generally have some way of interpreting assertions of
this sort so that these assertions are seen to be compatible with their theory of an
extratemporal God. They should feel free to interpret my assertions about God's actions
at particular times in the same way.

6. But, owing to our closure condition, He does not issue *only* those decrees; He
also decrees, at any given moment, any contingent proposition entailed by the totality
of that vast ensemble of decrees about individual particles. Or, at any rate, this follows
if we interpret our closure condition (which, as stated, does not refer to time) as having
this consequence: If, at t, God decrees certain propositions, and these propositions together entail the contingent proposition p, then at t, God decrees that p. Thus, at an
instant t, God then decrees every proposition that is true in all possible worlds in which,
at t, there are the same particles as there are in actuality and in which each of these
particles has at t the same causal powers it has in actuality.

We should note that the thesis that God decrees at t that a certain particle then exist
and then have certain causal powers does not entail that He decrees at t that it then be
at any particular place. "Let *that* now exist and have such-and-such causal powers" is
not the same decree as "Let *that* now exist and be *right there* and have such-and-
such causal powers." (A similar point applies to velocity and the higher derivatives of
displacement.) More generally: From the thesis that God at t is sustaining the universe,
it does not follow that He then decrees the particular *arrangement* of particles that in
fact obtains at that time. Here is an imperfect analogy. From the fact that a gardener is
now tending the flowers in a certain garden (and is thus in a sense now sustaining them
in existence) it hardly follows that he is now determining the way they are now arranged.
I return to this point in note 11.

event, in other words, is one such that, if someone asks of it, "Why did that happen?" the only right answer is: "There *is* no reason or explanation; it just happened."[7] But you must treat this statement charitably. I do not mean to imply that a "chance" event in this sense has no explanation of *any* sort. If Alice suddenly remembers that she had promised to buy a box of crayons for her son, and turns into an unfamiliar street in search of an appropriate shop, and is struck and killed by a car whose brakes have failed, her death may well be a "chance" occurrence in the sense I mean—someone who did not believe in divine providence would almost certainly say that it was—even though in one sense her death has an obvious explanation: She was struck by a car. But if her grieving husband were to cry in despair, "Why did she die?", it would be a cruel joke to tell him that she died because she was struck by a large, heavy vehicle moving at fifty miles an hour. That is not the sort of explanation he would be asking for. By calling an event a "chance" event, I mean that it has no explanation of the sort Alice's husband might ask for: It has no purpose or significance; it is not a part of anyone's plan.

It does seem that there are many events of this sort; some horrible, some benefic, some of no consequence to anyone. But there are people who believe that this seeming is mere seeming and that either there are no chance events in this sense, or, if there are, they are always events

---

7. Some philosophers believe that there are impersonal but intelligible "world-historical" processes, and that these processes somehow confer intelligibility or significance on certain of the events that issue from them. For such an event there would be an answer to the question, Why did that happen? If there are such world-historical processes, one would not want to call their products "chance" events, despite the fact that—assuming that the world-historical processes are not instruments of God's purpose—they are not a part of anyone's plan (unless it were the plan of a personified abstraction like History). The primary purpose of the qualification "It might very well not have been" is to deny the status of a "chance" event to an event—as it may be, the rise of capitalism—that is a necessary product of some impersonal but intelligible world-historical process like the Labor of the Concept or the Dialectic of History. Since the idea of such processes is a vague one, I will not attempt to be precise about the meaning of "It might very well not have been." I will explicitly and formally exclude only metaphysically necessary events (if such there be) and metaphysically necessary states of affairs from the category "might not have been." (Thus, if Spinoza is right, no event or state of affairs can be ascribed to "chance.") Readers for whom Spinozism, and historicism of the Hegel-Marx-Spengler variety, are not live options can safely ignore the qualification "It might very well not have been." In any case, the *theist* will say, first, that Spinozism is false, and secondly, that either there are no "world-historical" processes, or, if there are, their existence is ordained by God and any necessary product of such processes will therefore be a part of someone's plan. The theist, therefore, may ignore the qualification "It might very well not have been." I shall do so in the sequel.

that are of no consequence to anyone. I have in mind those people who believe in divine providence and who take a certain view, which I shall proceed to describe, of divine providence. Such people think that God not only *knows* of the fall of every sparrow, but that the fall of every sparrow is a part of God's plan for His creation. Presumably they think that the exact number of hairs on one's head is also a part of God's plan. Other people may find the attribution of every detail of the world to providence bizarre, but say that at any rate all those events that would be accounted important by human beings—Alice's death, for example—must have a place in God's plan. A person who takes this view will say that when Alice's grieving husband asks, "Why did she die?", there is an answer to this question, an answer that God knows even if no human being knows it. My purpose in the remainder of this essay will be to suggest that this is wrong. I want to suggest that much of what goes on in the world, even much of what seems important and significant to us, is no part of God's plan—and certainly not a part of anyone *else's* plan—and is therefore due simply to chance.

If there is chance in a world sustained by God, what are its sources? Where, as it were, does it "come from"? Let us recall our picture of God's relation to the world: The world consists of elementary particles, and God created the world by creating these particles simultaneously at some moment in the past; God sustains each of them in existence and continuously "supplies" each of them with its causal powers; following the Creation, the world evolved in a manner determined, insofar as it *was* determined, by the causal powers of its constituent particles; the causal powers supplied to a given particle are normally invariant, but God may, of His own good pleasure, momentarily supply certain particles with different sets of causal powers from the ones they normally receive from Him, and, if He does this, then a miracle occurs.

If God has this relation to the created universe, what is meant by His "plan" for the created universe? I believe that we should, as a first approximation, identify God's plan with the sum total of what He has decreed. (I say "as a first approximation" because I will presently qualify this definition.) Thus, if God has issued the decree "Let there be light," then the existence of light is a part of His plan. If He has *not* issued the decree "let there be lies," then lies are no part of His plan. We should remember that a plan—God's plan or anyone's—may take account of a certain possibility without requiring that that possibility be realized. For example, bank robbers planning their getaway may *plan for* the contingency of leaving the city by air—they have bought airline tickets—but not *plan to* leave the city by air. Leaving the city by air is not a part of their plan in the way that arriving at the bank at 3:00 P.M. is. We should also remember that the fact that God knows that something will happen does not mean that that thing is a part of His plan. God may, therefore, have known before there were any rational creatures that some of them would someday tell lies, and His plan for the world may contain measures for dealing with lies should any lies be told; but it does not follow from these things that lies are a part of His plan. Now here is the qualification of our definition of God's plan that I alluded to a moment ago. It may happen that God sometimes issues decrees in response to events that He has not decreed. For example, suppose that a young man is dying following a car wreck and that God had not decreed that that car wreck should occur. Suppose the young man's mother prays that his life be saved, and that God grants this prayer by performing a miracle in virtue of which the man recovers. We shall not count this miraculous recovery as a part of God's plan, since it was contingent on an event—the car wreck—that God had *not* decreed. We might call the decree God issued to bring about the man's recovery a *reactive* decree, since it was issued in reaction to an event that God did not bring about. We may define a reactive decree of God's as a decree He would not have issued had some event not decreed by Him not occurred. Our revised definition of God's plan is: God's plan consists of the totality of all His decrees other than reactive decrees.[8]

If this is the correct picture of God's relation to the created world and His plan for it, there would seem to be, within such a world, at

---

8. Or we might call this totality "God's unqualified plan" or "God's eternal plan" or "God's plan *ante omnia saecula*." We could also speak, for any contingent proposition *p*, of "God's plan given that *p*": If the conditional "if *p* then *q*" is a part of God's eternal plan, and if *p* is true, then *q* is a part of "God's plan given that *p*." If *q* is a part of God's plan given that *p*, and if *p* is not a part of God's unqualified plan, then *q* will be a part of God's plan given that *p*, but not a part of God's unqualified plan. If *q* is a part of God's plan given that *p* (but not a part of God's plan *ante omnia saecula*) and if *p* is a proposition that we all know to be true—or which we and all of our coreligionists believe to be true—it will be natural for us to speak of *q* as being "a part of God's plan"; in fact it would be inadvisable for anyone to speak otherwise, except (as in the present case) when engaged in highly abstract theological speculation. Thus, Christians may properly speak of the Incarnation as being "a part of God's plan," even if there would have been no Incarnation if there had been no Fall: for, surely, there is some contingent proposition *p* (perhaps "Man falls from his original perfection," or the conjunction of this and various other propositions) such that the Christian will believe that *p* is in fact true and also believe that "If *p*, then God becomes man" is a part of God's eternal plan.

We should note that God's eternal plan is not (at least according to orthodox Christian theology) a necessary product of the Divine Nature. "There is a created universe" is a part of God's eternal plan, but not, orthodoxy has it, a necessary truth.

least three possible sources of chance, or of events or states of affairs that are not a part of God's plan: the free will of rational creatures, natural indeterminism, and the initial state of the created world. (I call these *three* sources of chance, but I realize that proponents of various philosophical theories may hold that every instance of some one of these sources is also an instance of one of the other two. For example, a philosopher who holds that free will and determinism are incompatible will probably maintain that every instance of human free will is also an instance of natural indeterminism.)

Let us first consider human free will. I take it to be obvious that if God decrees (I do not mean *commands*) that a certain human being on a certain occasion behave in a certain way, then that human being loses his freedom of choice on that particular occasion. When, for example, God "hardened Pharaoh's heart," Pharaoh—at that particular moment—did not *freely* choose to forbid the Hebrews to leave Egypt. Thus, if there is such a thing as human free will, it cannot be that all of our choices are like Pharaoh's. And it is certainly not obviously the biblical picture of God's relation to man that all of our choices *are* of that sort. For example, Ecclesiasticus says of God (15:4): "He himself made man in the beginning, and then left him free to make his own decisions." (Admittedly, Christians have to deal with some difficult passages in Romans on this point.) If we have free will, therefore, the manner in which any particular person exercises this free will is no part of God's plan, and likewise the consequences of free acts, even if they occur thousands of years after the act, are no parts of God's plan. I must point out that this is not an attempt to *absolve* God of responsibility for the consequences of the free acts of creatures. After all, that an event is not part of one's plans does not necessarily mean that one is not responsible for it. If the man who fell among thieves had died beside the road from Jerusalem to Jericho, this would not have been a part of any plan of the priest or the Levite, but they would nonetheless have been responsible for his death. Whether God should be held responsible for the evils caused by the abuse of human free will—and He could certainly prevent most of these evils, if not all of them—is not the present question. I am arguing only that they are not part of His plan for the world, which is a relatively weak thesis.

A second source of chance in the world is natural indeterminism. Indeterminism is the thesis that the distribution of all the particles of matter in the universe at a given moment, and their causal powers at that moment, do not determine the subsequent behavior of the particles. In other words, an indeterministic universe is one in which a given state of affairs can have more than one outcome. The Greek atomists held that atoms—what are now called elementary particles—could swerve in the void, and something very much like this is true according to modern physics. If God's causal relations with the world are confined to continuously holding the elementary particles in existence and continuously supplying them with their causal powers, then He does not decree the outcomes of such "swerves in the void," since the "swerves" are not determined by the causal powers of the particles. And the consequences of such undetermined events can show up at the level of ordinary observation, if they are sufficiently amplified. A Geiger counter is an amplifier designed for this purpose. (Another effective amplifier can be found in the collisions of rolling spheres. Imagine a billiard table on which perfectly spherical, perfectly elastic billiard balls are in motion, without loss of kinetic energy to friction or to collisions with the sides of the table. Imagine a second billiard-table-and-balls setup that is as close to being an absolutely perfect duplicate of the first as the laws of nature allow. If the "laws of nature" are those of nineteenth-century physics, the second table will be an absolutely perfect duplicate of the first *sans phrase*, and the behavior of the balls on the second table will—presumably—duplicate exactly the behavior of the balls on the first table forever. Suppose, however, that a rolling billiard ball exhibits the position-momentum and time-energy uncertainties predicted by Heisenberg. For an object as big as a billiard ball, these uncertainties are minuscule indeed. Nevertheless, the capacity of the collisions of rolling spheres to magnify slight deviations is astounding: Within a few minutes the arrangements of balls on the two tables will be entirely different.)

Since the actual physical world seems in fact to be indeterministic, it is plausible to suppose that there are a great many states of affairs which are not part of God's plan and which, moreover, cannot be traced to the free decisions of created beings. I very much doubt that when the universe was (say) 10^{-45} seconds old, it was then physically inevitable that the earth, or even the Milky Way galaxy, should exist. Thus, these objects, so important from the human point of view, are no part of God's plan—or at least not unless their creation was due to God's miraculous intervention into the course of the development of the physical world at a relatively late stage. I see no reason as a theist, or as a Christian, to believe that the existence of human beings is a part of God's plan. This may seem a shocking statement. Let me attempt to palliate the shock. First, I do not claim to *know* that the existence of our species is not a part of God's plan. Secondly, I am sure that the existence of animals made in God's image—that is, rational animals having free will and capable of love—*is* a part of God's plan. I am simply not convinced that He had any *particular* species in mind. Thirdly, I do not deny God's omniscience. I do not deny that He knew from the beginning that humanity would exist; but what is foreknown is not necessarily what is planned. Fourthly, *having* come into existence, we are *now* in God's care and the objects of His love and the instruments of His purpose. Here is an analogy: When my wife and I decided to have a child, we did not decide with respect to some particular child to have *that* child, as a couple might decide with respect to some particular child to adopt *that* child. But now that our child is in existence, she, that very individual and no other, is in our care and is the object of our love. I concede that if God knows the future in every detail, then He knew before humanity existed that that particular species would exist; and my wife and I did not know of Elizabeth van Inwagen, before her conception, that she, that very individual, would exist. But if God knew from the beginning of time, or even "before all worlds," that humanity would exist, it does not follow that He decreed the existence of humanity; He may for all I know have issued no decree more particular than "Let there be a species in My image and likeness."

I now turn to the third source of chance in the world: the initial state of things. (I ignore the problem presented by the fact that, according to most of the current cosmological models, although the world has a finite age, there was no first instant of its existence—or if there was a first instant, the world was then of zero volume and infinite density, an idea that seems to make no sense.)

At the first moment of the existence of the physical universe there were, let us say, $(2.46 \times 10^{80}) + 2319$ particles,[9] each having a certain set of causal powers, a certain position in space, and a certain velocity. No doubt this "initial arrangement" (so to call it) suited God's purposes; if it did not, of course, there would have been some other initial arrangement. But is it conceivable that this was the only one out of all possible initial arrangements that suited God's purposes? Is it conceivable that God chose this arrangement because it was better for His purposes than *any* of the infinitely many alternatives? Well, I find that very hard to believe. I don't mean to deny that God could hold all of the infinitely many possible initial arrangements before His mind at once, and then say, "Let *that* one be." (Of course, this is mere picture-thinking, treating God as if He were just like a human being, with the

9. Or, better, think of a number of this order of magnitude that isn't mostly zeros.

minor difference that He is infinite. But picture-thinking is all we are capable of. When I say I don't mean to deny this, I am saying that I don't mean to deny that it's the best picture.) I do, however, doubt whether any *one* of the alternatives *could* be superior to all the others. To me that sounds as absurd as saying that, if an artist wants to draw a portrait in chalk, then one particular arrangement of calcium, carbon, and oxygen atoms, out of all the possible arrangements, must be the arrangement that would constitute the best possible piece of chalk for the job.

Well, suppose there are various alternative initial arrangements that would suit God's purposes equally well. Doubtless if there is more than one such arrangement there are infinitely many. But let us suppose for the sake of simplicity that there are just two, X and Y. We are supposing, that is, that for God's purposes to be accomplished, either X or Y must come into existence, but it makes no difference which; it is a matter of sheer indifference to Him. Now if God wishes either X or Y to come into existence, what decree shall He issue? There would seem to be three possibilities:

(1) "Let X be"

(2) "Let Y be"

(3) "Let either X or Y be."[10]

Leibniz, though he does not talk of things in exactly these terms, might be interpreted as saying, first, that (3) is impossible because God creates only "complete" states of affairs, fully detailed ones, "possible words"; secondly, that God cannot issue either (1) or (2), because that would be for God to act without a sufficient reason for His action; and, thirdly, that there must, therefore, be a *best possible* initial state, since there in fact is a created world.

I would deny the first of these assertions. It does not seem to me to be logically or metaphysically impossible that God should decree that either X or Y should be without decreeing that X should be and without decreeing that Y should be. Suppose God does decree that *either* X or Y exist; suppose Y thereupon comes into existence.[11] Then it is no part

10. We must be careful about what we mean by calling (1), (2), and (3) *three* possibilities, since, by our closure condition, if God issues either (1) or (2) He ipso facto issues (3). The three possibilities I mean to call attention to are: God issues (1); God issues (2); God issues (3) *without* issuing (1) or (2).

11. The moment Y comes into existence, there will, of course, be a particular number of particles and each will have a determinate position and velocity and complement of causal powers It is at *that* point that God must, if He is to sustain the world He has

of God's plan that *Y*—*as opposed to X*—exist, and the result of His decree might just as well have been the existence of *X*. We may therefore say that *Y* exists owing simply to chance, and that every result or consequence or *Y* that would not *also* be a result of *X* is due to chance. There could, therefore, be chance events even in a wholly deterministic world that was created and is sustained by God. If, moreover, we assume that God cannot, after all, decree that either *X* or *Y* exist except by decreeing that *X* exist or else decreeing that *Y* exist, this will not remove the element of chance from the world. It will simply locate the ultimate source of that chance within the internal life of God, rather

---

created, begin issuing "a vast number of decrees—as many as there are particles—of the form 'Let *that* now exist and have such-and-such causal powers'." Here is another imperfect horticultural analogy. Suppose I plant a tree in my garden. Within certain limits, it may not matter much to me where the tree is. I may, within these limits, choose a spot at random. But once I have planted the tree and it is firmly rooted at a particular spot, I must tend it where it is. It's no good watering a spot ten feet to the left of the tree, even if my purposes would have been as well served by planting the tree at that other spot.

I said in note 6 that it does not follow from the fact that God at *t* issues decrees that then sustain the universe in existence that He then decrees the current arrangement of particles. I will now go further and say that, if our model of God's relation to the world is anything like right, then at most *one* instant does He then decree the current arrangement of particles: the first. And if the decree of God that brings the universe into existence is indefinite (like "Let either *X* or *Y* be"), then at *no* instant does He then decree the current arrangement of particles. (Moreover, the existence of a first instant of time is a consequence of the limitations of our model: A more sophisticated model would allow for the possibility that, while the temporal sequence has a greatest lower bound, it has no earliest member.) It would, however, be possible for God to decree the arrangement of particles at *t* without *then* decreeing it. Suppose, for example, that at t_0 (the first moment of time), God then decrees a perfectly definite arrangement of particles; suppose that at every instant in the interval having t_0 as its earliest member and *t* as its earliest nonmember, He then decrees the existence of the same particles that existed at *t,* and also decrees a deterministic set of laws; and suppose that at *t* He then decrees the existence of the same particles that existed at t_0. Only one arrangement of particles at *t* will be consistent with this set of decrees and it therefore follows that God decrees the arrangement of particles at *t*. Since, however, He does not issue all of these decrees *at t,* we cannot say that *at t* He *then* decrees the current arrangement of particles. But, of course, if the theory presented in the text is correct, God does not, even in this sense, decree the arrangement of particles at any time: There are, in fact, possible worlds in which God has issued the same decrees He has issued in actuality, and in which no particle is where it is in actuality. Nevertheless, God may have (and if any revealed religion is true, *has*) decreed many of the features the universe has at any given moment: that it then contain living creatures, for example. It should be evident from what has been said in this note and in note 6 that we cannot validly deduce from the two premises: (i) God has decreed that at *t* there be living creatures, and (ii) at *t*, God then issues decrees that sustain in existence all the living creatures there are at that moment, the conclusion that at *t* God then issues the decree that there be living creatures at that moment.

than in the results of an indefinite decree. For if God must issue a decree that X exist or else issue a decree that Y exist, and if He has no reason to prefer one of these states of affairs to the other—if it is really, from God's point of view, six of one and half a dozen of the other—then there seems to be no way to avoid the conclusion that some analogue of a coin toss takes place within the Divine Nature. An analogy is provided by Buridan's Ass; this unfortunate animal, you remember, is forced to choose between two equally attractive and accessible piles of hay. If the poor creature is not to starve, it must make an arbitrary choice. And, presumably, within each animal—even within rational animals like ourselves—there exists some mechanism, some biological analogue of a coin toss, for making arbitrary choices. Occasional reliance upon such a mechanism is not beneath the dignity of an animal, even a rational animal, but I find it wholly incongruous to suppose that the Divine Nature contains anything remotely resembling a coin-tossing mechanism. To suggest this seems to be almost to suggest that the Lord of all is, as Zeus was said to be, one of the subjects of the goddess Tyche or Chance. I prefer to think that God is capable of decreeing that a certain indefinite condition be satisfied without decreeing any of the indifferent alternative states of affairs that would satisfy it. However this may be, the following result seems secure: If there are alternative initial arrangements of particles, any of which would have served God's purpose for His creation equally well, then certain features of the world must be due to mere chance. How pervasive these features may be, and how important they might seem to us, are, of course, further questions, questions that are not answered by anything that we have so far said. And this same result, the existence of states of affairs due to chance, follows from our consideration of human freedom and natural indeterminism. I do not doubt that all three sources of chance have in fact been in operation, and that many of the features of the actual universe are due to them—perhaps even features as prominent as the human race or the Local Group. I do not think that such a view of the place of chance in the formation of the universe is incompatible with the proposition that God is the Maker of all things, visible and invisible. Even if the planet Mars (say) is not a part of God's plan, it is entirely composed of particles which He made in the beginning and which exist from moment to moment only because He continues to hold them in existence and which continue from moment to moment to form a planet only because He is continuously supplying them with the causal powers by which they mutually cohere. I suppose that *we* exist only by chance, and yet it is in God that we live and move and have our being. And, as I have implied, creatures that, like us, exist by chance, may well be filling a divinely ordained *role*, and in that sense be serving God's purpose—rather as individual soldiers may be serving a general's purposes, even though the battle plan the general has drafted does not include any of their names. (But again, the analogy is imperfect, for the general, we may suppose, neither knows nor cares about individual private soldiers—even if he is concerned about their collective welfare—whereas God knows all about each of us, and loves each of us with a depth and intensity that are without human parallel.)

If what I have said so far is correct, then it seems very likely that among the events that are due simply to chance and not part of God's plan are certain evils; or perhaps even *all* evils. In the remainder of this essay I want to examine this idea and its consequences.

If much of the world is due to chance, and if much of the world is infected with evil, then it would be reasonable to suppose, on purely statistical grounds, that at least some evil is due to chance. Many theists, moreover, ascribe the very existence of evil to an abuse of the divine gift of free will by created beings. If that speculation is correct, then the very existence of evil is a matter of chance; that is, there is simply no answer to the question, Why is there evil? and it is not correct to say that God planned to create a world containing evil. Since people seem to be particularly likely to misunderstand the point of suggestions like this one, I will repeat something I have said before: This suggestion is in no way supposed to be a "solution to the problem of evil," since it is consistent with the proposition that before evil ever was, God knew that there would someday be evil and could have prevented it. I mention the point that (if evil is wholly due to the creaturely abuse of free will) evil is not a part of God's plan for His creation, simply to distinguish this point from the points I wish to discuss. The points I wish to discuss involve particular evils and their relation to God's plan.

What I want to say about particular evils is best made clear by illustration and example. I will consider two evils, one *very* particular—the accidental death of a particular person—and the other more general. I will discuss the more general evil first. I think that the existence of a certain disease will provide a good illustration of the point I want to make. For the sake of a concrete example, I will discuss rabies—an arbitrary choice, except that I have deliberately chosen a rather horrible disease. (A disease like rabies falls in the category that students of the problem of evil call "physical" or "natural" evil. But in what follows, I will make no explicit use of the distinction between natural and "moral" evil.) I see no reason to suppose that God has decreed the existence of rabies. In my view, the rabies virus simply evolved and it might not have. If the initial arrangement of things had been slightly different, or if the indeterministic course of the natural world had taken a slightly different turning in the remote past (on any of uncounted billions of occasions), the particular disease we call rabies would never have come into existence. (But other diseases might have. If the rabies virus had never evolved, the world's catalogue of diseases might have been a bit less horrible—or it might have been a bit more horrible.) Is there any reason a theist should want to deny this? Although *I* think that there is no explanation of the existence of evil—I don't deny that there is an explanation of the fact that God *permits* evil—I can see why a theist would want to say that there must be an explanation of the existence of evil. Although I think that there is no explanation of the fact that many people die in agony—I don't deny that there is an explanation of the fact that God *allows* people to die in agony—I can see why a theist would want to say that there must be an explanation of the fact that many people die in agony. Well, suppose there were explanations of these things. Suppose there were a good explanation of the fact that there is evil. Suppose there were a good explanation of the fact that some people die in agony. Why should the theist want or expect an explanation of the fact that one of the evils is the particular disease rabies, or of the fact that some of the agonizing deaths are due to that disease? By the same token, if there is an explanation of the fact that God *permits* the existence of evil and agonizing death (even if there is no explanation of the existence of these things), why should anyone want or expect an explanation of the fact that rabies is one of the evils or is one of the causes of the agonizing deaths that God permits? I think that this point is an important one, for theists are often challenged to produce an explanation—even a *possible* explanation—of the existence of this or that evil, or of God's permitting that evil to come to be or to continue. Any many theists, in their pride, construct fanciful explanations of particular evils as divine punishments. (Christians who explain particular evils—like the Bubonic Plague or the AIDS virus—as divine punishments are neglecting the story of the tower at Siloam and the story of the man born blind.) But there is no reason that the theist should believe that there are any such explanations. This point is even more important in connection with the misfortunes of individual persons, to which I now turn.

Let us consider again the case of Alice, who, by sheerest chance, turned into a certain street and was killed by a car whose brakes had failed. Let us borrow a term from the law and call her death an example of *death by misadventure*. Although I think that there is no explanation of the existence of death by misadventure—I don't deny that there is an explanation of the fact that God *permits* the existence of death by misadventure—I can see why a theist would want to say that there must be an explanation of the existence of death by misadventure. Well, suppose that there were an explanation of the fact that there are deaths by misadventure. Why should the theist want or expect an explanation of the fact that *Alice*, then and there, died by misadventure? By the same token, if there is an explanation of the fact that God *permits* the existence of death by misadventure, why should anyone want or expect an explanation of the fact that God permitted *Alice* to die by misadventure? Why should there be an answer to the question, "Why did *Alice* have to die that way?"? Suppose that the driver of the car had seriously considered having his brakes checked a few days ago, when he first noticed certain ominous symptoms, that he freely decided to put it off till he was less busy, and that, if his deliberations had gone the other way, Alice would now be alive and well. Suppose that God's relation to Alice and the driver and their circumstances was confined to sustaining certain elementary particles (such as those that composed Alice and the driver and the braking system in the latter's car) in existence and supplying those particles with their normal causal powers. God would, of course, have known that the accident was to occur and could have prevented it by a miracle—one unnoticed by any human being, if He wished. If it really is true that God has a general reason for permitting deaths by misadventure, need He have a particular reason for permitting *this* death by misadventure? Why?

It is clear that many theists think that He *must* have such a reason. Every now and then, in Billy Graham's newspaper column and similar places, one finds explanations—admittedly speculative—of how a particular death by misadventure (or robbery or rape or illness) might serve God's purposes. I am not, as some are, morally offended by these explanations, but I find them singularly unconvincing, even as speculations. I certainly do not want to deny that *sometimes* particular deaths by misadventure, and other misfortunes of individual persons, may be such that God has a special reason for allowing those very misfortunes. I do not want to deny that God sometimes miraculously intervenes in the course of nature—say, in answer to someone's prayer for a loved one's safety—to *prevent* such misfortunes. I do not wish to deny that God sometimes intervenes miraculously in the course of nature to *cause* individual misfortunes. I want to deny only that there is any reason to suppose that, for every individual misfortune, God has a reason for not preventing *that* misfortune. (The English word *misfortune* is rather a milk-and-water word. My use of it *faute de mieux* should not be allowed to obscure the fact that my thesis comprehends events like the sudden death of a young woman who, had she not *happened* to turn down a certain street, might well have lived a long, happy, and useful life. Some would use the word *tragedy* for such events, but, in my usage at least, the word 'tragedy' carries the inescapable implication that the event to which it applies is, above all, a *meaningful* event, the very implication I want to avoid.)

Why should a theist deny any of this? One reason might be a conviction that there could not be a *general* explanation of God's allowing deaths by misadventure unless there were, for each such event, an explanation of His allowing *it*. A conviction, that is, that a general explanation of God's allowing deaths by misadventure could only be the sum of the explanations of His allowing this one and that one and the other one. I see no reason to believe this. After all, most theists believe that there is a general explanation of God's allowing sin—as it may be, a refusal to interfere with the free choices of creatures—that is independent of such reasons as He may have for allowing this, that, or the other sin. If this belief is correct, then, even if God had *no* special reason for allowing Cain to murder Abel, *no* reason peculiar to that act, *no* reason beyond His general policy of not interfering with the free choices of His creatures, it would not follow that He had no general reason for allowing sin. By analogy we may speculate that even if God had *no* special reason for allowing Alice to be struck by a car, *no* reason peculiar to that event, *no* reason beyond His general policy of allowing deaths by misadventure (whatever exactly the reasons underlying that policy might be), it would not follow that He had no general reason for allowing deaths by misadventure.

Or a theist may feel that it is simply not *fair* to Alice that she should die young, and that this unfairness could be acceptable only if God had a special reason for allowing her premature death. (A complication arises here. Most theists believe in an afterlife, and thus may be inclined to say that, in theory at least, an early death is not necessarily a misfortune. But this complication is due to a feature of the example that is not essential to the problem; it would not have arisen if, instead of assuming that Alice died when struck by the car, we had assumed that she lived out her normal span, but crippled and in pain.) One might point out that, if God indeed does allow people to be subject to Fortune and her wheel, then He has given everyone the same chance. Suppose, moreover, that He has a good reason for allowing us to be (to some extent) at the mercy of Fortune. If Fortune's wheel is fair, how, then, can the losers say that they have been treated unfairly? If the twins Tom and Tim both wish to propose marriage to Jane, and they take this problem to their father, and he orders them (this is in the old days) to draw straws, and Tim loses, can he say that he was treated unfairly by his father because his father had no special reason for denying him the opportunity to propose to Jane? No, the situation demanded a lottery, and Tim has no complaint unless the lottery was unfair. It will probably occur to someone to protest that *life's* lottery is *not* fair and that everyone does *not* have the same chance. (For example, someone living in Beirut has a greater chance of sudden violent death than someone living in Zurich.) But whatever problem this fact may raise for the theist, it does not seem to have anything in particular to do with chance. It is simply a special case of whatever problem is raised for the theist by the fact that life's blessings are not distributed equally. People are not equal in wealth, intelligence, native strength of character, or physical constitution. No one supposes that these inequalities are always a matter of desert. (What could one do to deserve greater native strength of character than someone else?) It may be that there are good reasons, known to God, for these inequalities. But such good reasons would not make the inequalities *fair*—not unless the reasons in some way involved desert. The theist may say all sorts of things in response to this difficulty: that the potter may do as he likes with his clay, for example, or that we deserve little from God and that no one gets less than he deserves and that it is not unfair for some to get more than they deserve provided no one gets less. But whatever the theist says about inequalities in the distribution of, say, intelligence and strength of character, I don't see why he shouldn't say the same thing about inequalities in the distribution of (for example) the probability of sudden violent death. In a nutshell: If it is fair that we should all be subject to chance in some degree, then it would seem to be unfair that we should be subject to unequal chances only if unequal distribution of any sort of advantage or disadvantage is unfair. It might be good at this point to remember the words of the Preacher (Eccl. 9:11–12):

> I returned, and saw under the sun, that the race is not to the swift, nor the battle to the strong, neither yet bread to the wise, nor yet riches to men of understanding, nor yet favor to men of skill; but time and chance happeneth to them all.
> For man also knoweth not his time: as the fishes that are taken in an

evil net, and as the birds that are caught in the snare; so are the sons of men snared in an evil time, when it falleth suddenly upon them.

If what I have said is true, it yields a moral for students of the problem of evil: Do not attempt any solution to this problem that entails that every particular evil has a purpose, or that, with respect to every individual misfortune, or every devastating earthquake, or every disease, God has some special reason for allowing it. Concentrate rather on the problem of what sort of reasons a loving and providential God might have for allowing His creatures to live in a world in which many of the evils that happen to them happen to them for no reason at all.[12]

12. This essay owes a great deal to chap. 6, "The Ordainder of the Lottery," of P. T. Geach's *Providence and Evil* (Cambridge: Cambridge University Press, 1977). I doubt, however, whether Professor Geach would approve of everything I say. I do give "real assent to the doctrine that all events however trivial fall within the ordering of Providence" (p. 116); I do not, however, take that doctrine to entail that God has chosen the number of hairs on my head, or even that He chose Matthias over Joseph Justus to fill the vacant apostolate of Judas. As to the latter case, we have not been told anything about this; what we may presume is that God was content that Matthias should hold that office. I *think* that Geach believes something stronger than this. Proverbs 16:33, which Geach cites, refers (I believe) only to the rather special case of the sacred lots, and, in any event, "the way it falls out is from the Lord" is open to various interpretations.

This essay was read at a conference on the philosophy of religion at Cornell University in February 1987 and at a meeting of the Society of Christian Philosophers in Chicago in May 1987. On the latter occasion, the commentator was Alfred J. Freddoso, some of whose spirited animadversions I have addressed in notes 4 and 8. (Freddoso's essay in the volume in which this essay was originally published contains much that is relevant to note 4 and to other matters discussed herein.) I thank Norman Kretzmann, Eleonore Stump, Richard Swinburne, Lawrence H. Davis and, especially, William P. Alston for helpful criticisms.

An extremely interesting book (not yet published in the United States) has come into my hands too late to influence this essay: *God of Chance*, by D. J. Bartholomew (London: S.P.C.K., 1984). This book brings the expertise and perspective of a statistician to bear on the question of the relation of chance and God's action in the created world.

3

The Problem of Evil,
the Problem of Air,
and the Problem of Silence

IT used to be widely held that evil—which for present purposes we may identify with undeserved pain and suffering—was incompatible with the existence of God: that no possible world contained both God and evil. So far as I am able to tell, this thesis is no longer defended. But arguments for the following weaker thesis continue to be very popular: Evil (or at least evil of the amounts and kinds we actually observe) constitutes evidence against the existence of God, evidence that seems decisively to outweigh the totality of available evidence *for* the existence of God.

In this essay, I wish to discuss what seems to me to be the most powerful version of the "evidential argument from evil." The argument takes the following form. There is a serious hypothesis *h* that is inconsistent with theism and on which the amounts and kinds of suffering that the world contains are far more easily explained than they are on the hypothesis of theism. This fact constitutes a prima facie case for preferring *h* to theism. Examination shows that there is no known way of answering this case, and there is good reason to think that no way of answering it will be forthcoming. Therefore, the hypothesis *h* is (relative to the epistemic situation of someone who has followed the argument this far) preferable to theism. But if *p* and *q* are inconsistent and *p* is (relative to one's epistemic situation) epistemically preferable

First published in *Philosophical Perspectives,* Vol. *5: Philosophy of Religion 1991*, pp. 135–165.

to *q,* then it is not rational for one to accept *q.* (Of course, it does not follow either that it is rational for one to accept *p* or that it is rational for one to reject *q.*) It is, therefore, not rational for one who has followed the argument up to this point to accept theism.[1]

In Section I, I shall present the version of the evidential argument from evil I wish to discuss. In Section II, I shall explain why I find the argument unconvincing. These two sections could stand on their own, and this essay might have consisted simply of the proposed refutation of the evidential argument from evil that they contain. But many philosophers will find the proposed refutation implausible, owing to the fact that it turns on controversial theses about the epistemology of metaphysical possibility and intrinsic value. And perhaps there will also be philosophers who find my reasoning unconvincing because of a deep conviction that, since evil just *obviously* creates an insoluble evidential problem for the theist, a reply to any version of the evidential argument can be nothing more than a desperate attempt to render the obvious obscure. Now if philosophers are unconvinced by one's diagnosis of the faults of a certain argument, one can attempt to make the diagnosis seem more plausible to them by the following method. One can try to find a "parallel" argument that is obviously faulty, and try to show that a parallel diagnosis of the faults of the parallel argument can be given, a diagnosis that seems plausible, and hope that some of the plausibility of the parallel diagnosis will rub off on the original. For example, if philosophers find one's diagnosis of the faults of the ontological argument unconvincing, one can construct an obviously faulty argument that "runs parallel to" the ontological argument—in the classical case, an argument for the existence of a perfect island. And one can then attempt to show that a diagnosis parallel to one's diagnosis of the faults of the ontological argument is a correct diagnosis of the

---

1. My formulation of this argument owes a great deal to a recent article by Paul Draper ("Pain and Pleasure: An Evidential Problem for Theists," *Noûs* 23 [1989], 331–350). I do not, however, claim that the argument I shall present *is* Draper's intricate and subtle argument, or even a simplified version of it. (One important difference between the argument discussed in the present essay and Draper's argument is that the latter makes reference to the distribution of both pain and pleasure, while the former makes reference only to the distribution of pain.) Nevertheless, I hope that the version of the evidential argument from evil that I shall discuss is similar enough to Draper's that what I say about my version will at least suggest strategies that the theist can employ in dealing with Draper's argument. Draper (p. 332) credits Hume with being the first to ask the question whether there is "any serious hypothesis that is logically inconsistent with theism [and] explains some significant set of facts about evil . . . much better than theism does." (See *Dialogues Concerning Natural Religion,* Part XI.)

faults (which, one hopes, will be so evident as to be uncontroversial) of the parallel argument. It is worth noting that even if an application of this procedure did not convince one's audience of the correctness of one's diagnosis of the faults of the original argument, the parallel argument might by itself be enough to convince them that there must be *something* wrong with the original argument.

This is the plan I shall follow. In fact, I shall consider *two* arguments that run parallel to the evidential argument from evil. In Section III, I shall present an evidential argument, which I feign is addressed to an ancient Greek atomist by one of his contemporaries, for the conclusion that the observed properties of air render a belief in atoms irrational. In Section IV, I shall present an evidential argument for the conclusion that the observed fact of "cosmic silence" renders a belief in "extraterrestrial intelligence" irrational. Neither of these parallel arguments—at least this seems clear to me—succeeds in establishing its conclusion. In each case, I shall offer a diagnosis of the faults of the parallel argument that parallels my diagnosis of the faults of the evidential argument from evil.

Finally, in Section V, I shall make some remarks in aid of a proposed distinction between facts that raise *difficulties* for a theory and facts that constitute *evidence* against a theory.

I

Let 'S' stand for a proposition that describes in some detail the amount, kinds, and distribution of suffering—the suffering not only of human beings, but of all the sentient terrestrial creatures that there are or ever have been.[2] (We assume that the content of S is about what one would expect, given our own experience, the newspapers, history books, textbooks of natural history and paleontology, and so on. For example, we assume that the world was not created five minutes ago—or six

---

2. In Draper's argument, the role that corresponds to the role played by S in our argument is played by a proposition O that reports "both the observations one has made of humans and animals experiencing pain or pleasure and the testimony one has encountered concerning the observations others have made of sentient beings experiencing pain or pleasure" (p. 332). I find that the argument goes more easily if it is stated in terms of the probability (on various hypotheses) of the pattern of suffering that it is reasonable to believe the actual world exhibits, rather than in terms of the probability (on those hypotheses) of the observations and testimony on which our reasonable belief in that pattern rests. I do not think that this modification of Draper's strategy leaves me with an argument that is easier to refute than the argument that would have resulted if I had retained this feature of his strategy.

thousand years ago—"complete with memories of an unreal past," and we assume that Descartes was wrong and the cats really do feel pain.)

Let "theism" be the proposition that the universe was created by an omniscient, omnipotent, and morally perfect being.[3]

The core of the evidential argument from evil is the contention that there is a serious hypothesis, inconsistent with theism, on which S is more probable than S is on theism. (The probabilities that figure in this discussion are epistemic. Without making a serious attempt to clarify this notion, we may say this much: p has a higher epistemic probability on h than q does, just in the case that, given h, q is more *surprising* than p. And here 'surprising' must be understood as having an epistemic, rather than a merely psychological, sense. It is evident that the epistemic probability of a proposition is relative to the "epistemic background" or "epistemic situation" of an individual or a community: the epistemic probability of p on h need not be the same for two persons or for the same person at two times.)[4] That hypothesis is "the hypothesis of indifference" (HI):

> Neither the nature nor the condition of sentient beings on earth is the result of benevolent or malevolent actions performed by nonhuman persons.[5]

Here is a brief statement of the argument that is built round this core. We begin with an epistemic challenge to the theist, the presentation of a prima facie case against theism: The truth of S is not at all surprising, given HI, but the truth of S is very surprising, given theism. (For the following propositions, if they are not beyond all dispute, are at least highly plausible. Suffering is an intrinsic evil; A morally perfect being will see to it that, insofar as it is possible, intrinsic evils, if they are allowed to exist at all, are distributed according to desert; An omniscient and omnipotent being will be able so to arrange matters that the world contains sentient beings among whom suffering, if it exists at all, is apportioned according to desert; the pattern of suffering recorded in S is well explained—insofar as it can be explained: many instances of suffering are obviously due to chance—by the biological utility of pain, which is just what one would expect on HI, and has little if

3. Cf. Draper, p. 331. Perhaps we should add that this being has not ceased to exist, and has never ceased to be omniscient, omnipotent, or morally perfect.

4. Cf. Draper, pp. 333 and 349 (note 2). Some difficulties with the notion of epistemic probability are discussed in note 7 below.

5. Cf. Draper, p. 332.

anything to do with desert.) We have, therefore, a good prima facie reason to prefer HI to theism.

How shall the theist respond to this challenge? The "evidentialist" (as I shall call the proponent of the evidential argument from evil) maintains that any response must be of one of the following three types:

the theist may argue that S is much more surprising, given HI, than one might suppose

the theist may argue that S is much less surprising, given theism, than one might suppose

the theist may argue that there are reasons for preferring theism to HI that outweigh the prima facie reason for preferring HI to theism that we have provided.

The first of these options (the evidentialist continues) is unlikely to appeal to anyone. The third is also unappealing, at least if "reasons" is taken to mean "arguments for the existence of God" in the traditional or philosophy-of-religion-text sense. Whatever the individual merits or defects of those arguments, none of them but the "moral argument" (and perhaps the ontological argument) purports to prove the existence of a morally perfect being. And neither the moral argument nor the ontological argument has many defenders these days. None of the "theistic" arguments that are currently regarded as at all promising is, therefore, really an argument for *theism*.[6] And, therefore, none of them can supply a reason for preferring theism to HI.

The second option is that taken by philosophers who construct *theodicies*. A theodicy, let us say, is the conjunction of theism with some "auxiliary hypothesis" *h* that purports to explain how S could be true, given theism. Let us think for a moment in terms of the probability

---

6. It is a currently popular view that one can have reasons for believing in God that are of a quite different kind from "arguments for the existence of God." For a sampling of versions of this view, see the essays by the editors and the essay by William P. Alston in, *Faith and Rationality: Reason and Belief in God,* ed. Alvin Plantinga and Nicholas Wolterstorff (South Bend, Ind.: University of Notre Dame Press, 1983). My own position on this matter is that some version of this view is right, and that there are reasons for believing in God that are of the general kind described by Plantinga, Wolterstorff, and Alston. I believe, moreover, that these reasons not only can provide one with adequate justification for being a theist in the absence of a prima facie case against theism, but are strong enough to override any conceivable prima facie case against theism. (For a contrary view—which I believe rests on a misunderstanding—see Draper, pp. 347–348.) But I shall not defend this thesis here, since the point of the present essay is that the patterns of suffering that exist in the actual world do not constitute even a prima facie case against theism.

calculus. It is clear that if a theodicy is to be at all interesting, the probability of S on the conjunction of theism and h (that is, on the theodicy) will have to be high—or at least not too low. But whether a theodicy is interesting depends no only on the probability of S on the conjunction of theism and h, but also on the probability of h on theism. Note that the higher P(h/theism), the more closely P(S/theism) will approximate P(S/theism & h). On the other hand, if P(h/theism) is low, P(S/theism) could be low even if P(S/theism & h) were high. (Consider, for example, the case in which h is S itself: even if P(S/theism) is low, P(S/theism & S) will be 1—as high as a probability gets.) The task of the theodicist, therefore, may be represented as follows: find a hypothesis h such that P(S/theism & h) is high, or at least not too low, and P(h/theism) is high. In other words, the theodicist is to reason as follows. "Although S might initially seem surprising on the assumption of theism, this initial appearance, like many initial appearances, is misleading. For consider the hypothesis h. The truth of this hypothesis is just what one would expect given theism, and S is just what one would expect [would not be all that surprising] given both theism and h. Therefore, S is just what one would expect [would not be at all surprising] given theism. And, therefore, we do not have a prima facie reason to prefer HI to theism, and the evidential argument from evil fails."[7]

7. I prefer to formulate the evidential argument from evil in terms of epistemic surprise, rather than in terms of high and low epistemic probability. (Draper's essay suggested this use of the concept of "surprise" to me. Although his "official" formulation of his argument is in terms of epistemic probability, he frequently employs the notion of "surprise" in his informal commentary on the argument. Indeed, at one place—see p. 333—he comes very close to explaining epistemic probability as I did in the text: by equating 'has a lower epistemic probability' with 'is more surprising'.) Let me attempt to explain why I am uneasy about formulating the argument in terms of probabilities. If the argument is so formulated, it would appear to depend on the validity of the following inference-form: p; the probability of p on q is much higher than the probability of p on r; q and r are inconsistent; therefore, there exists a prima facie reason (viz., that p) for preferring q to r. The trouble with this inference-form is that the probability of p may be very low on q despite the fact that p is not at all *surprising* on q. For example, the probability of the hypothesis that the unobservable card that Alice is holding is the four of clubs is quite low on the hypothesis that she drew the card at random from a standard deck, but the former hypothesis is not at all surprising on the latter. Now let S be some true proposition that has a low probability on theism but is not at all surprising on theism. I should think that the proposition that states the exact number of dogs would do: in "most" possible worlds in which God exists, the number of dogs is not the actual number. It is clear that the following facts do not comprise a prima facie case for preferring 'S and God does not exist' to 'God exists': S; the probability of S on 'S and God does not exist' is much higher than the probability of S on 'God exists'; 'S and God does not exist' and 'God exists' are inconsistent.

These considerations show that the use of the language of high and low probabilities

But (the evidentialist concludes) the prospects of finding a theodicy that satisfies these conditions are not very promising. For any auxiliary hypothesis *h* that has actually been offered by the defenders of theism, it would seem that either no real case has been made for P(*h*/theism) being high, or else no real case has been made for P(S/theism & *h*) being high—or even not too low. Consider, for example, the celebrated Free Will Defense (FWD). Even if it is granted that P(FWD/theism) is high, there is every reason to think that P(S/theism & FWD) is low, since of all cases of suffering (a phenomenon that has existed for hundreds of millions of years), only a minuscule proportion involve, even in the most indirect way, beings with free will. And no one has the faintest idea of how to find a proposition that is probable on theism *and*, in conjunction with theism, renders S probable. Therefore, given the present state of the available evidence, our original judgment stands: we have a good prima facie reason to prefer HI to theism. And, as we have seen, we have no reason to prefer theism to HI that outweighs this prima facie reason. It is, therefore, irrational to accept theism in the present state of our knowledge.

II

It will be noted that the evidential argument consists not only of an argument for the conclusion that there is a prima facie case for preferring HI to theism, but also of a list of options open to the theist who wishes to reply to that argument: the defender of theism must either refute the argument or else make a case for preferring theism to HI that outweighs the prima facie case for preferring HI to theism; if the defender chooses to refute the argument, he must do this by producing a theodicy in the sense explained in Section I.

This list of options seems to me to be incomplete. Suppose that one were successfully to argue that S was not surprising on theism—and not because S was "just what one should expect" if theism were true, but because no one is in a position to know whether S is what one should expect if theism were true. (Suppose I have never seen, or heard a description of, Egyptian hieroglyphs, although I am familiar with Chinese characters and Babylonian cuneiform and many other exotic scripts. I am shown a sheet of paper reproducing an ancient Egyptian inscription, having been told that it displays a script used in ancient

in formulating the evidential argument from evil is a source of possible confusion. Since, however, my criticisms of the argument have nothing to do with this point, I shall continue to employ this language. But I shall employ it only as a stylistic device: anything I say in this language could easily be restated in terms of epistemic surprise.

Egypt. What I see cannot be described as "looking just the way one should expect a script used in ancient Egypt to look," but the fact that the script looks the way it does is not epistemically surprising on the hypothesis that it was a script used in ancient Egypt. I am simply not in a position to know whether *this* is the way one should expect a script that was used in ancient Egypt to look.)[8] If one could successfully argue that one simply could not know whether to expect patterns of suffering like those contained in the actual world in a world created by an omniscient, omnipotent, and morally perfect being, this would refute the evidentialist's case for the thesis that there is a prima facie reason for preferring HI to theism. If one is not in a position to assign any epistemic probability to S on theism—if one is not in a position even to assign a probability-range like 'high' or 'low' or 'middling' to S on theism—then, obviously, one is not in a position to say that the epistemic probability of S on HI is higher than the probability of S on theism.[9]

The evidentialist's statement of the way in which the defender of theism must conduct his defense is therefore overly restrictive: it is false that the defender must either make a case for theism or devise a theodicy. At any rate, another option exists as a formal possibility. But how might the defender of theism avail himself of this other option? Are there reasons for thinking that the assumption of theism yields no prima facie grounds for expecting a pattern of suffering different from that recorded by S?

I would suggest that it is the function of what have come to be called "defenses" to provide just such reasons. The word 'defense' was first employed as a technical term in discussions of the "logical" version of the argument from evil. In that context, a defense is a story according to which both God and suffering exist, and which is possible "in the

---

8. I can have *some* epistemically warranted expectations about how what I see displayed on the sheet of paper will look: it must in some sense "look like writing"—it can't be a detailed drawing of a cat or a series of a thousand identical marks. Similarly, I can have *some* epistemically warranted expectations about how suffering will be distributed if there is a God. I would suppose, for example, that it is highly improbable on theism that there be sentient creatures and that all of them be in excruciating pain at every moment of their existence.

9. Well, one might somehow know the probability of S on theism as a function of the probability of S on HI; one might know that the former probability was one-tenth the latter, and yet have no idea what either probability was. But that is not the present case. The evidentialist's argument essentially involves two independent probability-judgments: that the probability of S on HI is at least not too low and that the probability of S on theism is very low.

broadly logical sense"—or which is such that there is no reason to believe that it is impossible in the broadly logical sense. Let us adapt the notion of a defense to the requirements of a discussion of the evidential argument: a defense is a story according to which God and suffering of the sort contained in the actual world both exist, and which is such that (given the existence of God) there is no reason to think that it is false, a story that is not surprising on the hypothesis that God exists. A defense obviously need not be a theodicy in the evidentialist's sense, for the probability of a defense need not be high on theism.[10] (That is, a defense need not be such that its denial is surprising on theism.) In practice, of course, the probability of a defense will never be high on theism: if the defender of theism knew of a story which accounted for the sufferings of the actual world and which was highly probable on theism, he would employ it as a theodicy. We may therefore say that, in practice, a defense is a story which accounts for the sufferings of the actual world and which (given the existence of God) is true "for all anyone knows."

What does the defender of theism accomplish by constructing a defense? Well, it's like this. Suppose that Jane wishes to defend the character of Richard III, and that she must contend with evidence that has convinced many people that Richard murdered the two princes in the Tower. Suppose that she proceeds by telling a story—which she does not claim to be true, or even more probable than not—that accounts for the evidence that has come down to us, a story according to which Richard did not murder the princes. If my reaction to her story is, "For all I know, that's true. I shouldn't be at all surprised if that's how things happened," I shall be less willing to accept a negative evaluation of Richard's character than I might otherwise have been. (Note that Jane need not try to show that her story is highly probable on the hypothesis that Richard was of good character.) It would, moreover, strengthen Jane's case if she could produce not one story but many stories that "exonerated" Richard—stories that which were not trivial variants on one another but which were different in important ways.

---

10. Indeed, in *one* sense of probability, the probability of a defense may be very low on theism. We have said that a defense may not be *surprising* on theism, but, as we saw in note 7, there is a perfectly good sense of probability in which a proposition that is not at all surprising on theism may nevertheless be very improbable on theism. If the defender of theism had at his disposal a very large number of defenses, all of them inconsistent with the others and none of them epistemically preferable to any of the others, it is hard to see why he should not conclude that (relative to his epistemic situation) the probability of any given one of them was very low on theism.

This analogy suggests that one course that is open to the defender of theism is to construct stories which are true for all anyone knows—given that there is a God—and which entail both S and the existence of God. If the defender can do that, this accomplishment will undermine the evidentialist's case for the proposition that the probability of S is lower on theism than on HI. Of course, these stories will (presumably) be *false* for all anyone knows, so they will not, or should not, create any tendency to believe that the probability of S on theism is *not* lower than it is on HI, that it is about the same or higher. Rather, the stories will, or should, lead a person in our epistemic situation to refuse to make any judgment about the relation between the probabilities of S on theism and on HI.

I shall presently offer such a story. But I propose to simplify my task in a way that I hope is legitimate. It seems to me that the theist should not assume that there is a single reason, or tightly interrelated set of reasons, for the sufferings of all sentient creatures. In particular, the theist should not assume that God's reasons for decreeing, or allowing, the sufferings of nonrational creatures have much in common with His reasons for decreeing or allowing the sufferings of human beings. The most satisfactory "defenses" that have so far been offered by theists purport to account only for the sufferings of human beings. In the sequel, I will offer a defense that is directed toward the sufferings of nonrational creatures—"beasts," I shall call them. If this defense were a success, it could be combined with defenses directed toward the sufferings of human beings (like the Free Will Defense) to produce a "total" defense. This "separation of cases" does not seem to me to be an arbitrary procedure. Human beings are radically different from all other animals, and a "total" defense that explained the sufferings of beasts in one way and the sufferings of human beings in a radically different way would not be implausible on that account. Although it is not strictly to our purpose, I will point out that this is consonant with the most usual Christian view of suffering. Typically, Christians have held that human suffering is not a part of God's plan for the world, but exists only because that plan has gone awry. On the other hand:

Thou makest darkness that it may be night; wherein all the beasts of the forest do move.
The lions, roaring after their prey, do seek their meat from God.
The sun ariseth, and they get them away together, and lay them down in their dens. (Ps. 104:20–22)

This and many other biblical texts seem to imply that the whole subrational natural world proceeds according to God's plan (except insofar as we human beings have corrupted nature). And this, as the Psalmist tells us in his great hymn of praise to the order that God has established in nature, includes the phenomenon of predation.

I will now tell a story, a story that is true for all I know, that accounts for the sufferings of beasts. The story consists of the following three propositions:

(1) Every possible world that contains higher-level sentient creatures either contains patterns of suffering morally equivalent to those recorded by S, or else is massively irregular.

(2) Some important intrinsic or extrinsic good depends on the existence of higher-level sentient creatures; this good is of sufficient magnitude that it outweighs the patterns of suffering recorded by S.

(3) Being massively irregular is a defect in a world, a defect at least as great as the defect of containing patterns of suffering morally equivalent to those recorded by S.

The four key terms contained in this story may be explained as follows.

Higher-level sentient creatures are animals that are *conscious* in the way in which (*pace* Descartes) the higher nonhuman mammals are conscious.

Two patterns of suffering are *morally equivalent* if there are no morally decisive reasons for preferring one to the other: if there are no morally decisive reasons for creating a world that embodies one pattern rather than the other. To say that A and B are in this sense morally equivalent is not to say that they are in any interesting sense comparable. Suppose, for example, that the Benthamite dream of a universal hedonic calculus is an illusion, and that there is no answer to the question whether the suffering caused by war is less than, the same as, or greater than the suffering caused by cancer. It does not follow that these two patterns of suffering are not morally equivalent. On the contrary: unless there is some "nonhedonic" morally relevant distinction to be made between a world that contains war and no cancer and a world that contains cancer and no war (i.e., a distinction that does not depend on comparing the amounts of suffering caused by war and cancer), it would seem to follow that the suffering caused by war and the suffering caused by cancer *are*, in the present technical sense, morally equivalent.

It is important to note that A and B may be morally equivalent even if they are comparable and one of them involves *less* suffering than the other. By way of analogy, consider the fact that there is no morally decisive reason to prefer a jail term of ten years as a penalty for armed assault to a term of ten years and a day, despite the indubitable facts that these two penalties would have the same deterrent effect and that one is lighter than the other. I have argued elsewhere that, for any amount of suffering that somehow serves God's purposes, it may be that some smaller amount of suffering would have served them as well.[11] It may be, therefore, that God has had to choose *some* amount of suffering as the amount contained in the actual world, and could, consistently with His purposes, have chosen any of a vast array of smaller or greater amounts, and that all of the members of this vast array of alternative amounts of suffering are morally equivalent. (Similarly, a legislature has to choose *some* penalty as the penalty for armed assault, and—think of penalties as jail terms measured in minutes—must choose among the members of a vast array of morally equivalent

---

11. "The Magnitude, Duration, and Distribution of Evil: A Theodicy" (Essay 4 in this volume). See especially pp. 103–104. Failure to appreciate this consideration is a weak point in many versions of the evidential argument from evil. Consider, for example, William L. Rowe's much-discussed article, "The Problem of Evil and Some Varieties of Atheism" (*American Philosophical Quarterly 16* [1979], 335–341. In this article, Rowe employs the following premise:

> An omniscient, wholly good being would prevent the occurrence of any intense suffering it could, unless it could not do so without losing some greater good or permitting some evil equally bad or worse.

If there are alternative, morally equivalent amounts of (intense) suffering, then this premise is false. To make this point more concrete, let us consider Rowe's famous case of a fawn that dies in prolonged agony of burns that it suffers in a forest fire caused by lightning. God, I concede, could have miraculously prevented the fire, or miraculously saved the fawn, or miraculously caused its agony to be cut short by death. And, I will concede for the sake of argument, if He had done so, this would have thwarted no significant good and permitted no significant evil. But what of the hundreds of millions (at least) of similar incidents that have, no doubt, occurred during the long history of life? Well, I concede, He could have prevented any one of them, or any two of them, or any three of them . . . without thwarting any significant good or permitting any significant evil. But could he have prevented all of them? No—not without causing the world to be massively irregular. And, of course, there is no sharp cutoff point between a world that is massively irregular and a world that is not—just as there is no sharp cutoff point between a penalty that is an effective deterrent for armed assault and a penalty that is not. There is, therefore, no *minimum* number of cases of intense suffering that God could allow without forfeiting the good of a world that is not massively irregular—just as there is no shortest sentence that a legislature can establish as the penalty for armed assault without forfeiting the good of effective deterrence.

penalties.) Or it may be that God has decreed, with respect to this vast array of alternative, morally equivalent amounts of suffering, that *some* member of this array shall be the actual amount of suffering, but has left it up to chance which member that is.[12]

A *massively irregular world* is a world in which the laws of nature fail in some massive way. A world containing all of the miracles recorded in the New Testament would not, on that account, be massively irregular, for those miracles were too small (if size is measured in terms of the amounts of matter directly affected) and too few and far between. But a world would be massively irregular if it contained the following state of affairs:

> God, by means of a continuous series of ubiquitous miracles, causes a planet inhabited by the same animal life as the actual earth to be a hedonic utopia. On this planet, fawns are (like Shadrach, Meshach, and Abednego) saved by angels when they are in danger of being burnt alive. Harmful parasites and microorganisms suffer immediate supernatural dissolution if they enter a higher animal's body. Lambs are miraculously hidden from lions, and the lions are compensated for the resulting restriction on their diets by physically impossible falls of high-protein manna. On this planet, either God created every species by a separate miracle, or else, although all living things evolved from a common ancestor, a hedonic utopia has existed at every stage of the evolutionary process. (The latter alternative implies that God has, by means of a vast and intricately coordinated sequence of supernatural adjustments to the machinery of nature, guided the evolutionary process in such a way as to compensate for the fact that a hedonic utopia exerts no selection pressure.)

It would also be possible for a world to be massively irregular in a more systematic or "wholesale" way. A world that came into existence five minutes ago, complete with memories of an unreal past, would be on that account alone massively irregular—if indeed such a world was metaphysically possible. A world in which beasts (beasts having the physical structure and exhibiting the pain-behavior of actual beasts) felt no pain would be on that account alone massively irregular—if indeed such a world was metaphysically possible.

A *defect in a world* is a feature of a world that (whatever its extrinsic value might be in various worlds) a world is intrinsically better for not having.

---

12. See "The Place of Chance in a World Sustained by God" (Essay 2 in this volume).

Our story comprises propositions (1), (2), and (3). I believe that we have no reason to assign any probability or range of probabilities to this story. (With the following possible exception: if we have a reason to regard the existence of God as improbable, then we shall have a reason to regard the story as improbable.)

We should have reason to reject this story if we had reason to believe that there were possible worlds—worlds that were not massively irregular—in which higher-level sentient creatures inhabited a hedonic utopia. Is there any reason to think that there are such worlds? I suppose that the only kind of reason one could have for believing that there was a possible world having a certain feature would be the reason provided by a plausible attempt to "design" a world having that feature. How does one go about designing a world?

One should start by describing in some detail the laws of nature that govern the world. (Physicists' actual formulations of quantum field theories and the general theory of relativity provide the standard of required "detail.") One should then go on to describe the boundary conditions under which those laws operate: the topology of the world's space-time, its relativistic mass, the number of particle families, and so on. Then one should tell in convincing detail the story of cosmic evolution in that world: the story of the development of large objects like galaxies and stars and of small objects like carbon atoms. Finally, one should tell the story of the evolution of life. These stories, of course, must be coherent, given one's specification of laws and boundary conditions. Unless one proceeds in this manner, one's statements about what is intrinsically or metaphysically possible—and thus one's statements about an omnipotent being's "options" in creating a world—will be entirely subjective, and therefore without value. But I have argued for this view of the epistemology of modal statements (that is, of modal statements concerning major departures from actuality) elsewhere, and the reader is referred to those arguments. In fact, the argument of those essays should be considered a part of the argument of the present essay.[13]

Our own universe provides the only model we have for the formidable task of designing a world. (For all we know, in every possible world that exhibits any degree of complexity, the laws of nature are the actual laws, or at least have the same structure as the actual laws.

---

13. "Ontological Arguments" (Essay 1 in this volume). Review of *The Coherence of Theism* by Richard Swinburne, *Philosophical Review* 87 (1979), 668–672 (the relevant passages of this review are quoted in the introduction to this section of the volume, pp. 19–21). See also George Seddon, "Logical Possibility," *Mind* 81 (1972), 481–494.

There are, in fact, philosophically minded physicists who believe that there is only one possible set of laws of nature, and it is epistemically possible that they are right.) Our universe apparently evolved out of an initial singularity in accordance with certain laws of nature.[14] This evolution is not without its mysteries: the very early stages of the unfolding of the universe (the incredibly brief instant during which the laws of nature operated under conditions of perfect symmetry), the formation of the galaxies, and the origin of life on the earth are, in the present state of natural knowledge, deep mysteries. Nevertheless, it seems reasonable to assume that all of these processes involved only the nonmiraculous operation of the laws of nature. One important thing that is known about the evolution of the universe into its present state is that it has been a very tightly structured process. A large number of physical parameters have apparently arbitrary values such that if those values had been only slightly different (very, *very* slightly different) the universe would contain no life, and a fortiori no intelligent life.[15] It may or may not be the "purpose" of the cosmos to constitute an arena in which the evolution of intelligent life takes place, but it is certainly true that this evolution did take place, and that if the universe had been different by an all unimaginably minute degree it wouldn't have. My purpose in citing this fact—it is reasonable to believe that it is a fact—is not to produce an up-to-date version of the design argument. It is, rather, to suggest that (at least, for all we know) only in a universe very much like ours could intelligent life, or even sentient life, develop by the nonmiraculous operation of the laws of nature. And the

14. These laws, being quantum mechanical, are indeterministic. God could not, therefore, have "fine-tuned" the initial state of a universe like ours so as to render an eventual universal hedonic utopia causally inevitable. It would seem to be almost certain that, owing to quantum mechanical indeterminacy, a universe that was a duplicate of ours when ours was, say, 10^{-45} seconds old could have evolved into a very different universe from our present universe. (There is also the point to be considered that there probably *was* no initial state of the universe.) Would it be possible for an omniscient and omnipotent being to create a universe that evolved deterministically out of a carefully selected initial state into a hedonic utopia? This question raises many further questions, questions that mostly cannot be answered. Nevertheless, the following facts would seem to be relevant to an attempt to answer it: life depends on chemistry, and chemistry depends on atoms, and atoms depend on quantum mechanics (classically speaking, an atom cannot exist: the electrons of a "classical" atom would spiral inward, shedding their potential energy in the form of electromagnetic radiation, till they collided with the nucleus), and quantum mechanics is essentially indeterministic.

15. This fact has been widely remarked on. See, e.g., John Leslie, "Modern Cosmology and the Creation of Life" in *Evolution and Creation,* ed. Ernan McMullin, (South Bend, Ind.: University of Notre Dame Press, 1985), pp. 91–120.

natural evolution of higher sentient life in a universe like ours essentially involves suffering, or there is every reason to believe it does. The mechanisms underlying biological evolution may be just what most biologists seem to suppose—the production of new genes by random mutation and the culling of gene pools by environmental selection pressure—or they may be more subtle. But no one, I believe, would take seriously the idea that conscious animals, animals conscious as a dog is conscious, could evolve naturally without hundreds of millions of years of ancestral suffering. Pain is an indispensable component of the evolutionary process after organisms have reached a certain stage of complexity. And, for all we know, the amount of pain that organisms have experienced in the actual world, or some amount morally equivalent to that amount, is necessary for the natural evolution of conscious animals. I conclude that the first part of our defense is true for all we know: Every possible world that contains higher-level sentient creatures either contains patterns of suffering morally equivalent to those recorded by S, or else is massively irregular.

Let us now consider the second part of our defense: Some important intrinsic or extrinsic good depends on the existence of higher-level sentient creatures; this good is of sufficient magnitude that it outweighs the patterns of suffering recorded by S. It is not very hard to believe (is it?) that a world that was as the earth was just before the appearance of human beings would contain a much larger amount of intrinsic good, and would, in fact, contain a better balance of good over evil, than a world in which there were no organisms higher than worms. (Which is not to say that there could not be worlds lacking intelligent life that contained a still better balance of good over evil—say, worlds containing the same organisms, but significantly less suffering.) And then there is the question of extrinsic value. One consideration immediately suggests itself: intelligent life—creatures made in the image and likeness of God—could not evolve directly from worms or oysters; the immediate evolutionary predecessors of intelligent animals must possess higher-level sentience.

We now turn to the third part of our defense: Being massively irregular is a defect in a world, a defect at least as great as the defect of containing patterns of suffering morally equivalent to those recorded by S. We should recall that a defense is not a theodicy, and that we are not required to argue at this point that it is *plausible to suppose* that massive irregularity is a defect in a world, a defect so grave that creating a world containing animal suffering morally equivalent to the animal suffering of the actual world is a reasonable price to pay to avoid it. We are required to argue only that *for all we know* this judgment is correct.

The third part of our defense is objectionable only if we have some prima facie reason for believing that the actual sufferings of beasts are a graver defect in a world than massive irregularity would be. Have we any such reason? It seems to me that we do not. To begin with, it does seem that massive irregularity is a defect in a world. One minor point in favor of this thesis is the witness of deists and other thinkers who have deprecated the miraculous on the ground that *any* degree of irregularity in a world is a defect, a sort of unlovely jury-rigging of things that is altogether unworthy of the power and wisdom of God. Presumably such thinkers would regard *massive* irregularity as a very grave defect indeed. And perhaps there is something to this reaction. It does seem that there is something right about the idea that God would include no more irregularity than was necessary in His creation. A second point is that many, if not all, massively irregular worlds are not only massively irregular but massively *deceptive*. This is obviously true of a world which looks like the actual world but which began five minutes ago, or a world which looks like the actual world but in which beasts feel no pain. (And this is not surprising, for our beliefs about the world depend in large measure on our habit of drawing conclusions that are based on the assumption that the world is regular.) But it is plausible to suppose that deception, and, a fortiori, massive deception, is inconsistent with the nature of a perfect being. These points, however, are no more than suggestive, and, even if they amounted to proof, they would prove only that massive irregularity was a defect; they would not prove that it was a defect in any way comparable to the actual suffering of beasts. In any case, proof is not the present question: the question is whether there is a prima facie case for the thesis that the actual sufferings of beasts constitute a graver defect in a world than does massive irregularity.

What would such a case be based on? I would suppose that someone who maintained that there was such a case would have to rely on his moral intuitions, or, more generally, on his intuitions of value. He would have to say something like this: "I have held the two states of affairs—the actual sufferings of beasts and massive irregularity—before my mind and carefully compared them. My considered judgment is that the former is worse than the latter." This judgment presupposes that these two states of affairs are, in the sense that was explained above, comparable: one of them is worse than the other, or else they are of the same value (or disvalue). It is not clear to me that there is any reason to suppose that this is so. If it is *not* so, then, as we have seen, it can plausibly be maintained that the two states of affairs are morally equivalent, and a Creator could not be faulted on moral grounds for choosing either over the other. But let us suppose that the two states of affairs are comparable. In that case, if the value-judgment we are considering is to be trusted, then human beings possess a faculty that enables them correctly to judge the relative values of states of affairs of literally cosmic magnitude, states of affairs, moreover, that are in no way (as some states of affairs of cosmic magnitude may be) connected with the practical concerns of human beings. Why should one suppose that one's inclinations to make judgments of value are reliable in this area? One's intuitions about value are either a gift from God or a product of evolution or socially inculcated or stem from some combination of these sources. Why should we suppose that any of these sources would provide us with the means to make correct value-judgments in matters that have nothing to do with the practical concerns of everyday life? (I do think we must be able to speak of *correct* value-judgments if the problem of evil is to be of any interest. An eminent philosopher of biology has said in one place that God, if He existed, would be indescribably wicked for having created a world like this one, and, in another place, that morality is an illusion, an illusion that we are subject to because of the evolutionary advantage it confers. These two theses do not seem to me to add up to a coherent position.) Earlier I advocated a form of modal skepticism: our modal intuitions, while they are no doubt to be trusted when they tell us that the table could have been placed on the other side of the room, are not to be trusted on such matters as whether there could be transparent iron or whether there could be a "regular" universe in which there were higher sentient creatures that did not suffer. And if this true, it is not surprising. Assuming that there are "modal facts of the matter," why should we assume that God or evolution or social training has given us access to modal facts knowledge of which is of no interest to anyone but the metaphysician? God or evolution has provided us with a capacity for making judgments about size and distance which is very useful in hunting mammoths and driving cars, but which is no use at all in astronomy. It seems that an analogous restriction applies to our capacity for making modal judgments. How can we be sure that an analogous restriction does not also apply to our capacity for making *value*-judgments? My position is that we cannot be sure, and that for all we know our inclinations to make value-judgments are not veridical when they are applied to cosmic matters unrelated to the concerns of everyday life. (Not that our inclinations in this area are at all uniform. I myself experience no inclination to come down on one side or the other of the question whether massive irregularity or vast amounts of animal suffering is the graver defect in a world. I suspect that others do experience such inclinations. If they don't, of course, then I'm preaching to the converted.) But then there is no prima facie case for the thesis that the actual sufferings of beasts constitute a graver defect in a world than does massive irregularity. Or, at least, there is no case that is grounded in our intuitions about value. And in what else could such a case be grounded?

These considerations have to do with intrinsic value, with comparison of the intrinsic disvalue of two states of affairs. There is also the matter of extrinsic value. Who can say what the effects of creating a massively irregular world might be? What things of intrinsic value might be frustrated or rendered impossible in a massively irregular world? We cannot say. Christians have generally held that at a certain point God plans to hand over the government of the world to humanity. Would a massively irregular world be the sort of world that could be "handed over"? Perhaps a massively irregular world would immediately dissolve into chaos if an infinite being were not constantly making adjustments to it. We simply cannot say. If anyone insists that he has good reason to believe that nothing of any great value depends on the world's being regular, we must ask him why he thinks he is in a position to know things of that sort. We might remind him of the counsel of epistemic humility that was spoken to Job out of the whirlwind:

> Gird up now thy loins like a man; for I will demand of thee, and answer thou me.
> Where wast thou when I laid the foundations of the earth? Declare if thou hast understanding.
> Knowest thou it, because thou wast then born, or because the number of thy days is great?
> Canst thou bind the sweet influences of Pleiades, or loose the bands of Orion?
> Knowest thou the ordinances of heaven? Canst thou set the dominion thereof in the earth?[16]

I have urged extreme modal and moral skepticism (or, one might say, humility) in matters unrelated to the concerns of everyday life. If

16. This is not properly speaking a quotation; it is, rather, a selection of verses from chapter 38 of the book of Job. It comprises verses 3, 4, 21, 31, and 33.

such skepticism is accepted, then we have no reason to accept the evidentialist's premise that "an omniscient and omnipotent being will be able so to arrange matters that the world contains sentient beings among whom suffering, if it exists at all, is apportioned according to desert." More exactly, we have no reason to suppose that an omniscient and omnipotent being could do this without creating a massively irregular world; and, for all we know, the intrinsic or extrinsic disvalue of a massively irregular world is greater than the intrinsic disvalue of vast amounts of animal suffering (which, presumably, are not apportioned according to desert). If these consequences of modal and moral skepticism are accepted, then there is no reason to believe that the probability of S on HI is higher than the probability of S on theism, and the evidential argument from evil cannot get started. Even if we assume that the probability of S on HI is high (that the denial of S is very surprising on HI), this assumption gives us no reason to prefer HI to theism. If there were such a reason, it could be presented as an argument:

The probability of S on HI is high

We do not know what to say about the probability of S on theism

HI and theism are inconsistent

Therefore, for anyone in our epistemic situation, the truth of S constitutes a prima facie case for preferring HI to theism.

This argument is far from compelling. If there is any doubt about this, it can be dispelled by considering a parallel argument. Let L be the proposition that intelligent life exists, and let G be the proposition that God wants intelligent life to exist. We argue as follows:

The probability of L on G is high

We do not know what to say about the probability of L on atheism

G and atheism are inconsistent

Therefore, for anyone in our epistemic situation, the truth of L constitutes a prima facie case for preferring G to atheism.

The premises of this argument are true. (As to the second premise, there has been considerable debate in the scientific community as to whether the natural evolution of intelligent life is inevitable or extremely unlikely or something in between; let us suppose that "we" are a group of people who have tried to follow this debate and have been hopelessly confused by it.) But I should be very surprised to learn of someone who believed that the premises of the argument entailed its conclusion.

I will close this section by pointing out something that is not strictly relevant to the argument it contains, but is, in my view, of more than merely autobiographical interest. I have not accepted the extreme modal skepticism that figures so prominently in the argument of this section as a result of epistemic pressures exerted by the evidential argument from evil. I was an extreme modal skeptic before I was a theist, and I have, on the basis of this skepticism, argued (and would still argue) against both Swinburne's attempt to show that the concept of God is coherent and Plantinga's attempt to use the modal version of the ontological argument to show that theism is rational.[17]

III

Imagine an ancient Greek, an atomist who believes that the whole world is made of tiny, indestructible, immutable solids. Imagine that an opponent of atomism (call him Aristotle) presents our atomist with the following argument: "If fire were made of tiny solids, the same solids earth is made of, or ones that differ from them only in shape, then fire would not be Absolutely Light—it would not rise toward the heavens of its own nature. But that fire is not Absolutely Light is contrary to observation."[18] From our lofty twentieth-century vantage point, we might be inclined to regard Aristotle's argument as merely quaint. But this impression of quaintness rests on two features of the argument that can be removed without damage to what is, from one point of view anyway, its essential force. The two quaint features of Aristotle's argument, the idea that fire is a stuff and the idea of the Absolutely Light, can be removed from the argument by substituting air for fire and by substituting the behavior we nowadays associate with the gaseous state for the defining behavior of the Absolutely Light (that is, a natural tendency to move upward). The resulting argument would look something like this:

> Suppose air were made of tiny solid bodies as you say. Then air would behave like fine dust: it would eventually settle to the ground and become a mere dusty coating on the surface of the earth. But this is contrary to observation.

17. See the essay and review cited in note 13.
18. Cf. *De Cælo IV*, especially 309ª 18–310ª 13.

Well, what is wrong with this argument? Why *don't* the O_2, N_2, CO_2, and other molecules that make up the atmosphere simply settle to the ground like dust particles? The answer is that air molecules, unlike dust particles, push on one another; they are kept at average distances that are large in comparison with their own sizes by repulsive forces (electromagnetic in nature), the strength of these forces in a given region being a function of the local temperature. At the temperatures one finds near the surface of the earth (temperatures maintained by solar radiation and the internal heat of the earth), the aggregate action of these intermolecular forces produces the kind of aggregate molecular behavior that, at the macroscopic level of description, we call the gaseous state.

We can see where the improved version of Aristotle's argument goes wrong. (We can also see that in one minor respect it's better than an ancient Greek could know: if it weren't for intermolecular forces, air molecules would not simply settle slowly to the ground; they would drop like rocks.) But what about our imaginary ancient atomist, who not only doesn't know all these things about intermolecular forces and temperature and so on, but who couldn't even conceive of them as epistemic possibilities? What shall he say in response to the improved version of Aristotle's argument?

In order to sharpen this question, let us imagine that a Greek philosopher called A-prime has actually presented our atomist with the air-and-dust argument, and let us imagine that A-prime has at his disposal the techniques of a late-twentieth-century analytical philosopher. Having presented the atomist with the simple argument that I have given above (the primitive or "whence, then, is air?" version of the argument from air), he presses his point by confronting the atomist with a much more sophisticated argument, the *evidential* argument from air. "Let HI, the Hypothesis of Independence, be the thesis that there are four independent and continuous elements, air among them, each of which has sui generis properties (you can find a list of them in any reputable physics text) that determine its characteristic behavior. Let S be a proposition that records the properties of air. The simple air-and-dust argument is sufficient to establish that S is not surprising given HI, but is very surprising given atomism. There are only three ways for you to respond to this prima facie case against atomism: you may argue that S is much more surprising, given HI, than one might suppose; or that S is much less surprising, given atomism, than one might suppose; or that there are reasons for preferring atomism to HI that outweigh the prima facie reason for preferring HI to atomism that is provided by the air-and-dust argument. The first I shall not discuss. The third is unpromising, unless you can come up with something better than the very abstract metaphysical arguments with which you have attempted to support atomism in the past, for they certainly do not outweigh the clear and concrete air-and-dust argument. The only course open to you is to construct an *atomodicy*. That is, you must find some auxiliary hypothesis *h* that explains how S could be true, given atomism. And you will have to show both that the probability of S is high (or at least not too low) on the conjunction of atomism and *h* and that the probability of *h* on atomism is high. While you may be able to find a hypothesis that satisfies the former condition, I think it very unlikely that you will be able to find one that satisfies the latter. In any case, unless you *can* find a hypothesis that satisfies both conditions, you cannot rationally continue to be an atomist."

Whatever else may be said about this argument, A-prime is certainly right about one thing: it is unlikely that the atomist will be able to produce a successful atomodicy. Even if he were told the modern story about air, he could not do it. At least, I don't think he could. What is the epistemic probability on atomism (relative to the epistemic situation of an ancient Greek) of our complicated modern story of intermolecular forces and the gaseous state? What probability should someone who knew nothing about the micro-structure of the material world except that it was composed of atoms (it is, of course, our "elementary particles" and not our "atoms" or our "molecules" that correspond to the atoms of the Greeks) assign to the modern story? As far as I am able to judge, the only rational thing such a person could do would be to decline to assign any probability to the modern story on atomism. (The answer of modern science to the air-and-dust argument does not take the form of a story that, relative to the epistemic situation of an ancient Greek, is highly probable on atomism.)

Fortunately for the atomist, A-prime's demand that he produce an atomodicy is unreasonable. The atomist need do nothing more in response to the evidential argument from air than find a defense—or, better, several independent defenses. A defense, of course, is a story that explains how there could be a stuff that has the properties of air (those known to an ancient Greek), given that the material world is made entirely of atoms. A defense need *not* be highly probable on atomism. It is required only that, given atomism, the defense be true for all anyone (sc. any ancient Greek) knows.

Here is one example of a defense: air atoms (unlike earth atoms) are spheres covered with a "fur" of long, thin, flexible spikes that are, unless flexed by contact with another atom, perpendicular to the surface of the atom's "nucleus" (i.e., its central sphere); the length of the spikes is large in comparison with the diameters of nuclei, and their presence thus tends to keep nuclei far apart. Since, for all anyone (anyone in the epistemic situation of an ancient Greek) knows, some atoms have such features—if there are atoms at all—the observed properties of air are not surprising on the assumption of atomism. Since there are defenses that are true for all anyone (anyone in the epistemic situation of an ancient Greek) knows, no ancient Greek was in a position to say anything about the probability on atomism of S, the proposition that sums up the properties of air that were known to him. A-prime, therefore, is left with no better argument than the following:

The probability of S on HI is high

We do not know what to say about the probability of S on atomism

HI and atomism are inconsistent

Therefore, for anyone in our epistemic situation, the truth of S constitutes a prima facie case for preferring HI to atomism.

And this argument is manifestly invalid.

IV

We know how it is that air can be composed of molecules and yet not drift to the ground like dust. This knowledge provides us with a certain rather Olympian perspective from which to view the "Problem of Air." I wish next to examine the epistemic situation of those of our contemporaries who believe that the Milky Way galaxy (ours) contains other intelligent species than humanity. (Since they are our contemporaries, we cannot view their situation from any such Olympian perspective.) Let us confront them with an argument analogous to the argument from evil and the argument from air. The essence of this argument is contained in a question of Enrico Fermi's, a question as pithy as 'Whence, then, is evil?': Where are they?

If there are other intelligent species in the galaxy, the overwhelming probability is that at least one intelligent species existed at least a hundred million years ago. There has been life on the earth for at least thirty times that long, and there is nothing magical about the present time. The universe was just as suitable for intelligent life a hundred million years ago, and if the pace of evolution on the earth had been just three or four percent faster, there would have been intelligent life *here* a hundred million years ago. An intelligent and technologically able species will attempt to send messages to other species elsewhere in the galaxy (as we have begun to do). The most efficient way to do this is to send out self-reproducing robotic probes to other stars: when such a probe reaches another star, it makes two or more duplicates of itself out of local materials, and these duplicates proceed to further stars. Then it waits, perhaps for hundreds of millions of years, till it detects locally produced radio signals, at which point it reveals itself and delivers its message. (There are no fundamental technological barriers to this program. At our present rate of scientific progress, we shall be able to set such a process in motion within the next century.) It is not hard to show that the descendants of the original probes will reach every star in the galaxy within fifty million years. (We assume that the probes are capable of reaching one-tenth the speed of light.) But no such probe has revealed itself to us. Therefore, any nonhuman intelligence in the galaxy came into existence less than fifty million years ago. But it is statistically very unlikely that there are nonhuman intelligences *all* of which came into existence within the last fifty million years. (The reasoning is like this: if you know that such people as there are in the Sahara Desert are distributed randomly, and if you know that there are no people in the Sahara except, possibly, within a circular area one hundred miles in diameter that is hidden from you, you can conclude that there are probably no people at all in the Sahara.) Furthermore, it is not merely the absence of robotic probes that should disturb the proponent of "extraterrestrial intelligence." There are also the absence of radio signals from thousands of nearby stars and several of the nearer galaxies[19] and the absence of manifestations of "hyper-technology" like the wide-angle infrared source that would signal the presence of a star that has been surrounded with a "Dyson sphere." We may refer collectively to all of these "absences" as *cosmic silence*, or simply *silence*. (If there are other intelligent species in the galaxy, or

19. This latter fact is very important in the debate about extraterrestrial intelligence. If someone in our galaxy aimed a powerful signal at, say, the Andromeda galaxy, then, two million years later, anyone in the Andromeda galaxy who aimed a sensitive receiver precisely at our galaxy would detect that signal. When we aim a sensitive receiver precisely at the Andromeda galaxy, however, we detect no signal. Therefore, no one on any planet circling any of the hundred billion or more stars in the Andromeda galaxy was aiming a signal at the Milky Way galaxy two million years ago. (This argument actually depends on the false assumption that all of the stars in the Andromeda galaxy are equally distant from us, but the essential point of the argument is sound.)

even in the nearby galaxies, they are *species absconditae*.) The obvious implication of these observations is that we are alone.[20]

Let us call the thesis that there is intelligent life elsewhere in the galaxy *noetism*. The above argument, the argument from cosmic silence, provides materials from which the antinoetist may construct an evidential argument against noetism analogous to the evidential argument from evil: "Let the Hypothesis of Isolation (HI) be the hypothesis that humanity is the only intelligent species that exists or has ever existed in the Milky Way galaxy or any of the nearby galaxies. Let S be a proposition that records all of the observations that constitute a failure to discover any manifestation whatever of life, and, a fortiori, of intelligent life, elsewhere in the universe. The argument from cosmic silence is sufficient to establish that the truth of S (which, of course, is not at all surprising given HI) is very surprising, given noetism. There are only three ways for you to respond to the argument from cosmic silence: you may argue that S is much more surprising, given HI, than one might suppose; or that S is much less surprising, given noetism, than one might suppose; or that there are reasons for preferring noetism to HI that outweigh the prima facie reason for preferring HI to noetism that is provided by the argument from cosmic silence. The first is no more than a formal possibility. The third is unpromising, unless you can come up with something better than those facile arguments for the prevalence of life in the cosmos that are so popular with astronomers and physicists and so exasperating to evolutionary biologists.[21] The only course open to you is to construct a *noödicy*. That is, you must find some auxiliary hypothesis *h* that explains how S could be true, given noetism. And you will have to show both that the probability of S is high (or at least not too low) on the conjunction of noetism and *h* and that the probability of *h* on noetism is high. While you may be able to find a hypothesis that satisfies the former condition, I think it very unlikely that you will be able to find one that satisfies the latter. In any case, unless you *can* find a hypothesis that satisfies both conditions, you cannot rationally continue to be a noetist."

The antinoetist is no doubt right in supposing that it is very unlikely that the noetist will be able to construct a successful noödicy. One

20. For an excellent popular article on the search for extraterrestrial intelligence, see Gregg Easterbrook, "Are We Alone?" *The Atlantic*, August 1988, pp. 25–38.

21. See, for example, Ernst Mayr, "The Probability of Extraterrestrial Intelligent Life," in *Philosophy of Biology*, ed. Michael Ruse (New York: MacMillan, 1989), pp. 279–285.

example should suffice to make the point. Consider the elegantly simple, if rather depressing, Nuclear Destruction Scenario: intelligent species do not last long enough to make much of a mark on the cosmos; within at most a few decades of developing radio transmitters powerful enough to be detected across a distance of light-years (and long before they can make self-reproducing intersidereal robotic probes), they invariably destroy themselves in nuclear wars. It is clear that the Nuclear Destruction Scenario is a failure as a noödicy, for it is not highly probable on noetism. (That intelligent species invariably destroy themselves in nuclear wars is not highly probable on the hypothesis that intelligent species exist.) The proponents of extraterrestrial intelligence have provided a wide range of possible explanations of "cosmic silence" (intelligence does not necessarily imply technology; the desire to communicate with other intelligent species is a human idiosyncrasy; the most efficient means of intersidereal signaling, the one that all the extraterrestrials actually employ, is one we haven't yet thought of), but it is clear that none of these possible explanations should be regarded as *highly probable* on noetism. We simply do not know enough to make any such probability judgment. Shall the noetist therefore concede that we have shown his position to be irrational? No, for the antinoetist's demand that the noetist produce a noödicy is wholly unreasonable. The noetist need only produce one or more *defenses,* one or more explanations of the phenomenon of cosmic silence that entail noetism and are true for all we know. And this is just what the noetist has done. (I have already mentioned several of them.) Since there are defenses that for all anyone knows are true, no one knows what to say about the probability on noetism of S (the proposition that records all of our failed attempts to discover any manifestation of intelligent life elsewhere in the universe). The antinoetist has therefore failed to show that the truth of S constitutes a prima facie case in favor of preferring HI to noetism.

V

"This is all very well. But evil *is* a difficulty for the theist, and the gaseous state *was* a difficulty for the ancient atomist, and cosmic silence *is* a difficulty for the noetist. You seem to be saying that they can just ignore these difficulties."

Not at all. I have said that these difficulties (I accept the term 'difficulty') do not render their beliefs irrational—not even if they are unable to find arguments that raise the probabilities of their hypotheses relative to the probabilities of competing hypotheses that do not face the same difficulties, and are also unable to devise auxiliary hypotheses that enable them to construct "-dicies." It doesn't follow that they should simply ignore the difficulties.

"Well, what *should* they do?"

To begin with, they can acknowledge the difficulties. They can admit that the difficulties exist and that they're not sure what to say about them. They might go on to offer some speculations about the causes of the phenomena that raise the difficulties: mechanisms that would account for the gaseous state, possible conditions that would interfere with communications across light-years, reasons God might have for allowing evil. Such speculations need not be (they almost certainly will not be) highly probable on the "-ism" in whose defense they are employed. And they need not be probable on anything that is known to be true, although they should not be improbable on anything that is known to be true. They are to be offered as explanations of the difficult phenomena that are, *for all anyone knows,* the correct ones. In sum, the way to deal with such difficulties is to construct defenses.

"But if a phenomenon is a 'difficulty' for a certain theory, does that not mean that it is evidence against that theory? Or if it is not evidence against that theory, in what sense can it raise a 'difficulty' for the theory? Are you not saying that it can be right to accept a theory to which there is counterevidence when there are competing theories to which there is no counterevidence?"

That sounds good, but it is really a recipe for rejecting just about any interesting theory. Just about any interesting theory is faced with phenomena that make the advocates of the theory a bit uncomfortable, this discomfort being signaled by the tendency to speculate about circumstances consistent with the theory that might produce the phenomena. For any theory that faces such a difficulty, there will always be available another "theory," or at least another hypothesis, that does not face that difficulty: its denial. (The denial of an interesting theory will rarely if ever itself be an interesting theory; it will be too general and nonspecific.) Your suggestion would therefore appear to constrain us never to accept any interesting theory, but always either to accept its denial or else neither the theory nor its denial. The latter will be the more common result, since the denial of a theory can usually be partitioned into interesting theories that face individual difficulties. (For example, the denial of atomism can be partitioned into the following hypotheses: matter is continuous; matter is neither continuous nor atomically structured; matter does not exist. Each of these hypotheses faces difficulties.) This result might be avoided if you placed some sort of restriction on what counted as a "competing theory," but it is not clear what sort of restriction would be required. It will not do simply to rule out the denial of a theory as a competing theory, for contraries of the theory that were very general and nonspecific could produce equally counterintuitive results. If, moreover, you did produce a satisfactory solution to this problem, it is not clear what consequences your solution might have for the evidential argument from evil. Consider, for example, the Hypothesis of Indifference. This is not a very specific thesis: it tells us only that the nature and condition of sentient beings on earth do *not* have a certain (very narrowly delineated) cause. Perhaps it would not count as a proper "competitor" with the quite specific thesis we have called 'theism'. Perhaps it would be a consequence of your solution that only some proposition more specific than HI, some proposition that entailed but was not entailed by HI, could properly be in competition with theism. And this proposition might face difficulties of its own, difficulties not faced by HI.

But we may answer your question more directly and simply. A difficulty with a theory does not necessarily constitute evidence against it. To show that an acknowledged difficulty with a theory is not evidence against it, it suffices to construct a defense that accounts for the facts that raise the difficulty. (This thesis by no means provides an automatic "out" for a theory that is confronted with some recalcitrant observation, for a defense is not automatically available to the proponents of every theory that is confronted with a recalcitrant observation. A defense may not be improbable, either on the theory in whose cause it is employed or on anything we know to be true. In a particular case, it may be that no one can think of any hypothesis that satisfies these two conditions, and what was a mere difficulty for a theory will thereby attain to the status of evidence against the theory. It is perhaps worth pointing out that two or more difficulties may jointly constitute evidence against a theory, even if none of them taken individually counts as evidence against it. This could be the case if the defenses that individually "handle" the difficulties are inconsistent, or if—despite the fact that none of the defenses taken individually is improbable—their conjunction is improbable.)

The central thesis of this essay may be usefully summarized in the terminology that has been introduced in the present section: While the patterns of suffering we find in the actual world constitute a *difficulty* for theism and do not constitute a difficulty for the competing hypothesis HI, they do not—owing to the availability of the defense[22] I have

22. Are there other defenses—other defenses that cover the same ground as the defense I have presented in Section II? I should like to think so, although I have not had

outlined—attain to the status of *evidence* that favors HI over theism. It follows that the evidential argument from evil fails, for it is essential to the evidential argument that those patterns of suffering be evidence that favors HI over theism.[23]

---

any very interesting ideas about how additional defenses might be constructed. I should welcome suggestions.

23. This essay was read at Brandeis University. The author wishes to thank the members of the Brandeis Philosophy Department, and especially Eli Hirsch, for their helpful comments and criticisms.

4

The Magnitude, Duration, and Distribution of Evil: A Theodicy

In his work on the problem of evil, Alvin Plantinga has made a useful distinction between "giving a theodicy" and "giving a defense." To give a theodicy is to "answer in some detail the question 'What is the source of the evil we find, and why does God permit it?'"[1] To give a defense is to construct a story according to which both God and evil exist and to attempt to show that this story is "possible in the broadly logical sense."[2] The purpose of giving a theodicy is "to justify the ways of God to men." The purpose of giving a defense is, in the first instance, to show that the coexistence of God and evil is possible. (In the first instance. But one might have further projects in mind—such as the project of showing that the existence of God is not improbable on some body of evidence that includes a description of the amounts and kinds of evil that actually exist.)

Plantinga is rather down on theodicies. I have heard him say that to give a theodicy is "presumptuous." I propose, nevertheless, to offer a theodicy. I propose to explain God's ways—or at least to offer a partial and speculative explanation of those ways. I am sufficiently sensitive

First published in *Philosophical Topics* 16, no. 2 (1988), 161–187.

1. The characterization is Plantinga's. See his "Self-Profile," in *Alvin Plantinga*, ed. James E. Tomberlin and Peter van Inwagen (Dordrecht: D. Reidel, 1985), p. 42.

2. The characterization is mine. The phrase "possible in the broadly logical sense," however, is Plantinga's. See, e.g., *The Nature of Necessity* (Oxford: Clarendon Press, 1974), p. 2.

to the merits of Plantinga's charge of presumption, however, to wish to say something in response to it. I will make three points.

(1) I do not claim that the theodicy I shall offer is *comprehensive*. That is, while I shall ascribe to God certain reasons for allowing evil to exist, I do not claim to give *all* of His reasons, or even to claim that the reasons I shall give are His most important reasons. For all I know, God has reasons for allowing evil to exist that no human being could understand; perhaps, indeed, He has hundreds of perfectly good reasons that no *possible* creature could understand. What I claim for the theodicy presented in this essay is this: it alleges a reason, or an interconnected set of reasons, that God has for allowing evil—of the amounts and kinds we observe—to come to be and to continue; if these were the only reasons God had for permitting evil, they would by themselves justify this permission.

(2) The theodicy I shall present is not in any large part my own invention. I do not claim to be the first human being in history to have fathomed God's purposes. Nor do I claim to be the recipient of a special revelation from God: I do not claim to be a prophet whom God has charged with the task of disseminating an explanation of His ways. The method of this essay is simply philosophical reflection on the data of Christian revelation—or, more exactly, on what one tradition holds (in my view, correctly) to be the data of Christian revelation. (Those who do not share my allegiance to these data may wish to regard this essay as providing one more defense, in Plantinga's sense.)

(3) Insofar as anything in this essay is original, it is speculative. I do not claim that what is unique to this essay has any authority over those who accept the data of Christian revelation referred to above. But I claim more for these speculations than that they are "possible in the broadly logical sense." I offer them as consonant with and a plausible elaboration of the data of Christian revelation. (This, by the way, could not be claimed for them if they contained any element that was improbable on the known facts of science and history. I therefore explicitly claim that no proposition contained in the theodicy presented in this essay is improbable on the whole set of propositions endorsed by the special sciences.) One might object that someone who offers a theodicy in such a tentative fashion as this is not really "giving a theodicy" in Plantinga's sense. To "give a theodicy," one might argue, is to represent oneself as *knowing* that every proposition one puts forward is true.

Perhaps there is some justice in this protest. If so, however, there is certainly *room* for the kind of thing I propose to do. There seems to be no reason to require that everyone who tells a story about God and evil must either claim to know this story to be true or else claim only that it is possible in the broadly logical sense. And I think that if one does put forward an admittedly speculative but (or so one believes) plausible account of God's reasons for allowing the existence of evil, one is not abusing language if one describes one's offering as a theodicy.

These three points, it seems to me, are sufficient to disarm the charge of presumption.

I

It is generally, but not universally, conceded by Christians that the existence of evil has something to do with free will. The theodicy I shall present is of the "free will" type. That is to say, it proceeds by extending and elaborating the following story:

> God made the world and it was very good. An important part of its goodness was that it contained creatures made in His own image—that is, created beings capable of understanding (to some degree) their own nature and their place in the scheme of things entire; creatures, moreover, that were fit to be loved by God and to love Him in return and to love one another. But love implies freedom: for *A* to love *B* is for *A* freely to choose to be united to *B* in a certain way.[3] Now even an omnipotent being cannot *ensure* that some other being *freely* choose *x* over *y*. For God to create beings capable of loving Him, therefore, it was necessary for Him to take a risk: to risk the possibility that the beings He created would freely choose to withhold their love from Him.
>
> To love God and to desire to submit to His will are very closely related—at least as closely as the love of one's offspring and the desire to nurture and protect and raise them. God's free creatures—or some of

---

3. At any rate this is true for certain sorts of love (I concede that the word 'love' may sometimes refer to a mere feeling), and it is love of these sorts that is meant. Anyone who is doubtful that there are kinds of love that have this feature should meditate on Ruth 1:16–17 and the Anglican wedding vow:

And Ruth said, Entreat me not to leave thee, or to return from following after thee, for whither thou goest, I will go; and where thou lodgest, I will lodge: thy people shall be my people and thy God my God: Where thou diest, will I die, and there will I be buried.

I M. take thee N. to my wedded wife, to have and to hold from this day forward, for better for worse, for richer for poorer, in sickness and in health, to love and to cherish, till death us do part, according to God's holy ordinance; and thereto I plight thee my troth.

them—instead of loving Him and submitting to His will, chose to turn away from Him and "to follow instead the devices and desires of their own hearts." It was thus that evil entered the world. A husband and father who turns away from his wife and children and suppresses his natural desire to live with and to love and protect them, and chooses instead to indulge a desire for fame or sexual adventure or "self-realization," turns himself into something unnatural and harmful. Likewise, a creature who turns away from God turns himself into something unnatural and harmful. Having turned away from God, His creatures laid violent hands on the created world. They snatched it out of His grasp and turned it to their own purposes. We are now living with the catastrophic consequences of that act.

This is the beginning of our theodicy. At its heart is what is a familiar "move" in discussions of the problem of evil, the insistence that even an omnipotent being cannot ensure that someone *freely* do one thing rather than some contemplated alternative. Some philosophers have said that the proposition

> An omnipotent being cannot ensure that a creature who has a free choice between x and y choose x rather than y

is false—and, of course, necessarily false, for, owing to its modal character, this proposition is necessarily false if it is false at all. The issues raised by this contention have been extensively debated, and I have nothing new to say about them. I shall simply assume that this proposition is true.

I proceed now to elaborate the above very sketchy narrative of the origin of evil. It is obvious that this must be done. As it stands, the narrative accounts for the existence of only, as we might say, "some evil or other." It says nothing about evil of the kinds or in the amounts we actually observe, or anything about its duration—thousands upon thousands of years—or anything about the fact that its worst effects are distributed apparently at random and certainly without regard for desert. I shall elaborate this narrative with certain propositions drawn from Christian theology. All Christian theologians who could lay any claim to the titles "orthodox," "Catholic," or "traditional" would accept the following theses:

> *All* evil is the result of the primordial act of turning away from God; there is no source of evil other than creaturely rebellion.

> The creatures who committed the initial act of rebellion received sufficient warning that their act would lead to disaster. While they may have been

unlike us in many ways, they were not children and were at least as intelligent as we; they fully understood the warning and the wisdom and authority of its Source.

Among the creatures who rebelled were an entire generation of human beings, all of the human beings who were alive at some particular moment. [In my view, it was the *first* generation of human beings. But I shall not build this into our theodicy because (a) it is not necessary, and (b) to argue that the proposition that there *was* a first generation of human beings is compatible with what we know about our evolutionary history would require a lengthy digression. The digression would involve the removal of two sorts of misunderstanding: misunderstandings about what it would be for there to be a first generation of human beings, and misunderstandings about what scientific study of the evolutionary history of our species has actually shown.] Before this rebellion, there was no evil—or at any rate none that affected human beings.[4]

In turning away from God, our ancestors ruined themselves; they became unable to turn back to Him of their own power, as someone who ignores a warning not to go too near the edge of a pit may fall into it, injure himself, and be unable to climb out. Thus, the act of rebellion, or its immediate consequences, may be called "the Fall."

Their ruin was in some way inherited by all of their descendants. [This does not necessarily mean that their genes were altered by the Fall. I believe that it is possible to construct models of the Fall according to which its hereditary aspect is due to the effects of unaltered genes operating under conditions for which they were not "designed"—namely, conditions attendant upon separation from God. But I will not argue for

---

4. To allay the possible curiosity of some readers, I will mention that I regard the story of Adam and Eve in Genesis as a myth, in the sense that, in my view, it is not a story that has come down to us via a long historical chain of tellings and retellings that originated with the testimony of participants in the events it describes. In my view, the rebellion of creatures against God happened far too long ago for any historical memory of it to have survived to the present day. (There are not even any surviving stories of the last glaciation, and the rebellion of our species was certainly before that.) I believe, however, that the development of this myth in the ancient Middle East and its eventual literary embodiment in Genesis took place under the guidance of the Holy Spirit; and I believe that, within certain limits, Genesis can be used as a guide to what actually happened. The key to observing these limits is to concentrate on the spiritually relevant features of the story, and to remember that the Bible is addressed equally to the people of all epochs and cultures and that a story of those remote events that satisfied modern standards of historical accuracy would probably have to involve concepts and facts that would render it inaccessible to the people of most epochs and cultures.

this here.] Thus, evil is a persisting and—by any natural means—unalterable fact of history.[5]

God has not left His creatures to their misery—not, at any rate, His human creatures. He has inaugurated a plan whose workings will one day eventuate in the Atonement (at-one-ment) of His human creatures with Himself. (Or, at least, the Atonement of some of His human creatures with Himself. It may be that some of His creatures will, by their own free choice, resist Atonement forever.) In order to achieve Atonement with God, a ruined creature must turn to God and ask for His help and accept that help. The undoing of creaturely ruin must be a cooperative endeavor. The creature cannot accomplish it for himself, and even an omnipotent being cannot effect the required sort of regeneration of a creature if the creature refuses to be regenerated. Any aspect of the creatures' environment that would tend to discourage them from turning to Him and asking for His help would therefore be an obstacle to the completion of His plan.[6]

Every human being has an eternal future (and, therefore, the human species has an eternal future). We are now living, and have been living, throughout the archaeologically accessible past, within a temporary

5. This is not a popular view among theologians just at present. The following passage by the late Lord Ramsey is typical: "The acceptance by Christian teachers of . . . the findings of evolutionary biology . . . [has] radically altered . . . the doctrine of the creation and fall of man. . . . [T]here is a radical reappraisal of the fall of man, so radical that the use of the word 'fall' is questionable. No longer is it thought that mankind's first parents lapsed from a state of innocence bringing pain and death as a punishment" (Michael Ramsey, *Jesus and the Living Past* [Oxford: Oxford University Press, 1980], pp. 20–21). If these words were simply a description of the reaction of nerveless academic theologians, carried about with every wind of doctrine, to what they believe to be the findings of evolutionary biology, they would, unfortunately, be unobjectionable. But what they are in fact are a statement of the way theologians *ought* to react to the findings of evolutionary biology. To this statement I can only say (borrowing from Russell) that I should not believe such a thing if it were told to me by the Archbishops of Canterbury *and* York. What one does not find in the writings of theologians like Lord Ramsey is a clear statement of what they take the "findings of evolutionary biology" to be, and an argument to show that acceptance of these "findings" requires a radical alteration of the doctrine of the Fall. But my strong feelings on this matter should not be allowed to give the impression that I think that the theodicy I present in this essay could not possibly be modified to accommodate a "radically revised doctrine of the fall." I leave that an open question, one to be investigated when it becomes clear that there is some reason to attempt such a revision.
6. These words are consistent with the heretical doctrine called semi-Pelagianism (i.e., the doctrine that the ruin of those creatures who separated themselves from God was not so complete as to deprive them of the power of turning to Him and asking for His help), but they by no means entail it.

aberration in human history, an aberration that is a finite part of an eternal whole. When God's plan of Atonement comes to fruition, there will never again be undeserved suffering or any other sort of evil. The "age of evil" will eventually be remembered as a sort of transient "flicker" at the very beginning of human history.

I have said that I have drawn these points from Christian theology. But I have stated them so abstractly that, I think, at least some Jews and Muslims would agree with most of them. (The major point of disagreement would probably be over my inclusion among them of the doctrine of Original Sin; that is, the doctrine of hereditary ruin.) Now the body of Christian theology deals with what we may call—from our present vantage point of lofty abstraction—the *details* of (what Christians believe to be) God's plan of Atonement. But in the present essay I shall hardly mention such matters as God's calling of Israel to be His people, the giving of the Law, the Incarnation, the ministry of Jesus, the institution of the Eucharist, the Crucifixion, the Resurrection, the Ascension, the Descent of the Holy Spirit, or the one, holy, Catholic, and Apostolic Church. It will be enough for my purposes to include in my theodicy the proposition that God has *some* plan of Atonement and that it will someday succeed in reuniting to Him all who choose to be reunited.

I added the above flesh to the skeleton provided by the standard "free-will" account of the origin of evil because it was clear that that skeleton was no theodicy. The skeleton, however, will require more flesh than this. We have still not got a finished theodicy. If we claimed that we had, a skeptic might, quite properly, respond along the following lines.

"God, you say, has set in motion a plan of Atonement. But why is it taking so long for His plan to work out? It's all very well to tell a tale that represents 'the age of evil' as a 'transient flicker at the very beginning of human history.' But every finite period is a mere flicker in Eternity. Nothing has been said to challenge the obvious proposition that God would not allow 'the age of evil' to go on any longer than necessary. Why, then, is 'this long' necessary?

"And why is there so *much* evil at any given time? Evil may be, as you say, the result of the creaturely abuse of free will. But the amount of evil could have been far less. For example, God, without in any way diminishing Cain's free will, could have warned Abel not to turn his back on him. If the implied general policy had been put into effect, a vast amount of evil would have been avoided.

"And why does God allow evil to be so unfairly distributed? Why is it so often the innocent—small children, for example—who suffer? Why is it so often the wicked who prosper?

"And what about 'physical' or 'natural' evil? How can the effects of the Bubonic Plague or the Lisbon earthquake be a result of creaturely free will?

"To roll all of these questions into one, Why has it been for thousands and thousands of years that enormous numbers of uncomprehending children have died as a result of epidemic disease and famine and natural disaster—while many a tyrant has died in bed? How could evil of such types and quantity and duration and distribution be necessary to God's plan of Atonement? Or, if all this evil is *not* necessary to God's plan, why does He not eliminate most of it and make do with that residue of evil that is really necessary?"

II

I will continue to flesh out our skeletal theodicy by attending to the questions posed by our imaginary skeptic. I will address the last of them first.

The question presupposes that if there are evils that are not required by God's plan of Atonement, then there is such a thing as "that residue of evil that is really necessary," the minimum of evil that is required for God's plan to succeed. But this is not a very plausible thesis. It is not very plausible to suppose that there is a way in which evil could be distributed such that (i) that distribution of evil would serve God's purposes as well as any distribution could and (ii) God's purposes would be less well served by *any* distribution involving less evil. (One might as well suppose that if God's purposes require an impressively tall prophet to appear at a certain place and time, there is a minimum height such a prophet could have.) But if there is no minimum of evil that would serve God's purposes, then one cannot argue that God is unjust or cruel for not "getting by with less evil"—any more than one can argue that a law that fines motorists $25.00 for illegal parking is unjust or cruel owing to the fact that a fine of $24.99 would have an identical deterrent effect. The same point can be made in relation to time. If there is a purpose that is served by allowing "the age of evil" to have a certain duration, doubtless the same purpose would be served if the age of evil were cut short by a day or a year or even a century. But we would not call a judge unjust or cruel for imposing on a criminal a sentence of ten years on the ground—doubtless *true*—that a sentence of ten years less a day would have served as well whatever end the sentence was designed to serve. It is obvious that if, for any amount of evil that would have served God's purposes, slightly less evil would have served His purposes just as well—a very plausible assumption—then the principle that God should have got by with less evil, if less would have served, entails the (*ex hypothesi* false) conclusion that God should have got by with no evil at all. It may be a difficult problem in philosophical logic correctly to diagnose the defect in illegitimate sorites arguments, but it is certainly evident that such a defect exists.

The important things to recognize about these two points are, first, that they are valid and that to ignore them is to court confusion, and, secondly, that, valid though they be, they do not really meet the essence of the difficulty perceived by the skeptic, the difficulty that prompts him to ask, Why so much? Why so long? To revert to our legal and judicial analogy, there may be no minimum appropriate fine for illegal parking, but (most of us would agree) if a fine of $25.00 would serve whatever purposes a fine for illegal parking is supposed to serve—deterrence, presumably—then it would be wrong to set the fine at five thousand dollars. Similarly, if an "age of evil" of twenty years' duration, an age during which there were a few dozen broken bones and a score or so of very bad cases of influenza, would have served God's ends as well as the actual evil of human history serves them, then the enormity of His achieving these same ends by allowing the existence of "actual evil" passes all possibility of adequate description.

What the theodicist must do, given the facts of history, is to say what contribution—what essential contribution—to God's plan of Atonement is made by the facts about the types, magnitude, duration, and distribution of evil that are made known to us by historians and journalists (not to mention our own experience).

It will be useful to divide this problem facing the theodicist—and why not call it simply the problem of evil?—into several subproblems. One division of the problem of evil is well known: the division of the problem into "the problem of moral evil" and "the problem of natural evil." A second division, one that will be particularly useful in our project of fleshing out our skeletal theodicy so as to meet the questions of the imaginary skeptic, cuts across the first. It divides the problem into three:

the problem of the magnitude of evil

the problem of the duration of evil

the problem of the distribution of evil.

III

I assume that we already have an adequate answer to the problem of moral evil. I am not much interested in treating the problem of natural evil; my main interest in the present essay is the subproblems generated by the second division. I shall, accordingly, treat the problem of natural evil in a rather perfunctory way. I shall suggest the broadest outlines of a solution and leave the details for another time—or another writer. (But some of the things said in the course of our later discussion of the distribution problem will have some relevance to questions about the role in God's plan of natural evil.)

Natural evil is often cited as a special problem for those who say that evil entered the world through the creaturely abuse of free will, since tornadoes and earthquakes are obviously not caused by the acts— free or unfree—of human beings. The evil that results from tornadoes and earthquakes must nevertheless be treated in any theodicy of the "free will" type as somehow stemming from creaturely free will. One notorious way of doing this is to postulate that tornadoes and earthquakes are caused by malevolent nonhuman creatures. Another way (the way I shall take) proceeds from the observation that it is not earthquakes and tornadoes per se that are evil, but rather the suffering and death that they cause. Consider the following tale.

"Earthquakes all occur in one particular region called Earthquake Country, a region that was uninhabited (because everyone knew about the earthquakes and had no reason to go there) until twenty years ago. At that time, gold was discovered on the borders of Earthquake Country and the geological indications were that there was much more inside. Motivated solely by a desire to get rich, many people—people by no means in want—moved to Earthquake Country to prospect for gold. Many took their families with them. Some of them got rich, but many of them were killed or maimed by earthquakes."

This tale may not be true, but it demonstrates that earthquakes need not be caused by the actions of creatures for the suffering and death caused by earthquakes to be a result of the actions of those creatures.

Our theodicy, as we have so far stated it, entails that at one time— before the Fall—our ancestors lived in a world without evil. This, I suppose, entails that they were not subject to the baleful effects of earthquakes and tornadoes. But why not? Well, for the purposes of a *perfunctory* treatment of the problem of natural evil, we need assume only that there was *some* reason for this, a reason that became inoperative when our ancestors separated themselves from God. We *might* suppose, for example, that the old tradition (it is without biblical warrant) that Adam and Eve possessed "preternatural powers" is substantially correct, and that these powers included certain cognitive powers; we might suppose that our unfallen ancestors knew (and pretty far in advance) whether an earthquake or tornado would strike a particular spot—and when. And we might suppose that their being able to know such things depended on their union with God and was lost as a natural consequence of their separating themselves from God. We must remember that, according to Christianity, human beings were designed for union with God, in the same sense as that in which they are designed to live in community with one another and to use language. A "feral child" is a ruined human being—though he is no less our brother than is Homer or Leonardo—and his ruin entails a grave diminution of his cognitive powers. According to Christianity, we have all been ruined by our separation from God, just as the feral child has been ruined by his separation from the human community. (The feral child's ruin is thus a ruin within a ruin, a second, individual ruin of an already ruined common human nature.) And the ruin of human nature consequent on our separation from God may have involved a grave diminution of our cognitive powers. According to the "just-so story" I am telling,[7] we were designed by God to be able to protect ourselves from earthquakes and tornadoes—if you think that it would be possible to design a planet, and a universe to contain it, that was both capable of supporting human life and contained no earthquakes or tornadoes, I can only point out that you have never tried[8]—and that the loss of this power is as natural a consequence of our ancestors' separation from God as is the loss of the capacity to acquire language a natural consequence of the feral child's separation from the human community. (Expansion of this just-so story to cover tigers and droughts and epidemic disease and so on is left as an exercise for the reader.) Doubtless we could tell many tales of speculative theological fiction having the feature that our being subject to the destructive forces of nature is ultimately a consequence of the creaturely abuse of free will. For our purposes, as I have said, it will suffice to assume that one of the tales that fits this abstract description is true.

This is all I have to say about natural evil, but I wish to remind the

7. I have borrowed this use of "just-so story" from Daniel Dennett. (See his *Elbow Room: The Varieties of Free Will Worth Wanting* [M.I.T. Press: Cambridge, 1980], p. 38.) Dennett's just-so stories are tales told to illustrate possibility, tales told against a background that may be described as the standard model of evolution. My just-so story is of a similar sort, but the "background" is provided by what I have described as "the data of Christian revelation."

8. Before you try, you should read "Logical Possibility" by George Seddon (*Mind* [1972], 481–494). See also my discussion of possibility and consistency in "Ontological Arguments" (Essay 1 in this volume), pp. 31–35 in particular, and my review of Richard Swinburne's *The Coherence of Theism*, quoted in the introduction to this section.

reader that if all human beings were wise and good, our sufferings would be vastly less than they are; and it is probably not true that we should be much better off for a complete elimination of natural evil. Doubtless there would be human beings more than willing to take up the slack. Our ancestral ruin is *primarily* a moral, as opposed to a cognitive, ruin. But ruins we are. If two explorers—who have never seen such a thing—come upon a ruined temple in the jungle, and if one of them thinks that it is a natural geological formation and the other that it is a building that is just as it was designed to be, neither will understand its shape. From the Christian point of view, it is impossible for one to understand humanity if one thinks of a human being as either a product of natural forces behind which there is no Mind or as the work that a Mind intended to produce. Both naturalism and deism (Christianity holds) go wrong about our nature right at the outset, and neither can yield an understanding of that nature.

We thus have some basis for understanding both "moral" and "natural" evil. (In a sense, the theodicy I am proposing entails that there is no fundamental distinction between them: natural evil is a special category of moral evil.) That is, we have a basis for understanding why God would allow such things to come to be. (This is a very abstract statement. Remember, we have not yet said anything about the magnitude, duration, or distribution of either sort of evil.) We may, to sum up, add the following statement to our theodicy.

Our unfallen ancestors were somehow able to protect themselves from earthquakes and tornadoes and wild beasts and disease and so on. This ability depended on their union with God, and was lost when they separated themselves from Him.

I now turn to my primary interests in offering a theodicy: The magnitude, duration, and distribution of evil.

IV

"Our ancestors turned away from God and ruined themselves both morally and intellectually—and thus they began to harm one another and they lost their aboriginal power to protect themselves from the potentially destructive forces of nonhuman nature. This condition— their wickedness and helplessness—has persisted through all the generations, being somehow hereditary. But God has set a chain of events in motion that will eventually being this state of affairs to an end."

The theodicist who wishes to add to this story elements that will account for evil as we actually find it must consider the questions about the magnitude, duration, and distribution of evil that we have put into the mouth of our imaginary skeptic. It will aid my order of exposition—and not, I think, unfairly modify the skeptic's case—if we recast the skeptic's three questions as four questions. The first and third have to do with the duration of evil, the second with its magnitude, and the fourth with its distribution.

Question 1. Why didn't God immediately restore His fallen creatures to their original union with Him?

Question 2. Why doesn't God protect His fallen creatures from the worst effects of their separation from Him: the horrible pain and suffering?

Question 3. Why has God allowed "the age of evil" to persist for thousands and thousands of years?

Question 4. Why do the innocent suffer and the wicked prosper?

Question 1

What would doing that actually have involved? Suppose that two brothers quarrel. Suppose that the quarrel becomes violent and then bitter and that finally they come to hate each other. Suppose that their mother prays to God that He restore their mutual love—and not by any gradual process, but immediately, right on the spot. What is she asking God to do? I can think of only one thing: to grant her request, God would have to wipe away all memory of everything that had happened between them since just before the moment they quarreled. Any philosopher worth his salt will probably be able to think of several conceptual difficulties that would attend this plan, but (assuming they could be overcome by omnipotence) God would not do such a thing, because, as Descartes has pointed out, God is not a deceiver, and such an act would constitute a grave deception about the facts of history. (I have no memory of a violent, bitter quarrel with Eleonore Stump, and thus my memory represents the past to me as containing no such quarrel. I have the best epistemic warrant for believing that no such quarrel has ever occurred. If she and I *have* so quarreled and if God has "deleted" my memories of it—and has somehow rendered the resulting set of memories coherent—then He has deceived me about the past.) I cannot see how God could simply, by sheer fiat, immediately have restored fallen humanity other than by a similar grave deception. And, we may add, if He did, what would happen next? What would prevent the Fall from immediately recurring?

V

Question 2

Consider the parable of the Prodigal Son. (Those whose memory of this story is dim will find it in the Gospel according to St. Luke, 15:11–32.) Suppose the father of the Prodigal had foreseen the probable effects of his son's rash use of his patrimony, and had hired actors to represent themselves as gamblers and deliberately to lose substantial sums to the Prodigal; and suppose that he had further arranged for his agents to bribe prostitutes to tell the Prodigal that they had fallen in love with him and wanted to give him all their earnings (following which declaration they are to pass on to him monies provided by his father); and suppose that the father's agents, on his instructions, had followed the Prodigal about in secret to protect him from the dangers attendant on the night life of the ancient Middle East.

What would have been the effects of this fatherly solicitude? Certainly the son could have continued to squander his substance indefinitely and with impunity. But here the word impunity must be understood in a rather superficial sense: for the son will be living a life of illusion (and that is a misfortune), and it is hard to see what could ever induce him to consider returning to his father (and I am inclined to think that that would also be a misfortune).

This modification of the story of the Prodigal Son suggests why it is that God does not simply "cancel"—by an almost continuous series of miracles—the pain and suffering that our separation of ourselves from Him has led to. First, if He did so, He would be, no less than in the case of the deleted memories, a deceiver. If He did so, we should be living in a world of illusion. Our lives would be invisibly "propped up" by God, but we should—justifiably—think that we were living successfully simply by the exercise of our native powers. This, it seems to me, would reduce our existence to something worse than meaningless: We should be, every one of us, *comic* figures. (If there were a novel whose plot was the "revised" life of the Prodigal Son sketched above, he could not be its hero or even a sympathetic character. The novel would be a low comedy and he would be the butt of the joke.) Now illusion of this sort is a bad thing in itself, but it would have consequences even worse than its intrinsic badness. If God did what is proposed, we should all be satisfied with our existence—or at least a lot closer to being satisfied than most of us are now. And if we are satisfied with our existence, why should we even consider turning to God and asking for His help? An essential and important component of God's plan of Atonement—this constitutes an addition to our theodicy—is to make us *dissatisfied* with our state of separation from Him; and not by miraculously altering our values or by subjecting us to illusion or by causing us suffering that has no natural connection with our separation, but simply by allowing us to "live with" the natural consequences of this separation, and by making it as difficult as possible for us to delude ourselves about the kind of world we live in: a hideous world, much of whose hideousness is quite plainly traceable to the inability of human beings to govern themselves or to order their own lives. Let us expand our theodicy:

> As essential part of God's plan of Atonement for separated humanity is for human beings to perceive that a natural consequence of human beings' attempting to order their own lives is a hideous world—a world that is hideous not only by His standards, but by the very standards they themselves accept.

Why is it important for human beings to perceive the hideousness of the world? Well, first, because that's how things are. That's what "man on his own" *means*. Look at the world around you—the world of violence, starvation, hatred, the world of the death camps and the Gulag and (quite possibly) thermonuclear or ecological catastrophe. (These are not the worst features of separated human life in the eyes of God, for these are all finite evils, and He can see quite plainly that each of us daily risks an infinite evil, the loss of the end for which he was made. But they really are hideous and they are recognizable as hideous by almost everyone, no matter what his beliefs and values may be.) These are natural effects of our living to ourselves, just as a literally feral existence is a natural effect of an infant's separation from the human community.

People who do not believe in God do not, of course, see our living to ourselves as a result of a prehistoric separation from God. But they can be aware—and it is a part of God's plan of Atonement that they *should* be aware—that something is pretty wrong and that this wrongness is a consequence of the intrinsic inability of human beings to devise a manner of life that is anything but hideous. (They *can* be aware. Few are. Part of the reason is that various myths[9] have been invented[10] for

9. 2 Timothy 4:3–4.
10. Ephesians 6:12.

the purpose of obscuring the intrinsic incapacity of human beings to live successfully even by their own standards. The myths of Enlightenment, Progress, and the Revolution are the most prominent of these. Such myths in the end refute themselves by leading to ever deeper human misery; but, unfortunately, only in the end.) The broad psychological outlines of this feature of the plan that our theodicy ascribes to God are not hard to fathom. The realization that undirected human life is bound to be a failure even in secular terms may possibly set people to wondering whether there may not be some direction somewhere. But people who still think that the obvious hideousness of our world is caused by some accidental feature of human life—superstition, technological backwardness, primitive economic organization—one that we shall presently get round to altering, are probably not going even to consider turning to God. It is a commonplace that religious belief is more prevalent in South America and the Middle East and Africa than in the English-speaking countries and Western Europe. One possible explanation of this fact is that miserable and uneducated people turn to religious institutions as a man with a painful and incurable illness turns to quacks (and he is all the more likely to fall prey to quacks if he is uneducated). Here is another possible explanation. In the relatively prosperous and well-ordered West, people—middle-class people, anyway—are subject to an illusion about human nature and the conditions of human life. Although the prosperity and order in their lives is due to a special, fragile, and transient set of circumstances, they foolishly regard the kind of life they lead as the sort of thing human nature can be trusted to produce. The "wretched of the earth," on the other hand, see human nature as it really is. Many of them may be uneducated, in the sense of lacking the cognitive skills necessary to construct and operate a machine-based civilization, but they are far better educated than middle-class Europeans and Americans as regards the most general and important features of human nature. If an analogy involving medical quackery is wanted, we may say that a typical "postreligious" American or European is like a desperately sick man who has got his hands on some temporary panacea and who, as a consequence, has decided that the doctors who attempted to impress upon him the gravity of his condition are all quacks.

God's refusal to "cancel" the suffering that is a natural consequence of the Fall by providing separated humanity with a vast set of miraculous and invisible props can (according to the theodicy I propose) be understood on the model of a doctor who refuses to prescribe a painkiller (say, for angina), on the ground that he knows that his patient will curtail some beloved but self-destructive activity—long-distance running, say—only if the patient continues to experience the pain that his condition signals. Now this sort of behavior on the part of a *doctor* may well be morally objectionable. The doctor is the patient's fellow adult and fellow citizen, and, or so it can plausibly be argued, it would be presumptuous of him to act in such a paternalistic way. One might even say that in so acting the doctor would be "playing God." But we can hardly accuse *God* of playing God. God is justifiably paternalistic because He is our Father and because He is perfect in knowledge and wisdom and because, or so I would argue, He has certain rights over us. These rights, as I see it, derive from the following facts: He made up the very idea of there being creatures like us out of the thought of His own mind, and He made us out of nothing to meet the specifications contained in that idea; everything we have—including the intellectual and moral faculties by means of which we make judgments about paternalism—we have received from Him; He made us for a certain purpose (to glorify Him and to enjoy Him forever) and we threaten to prevent that purpose from being fulfilled.

I have suggested that the initial stage of God's plan of Atonement essentially involves His separated creatures' being aware of the hideousness of their condition and of its being a natural result of their attempting to order their own lives. I would also suggest that the *outcome* of His plan of Atonement, the unending union of creatures with Himself, will essentially involve the *memory* of that hideousness. A student of mine, a Christian, once told me of a professor of philosophy who had questioned him somewhat as follows. "You Christians believe that in the beginning man was in Paradise, and that in the end man will be in Heaven. In each of these states, man is in perfect union with God. So what is the difference between Paradise and Heaven? By abusing his free will, you say, man lost Paradise. And, you say, Heaven will be forever. But how can you know that man, having attained Heaven, won't proceed to lose it again by abuse of his free will?" There is a very simple answer to this question. The human beings in Heaven (that is, those whom God has rescued and restored to union with Himself; 'Heaven' is not the name of a place but of a condition) will know what it's like to be separated from God. They will remember the hideousness of their lives before the restoration of their union with God, and their continuing in their restored state will be no more puzzling than the refusal of the restored Prodigal Son to leave his father's house a second time. (Christian theologians have generally held that the inhabitants of Heaven—unlike the inhabitants of Paradise—are *unable* to sin. If the considerations of the present paragraph are combined with the theses on the nature of free will that I have argued in my essay "When Is the Will Free?"[11] it is easy to see why this should be so.) Theologians have also held that the happiness of those in Heaven will essentially involve, will perhaps be identical with, an immediate, intuitive knowledge of God, generally called the Beatific Vision. We might speculate that this Vision will have as a component an awareness of God's opposite, an awareness best revealed in the memory of separation from Him. Reflection on reunited lovers or returned exiles suggests why this might be the case.

Let us formally add these ideas to our theodicy:

The perception by human beings of their incapacity to "live to themselves" is essential to God's plan of Atonement because, first, without this perception few if any human beings would consider turning to God. (If, therefore, God were miraculously to "cancel" the natural consequences of separation from Himself, He would not only be a deceiver but would remove the only motivation fallen human beings have for turning to Him.) And because, secondly, memory of the hideousness of separated human life will be an important, perhaps an essential, component of the final state of restored humanity. Among the natural consequences of separation from God is the vast quantity of pain and suffering that we observe.

VI

Question 3

I am uncertain about what to say about the duration of the "age of evil." I suggest some speculations that seem to me to be plausible.

—Perhaps God wants the final community of those in union with Him to be rather *large*. (Couldn't God allow an increase in the human population to occur *after* His plan of Atonement has been completed? Well, there is certainly the point to be considered that people born after the completion of God's plan would not remember the "age of evil" and thus would be just as liable to sin as their remote ancestors in Paradise; and it might be, as I have speculated, that memory of a world separated from God will be an essential part of the final condition of restored humanity.)

—Perhaps God wants the final community of those in union with Him to be rather *diverse*. It seems plausible to suppose that if God had

11. *Philosophical Perspectives* 3, 1989, 399–422. I owe this point to Eleonore Stump.

brought the age of evil to an end in, say, A.D. 1000, the final human community would have been very unlike what it would be if He brought that age to an end tomorrow. In the latter case the final community would contain men and women whose cast of mind and world-view were radically unlike those of the members of any earlier age or culture. One might speculate that the members of a community composed of people born in diverse periods and cultures would be able to perceive and to communicate to one another aspects of the Divine Nature that the members of a community of less heterogeneous cultural origins would have been blind to.

—Various important stages in God's plan of Atonement may require particular levels of social and cultural development. The unhappy first generation of separated human beings must have been in a truly miserable state, having lost the smoothly functioning behavioral instincts of their purely animal ancestors, but without the learned social organization, custom, and tradition by which human beings—as we know them—maintain themselves in an environment indifferent to their welfare. (Perhaps they were even without an actual language: a population of feral children, as it were. I suppose no one claims to know what would happen to a closed population of feral children over many generations?) Or even if they were never wholly without a culture and social organization, we can hardly suppose them to have had anything but a tribal culture. It may well be that God's plan of Atonement requires that at certain points in history some people belong to a more "advanced" culture than a tribal culture. If we consider the Christian account of God's plan of Atonement, for example, we shall see that it is evident that the ministry of Jesus (an essential part of God's plan) could not have taken place in a culture much different from that of first-century Palestine; certainly it could not have taken place in a tribal culture, or in a "normal" culture of the ancient Mediterranean world, a pagan polytheism. A "specialized" culture like that of ancient Judaism cannot appear overnight. Even if one does not believe the biblical account of God's long interaction with Israel, one must grant that the Hebrew culture of two thousand years ago embodied a long history. (God doubtless had the power to "raise up children for Abraham from these stones," but if He had exercised that power He would have been a deceiver; vivid and detailed memories of the long history of their people were an essential part of the reaction of Jesus' Hebrew audience to His preaching.) And, of course, the rapid and accurate spread of the news about Jesus (also an essential part of God's plan, according to

Christians) could hardly have happened except within the setting of a vast, cosmopolitan empire.

—Creatures like ourselves, sunk deep in self-will, take a long time to respond to any sort of guidance, particularly if it appeals to considerations higher than power and wealth. It may be hard to kick against the goad, but it is certainly done.

Question 4

Let us not discuss cases of the suffering of the innocent that depend on human wickedness or folly or corrupt institutions. Let us instead examine cases in which there are no oppressors but only victims. These would seem to raise all of the difficulties for the theodicist that are raised by cases in which an oppressor is present, and to be amenable to a smaller class of solutions; they are not, for example, amenable to any solution that involves a concern for the ultimate spiritual welfare of the oppressor or respect for his free will or anything of that sort.

A young mother dies of leukemia. A school bus full of children is crushed by a landslide. A child is born without limbs. A wise and good man in the prime of life suffers brain damage and spends the remaining thirty years of his life in a coma. I do not know of a good general term for such events. Journalists often call them tragedies. But this word is properly applied only to events that are in some sense meaningful, and I know of no reason to think that such events *always* have a "meaning." I will call them *horrors*.

Why do horrors happen? I want to suggest that horrors happen for no reason at all, that when, for example, a child is born without limbs, the only answer to the question, "Why did that happen?" is "There is no reason or explanation; it just happened." Or, at any rate, I want to suggest that this is sometimes the case. (Whether some horrors are brought about by God for special purposes is a question I shall not attempt to answer.[12] If *some* horrors are brought about by God, and thus have a purpose and a meaning known to God but not to us, I have no opinion as to what proportion of the whole they might constitute.) But are not *all* events ordered by God, and must not *all* events

---

12. I shall not attempt to answer it because I do not think there is any way to get a purely philosophical grip on it. Any useful discussion of this question must presuppose an agreed-upon deposit of divine revelation, of God's statements to us about His purposes. The relevant biblical texts are very numerous. (Many of them, obviously, are contained in the book of Job.) Two important texts, which I choose almost at random, are Jeremiah 45:1–5 and John 9:1–3.

therefore have some sort of meaning? Christians and other theists are, I believe, committed to the truth of the following proposition:

> God is the maker of all things, visible and invisible (other than Himself); He sustains all created things in existence from moment to moment, and continuously supplies them with their causal powers.

In a previous essay,[13] in which I presented an account of God's action in the world, I argued that this proposition is consistent with the proposition that there are events having the following feature: If one asks concerning one of these events, "Why did that happen?" the only answer to one's question is, "There is no reason or explanation for that event. God did not cause it to happen or intend it to happen. It is not a part of God's plan for the world or anyone else's plan for anything. It just happened, and that's all there is to say about it." (Let us say of such events that they are *due to chance*.) I will not reproduce my arguments. Interested readers may turn to the earlier essay, to which the present essay is a sequel (although I have tried to make it self-contained). Now to say that there is no answer to the question, Why did X occur? is not to say there is no answer to such questions as Why did God allow X to occur? or Why did God not prevent X? I ended the earlier essay with these words:

> If what I have said is true, it yields a moral for students of the problem of evil: Do not attempt any solution to this problem that entails that every particular evil has a purpose, or that, with respect to every individual misfortune, or every devastating earthquake, or every disease, God has some special reason for allowing it. Concentrate rather on the problem of what sort of reasons a loving and providential God might have for allowing His creatures to live in a world in which many of the evils that happen to them happen to them for no reason at all.

I will now take my own advice and present my solution to this problem. God's reason for allowing His creatures to live in such a world is that their living in such a world is a natural consequence of their separation from Him. Consider again our earlier sketchy account of natural evil: in separating ourselves from God, we have somehow deprived ourselves of our primordial defenses against such potentially destructive things as tigers and landslides and tornadoes. But if, by our rebellion and folly, we have allowed the destructive potential of these things to be-

---

13. Essay 2 in this volume.

come actual, how shall we expect the effects of that actuality to be distributed? At random, surely? That is, with no correlation between these things and the innocence or wickedness of the people they impinge on—since the operations of these things in no way depend upon the moral qualities of the people they interact with? In fact, there is little correlation between the manner in which these things operate and *any* factor under human control (although civilization does what it can to try to induce correlations of this type).

Suppose that a certain man chooses, of his own free will, to stand at spot x at time t. His arrival at that place at that time converges with the arrival of an avalanche. Let us suppose that God did not miraculously cause the avalanche, and that He did not "move" the man to be at that place at that time. And let us also suppose that neither the man's arrival at x at t nor the avalanche's arrival at x at t was determined by the laws of nature and the state of the world, say, one hundred years earlier. (This is a plausible assumption on scientific grounds. Quantum mechanics has the following astounding consequence: Imagine a billiard table, one not subject to external influence other than constant, uniform gravitation, on which there are rolling perfectly spherical and perfectly elastic balls that—somehow—do not lose energy to the walls of the table in collision or to its surface in friction; the position of the balls a minute or so in the future is not even approximately determined by the laws of nature and the present physical state of the balls. This example strongly suggests that the precise moment at which an avalanche occurs is not determined a hundred years in advance.)

The man's death in the avalanche would seem to be in every sense due to chance, even though (the theist must suppose) God knew in advance that he would be killed by the avalanche and could have prevented it. In fact, the theist must suppose that, during the course of that event, God held all of the particles that composed the man and the moving mass of snow and ice in existence and continuously decreed the operation of the laws of nature by which those particles interacted with one another.

Why did God not miraculously save the man? We have seen the answer to this question already. He might very well have. Perhaps He sometimes does miraculously save people in such situations. but if He *always* did so, He would be a deceiver. If He always saved people about to be destroyed by a chance encounter with a violent phenomenon of nature, He would engender an illusion with the following propositional content:

It is possible for human beings to live apart from God and not be subject to destruction by chance.

To live under this illusion would be a bad thing in itself, but, more importantly, it would have harmful effects. This illusion would be, as it were, a tributary of illusion feeding into a great river of illusion whose content was, "Human beings can live successfully in separation from God."

In our current state of separation from God, we are continually blundering into "lines of causation" (the descent of an avalanche; the evolution of the AIDS virus; the building up of tension along a geological fault) that perhaps have no purpose at all and certainly have no purpose in relation to us. (It is simply a part of the mechanics of nature that intrinsically harmless but potentially destructive things like avalanches or viruses or earthquakes should exist. As I remarked above, if you think that you can design a world which does not contain such things and which can also serve as a home for human beings, you have never tried. Such things are a part of God's design in the sense that the ticking sound made by a clock is a part of the watchmaker's design: not intended, necessitated by what *is* intended, foreseen, and allowed for. What is not in any sense a part of God's design is *this* avalanche, *this* virus, and *this* earthquake. These are—sometimes, at any rate— due to chance.) If we had never separated ourselves from God, we should have been able to avoid such blunders. No longer to be able to avoid them is a natural consequence of the Fall. It is as if God had had—for some purpose—to cover the earth with a certain number of deep pits. These pits (we may stipulate) were not dangerous, since they could easily be seen and avoided; but we frustrated God's providence in this matter by deliberately making ourselves blind; and now we complain that some of us—quite often the good and wise and inno- cent—fall into the pits. God's response to this complaint, according to the theodicy I propose, is this: "You are the ones who made yourselves blind. If you make yourselves blind, some of you will fall into the pits, and, moreover, *who* falls into a pit and *when* will be wholly a matter of chance. Goodness and wisdom and innocence have no bearing on this matter. That's part of what being blind means." Or, rather, this is what we might imagine God's response to be in our simple "world of pits." In the real world, we should have to picture God as saying some- thing more complex, something like the following.

"Even I can't make a world which is suitable for human beings but which contains no phenomena that would harm human beings *if* they were in the wrong place at the wrong time. The reasons for this are complicated, but they turn on the fact that the molecular bonds that hold you human beings together must be weaker by many orders of magnitude than the disruptive potential of the surges of energy that must happen here and there in a structurally and nomologically coherent world complex enough to contain you. My providence dealt with this fact by endowing you with the power never to be in the wrong place at the wrong time, a power you lost when you ruined yourselves by turning away from Me. That is why horrors happen to some of you: you simply blunder into things. If I were to protect you from the consequences of your blindness by guiding you away from potentially destructive phenomena by an unending series of miracles—and I remind you that for all you know I *sometimes* do guide you out of harm's way—I should be deceiving you about the meaning of your separation from Me and seriously weakening the only motivation you have for returning to Me."

We may add the following proposition to our theodicy:

> Among the natural consequences of the Fall is the following evil state of affairs: Horrors happen to people without any relation to desert. They happen simply as a matter of chance. It is a part of God's plan of Atonement that we realize that a natural consequence of our living to ourselves is our living in a world that has that feature.

This completes my presentation of the theodicy I propose.[14] I have fleshed out the well-known story about how evil entered the world

---

14. It is often contended that a theodicy is a mere intellectual exercise; that the theodicist has nothing to say that would profit or comfort or even interest a religious believer who was undergoing, or watching a loved one undergo, terrible suffering, and who cried out to God for an explanation. The usual response to this contention is rather defensive: A distinction is made between intellectual and pastoral concerns and it is declared that a theodicy purports to be a solution only to the intellectual problems that human suffering raises for the theist. I believe, however, that there is a closer connection between intellectual and pastoral concerns than this response suggests. One is certainly asking too much of a work of theodicy if one demands that it should be capable of being read with profit by someone in terrible pain or distress. But one is not asking too much of a work of theodicy if one demands that it should be capable of being read with profit by someone whose vocation it is to minister to those in terrible pain or distress. By way of illustration, I should like to quote, with the writer's permission, a paragraph from a letter I have received (concerning Essay 2) from Dr. Stephen S. Bilynskyj, who is both a trained philosopher and the lead pastor of the First Evangelical Covenant Church of Lincoln, Nebraska: "As a pastor, I believe that some sort of view of providence which allows for genuine chance is essential in counseling those facing what I often call the 'practical problem of evil.' A grieving person needs to be able to trust in God's direction of her life and the world, without having to make God directly responsible for every

through the abuse of the divine gift of free will; I have fleshed it out in such a way as to provide plausible—at any rate, I find them plausible—answers to four pointed questions about the magnitude, duration, and distribution of evil. But in a sense it is not possible effectively to present a theodicy in a single piece of work by one author. Various elements in any proposed theodicy are bound to be thought false or felt to be implausible by some people. An essential part of presenting a theodicy is meeting the objections of those who have difficulties with it, or perhaps refining it in the face of their objections. A theodicy is a dialectical enterprise. The present essay, therefore, is best regarded as the "open-

---

event that occurs. The message of the Gospel is not, I believe, that everything that occurs has some purpose. Rather, it is that God's power is able to use and transform any event through the grace of Jesus Christ. Thus a person may cease a fruitless search for reasons for what happens, and seek the strength that God offers to live with what happens. Such an approach is very different from simply assuming, fideistically, that there must be reasons for every event, but we are incapable of knowing them." In addition to illustrating the point I wished to make, this paragraph raises an important further point. Dr. Bilynskyj's words suggest that God will at least sometimes use the sufferings that come to us—whether they come by chance or by providential design—not only for the general spiritual benefit of separated humanity, but for the individual spiritual benefit of the sufferer himself (at least if the sufferer submits to God's will and cooperates). I myself believe this, as, I suppose, do all Christians. I have not, however, incorporated this thesis into the theodicy I have presented. There are three reasons for this. First, a plausible discussion of the spiritual benefits of suffering would require a far longer essay than this one, and it would radically alter the character of the essay: it would necessitate an essay that contained a great deal more specifically Christian soteriology than the present essay. Secondly, I think that the theodicy I have presented gives, as it stands, an *adequate* explanation of the magnitude, duration, and distribution of suffering and other sorts of evil; I do not claim to have presented a complete account of the use God makes of evil. Thirdly, and most importantly, I see no reason whatever to believe that God does make use of *every* instance of suffering in a way that benefits the sufferer. And if there are any cases of suffering that do not benefit the sufferer, these are the "hard" cases and are therefore the ones that a theodicy (especially one that makes no claim to completeness) should concentrate on. If, however, anyone wishes to add to the theodicy I have presented the thesis that in at least some cases, *perhaps* in all cases, God uses suffering to bring important spiritual benefits to the sufferer himself, I shall certainly regard that as a "friendly amendment."

While we are on the subject of pastoral concern, I will briefly mention one other objection that has been made to the theodicy I have given, an objection that I think is best classified as "pastoral." A friend has told me that I have represented God as a lofty Benthamite deity who coldly uses suffering as a tool with which to manipulate His creatures (albeit for their own good). I don't see it. I will leave aside the point that as a Christian I believe that God is Himself a human being and was once tortured to death (a peculiar kind of loftiness). I will only record my conviction—a conviction that seems to me to be in no sort of tension with the theodicy presented in the text—that when we no longer see through a glass darkly, when we know as we are known, when God's sorrows are made manifest to us, we shall see that *we* have never felt anything that we could, without shame, describe as sorrow.

ing move" in such an enterprise, rather than a finished product. In closing, I wish to answer one objection to the theodicy I have presented, an objection that has been raised in conversation and correspondence by Eleonore Stump. Professor Stump objects that the theodicy I have presented represents God as allowing people to suffer misfortunes that do not (even in the long run) benefit *them*. An example may make the point of this objection clear. Suppose that God allows a horrible, disfiguring accident to happen to Alice (a true accident, an event due entirely to chance, but one that God foresaw and could have prevented). And suppose that the only good that is brought out of this accident is embodied in the following state of affairs and certain of its remote consequences: The accident, together with an enormous number of similar horrors, causes various people to realize that one feature of a world in which human beings live to themselves is that in such a world horrors happen to people for no reason at all. But suppose that Alice herself did not need to realize this; suppose that she was already fully aware of this consequence of separation from God. And suppose that many of the people who do come to realize this partly as the result of Alice's accident manage (owing mainly to luck) to get through life without anything very bad happening to them. According to Stump, these suppositions—and it is pretty certain that there *are* cases like this if our theodicy is correct—represent God as violating the following moral principle:

> It is wrong to allow something bad to happen to X—without X's permission—in order to secure some benefit for others (and no benefit for X).

I do not find this principle particularly appealing—not as a *universal* moral principle, one that is supposed to apply with equal rigor to all possible moral agents in all possible circumstances. The circumstances in which it seems most doubtful are these: The agent is in a position of lawful authority over both X and the "others" and is responsible for their welfare (consider, for example, a mother and her children or the state and its citizens); the good to be gained by the "others" is considerably greater than the evil suffered by X; there is no way in which the good for the "others" can be achieved except by allowing the evil in question to happen to X or to someone else no more deserving of it than X; the agent knows these things to be true. By way of example, we might consider cases of quarantine or of the right of eminent domain. Is it not morally permissible for the state to restrict my freedom of movement and action if I am the carrier of a contagious disease, or to force me to move if my house stands in the way of a desperately needed irrigation canal (one that will not benefit *me* in any way)? It is not to the point to protest that these cases are not much like cases involving an omnipotent God, who can cure diseases or provide water by simple fiat. They are counterexamples to the above moral principle, and, therefore, that moral principle is false. What is required of anyone who alleges that the theodicy I have proposed represents God as violating some (correct) moral principle is a careful statement of that moral principle. When we have examined that carefully stated moral principle, and have satisfied ourselves that it is without counterexample, we can proceed with the argument.

PART II

The Bible, the Church, and Modern Knowledge

Introduction

EACH of the essays in this section is self-contained, and there is little that need be said about them as a group beyond what was said in the General Introduction. If I were to choose an epigraph for this section, it would be a remark of Wittgenstein's: "The philosopher belongs to no climate of opinion. That is what makes him a philosopher." This remark must, of course, be regarded as a description of the ideal case: most people who are paid by universities to teach and write about philosophy belong to climates of opinion of which they not only are uncritical but seem to be entirely unaware. I am no exception to this sad generalization. (Or so I would suppose: I am of all people the least fitted to form any judgment about the way in which the generalization applies to me.) I do think, however, that I have managed to separate myself from one climate of opinion, the "great secular consensus" to which most university teachers in Europe and the English-speaking countries bear allegiance. I am not, however, what is called by that consensus a fundamentalist. If a fundamentalist is defined as someone who believes that about six thousand years ago the earth and all its furniture were created in six successive twenty-four-hour periods, then "fundamentalists" will tell me that I am indeed a member of the great secular consensus—or that my beliefs are an incoherent jumble of elements drawn from biblical Christianity and elements drawn from the dogmas of the secular consensus. Fundamentalism (in this sense) I regard as one more climate of opinion, although one I have a good deal more respect for than I do for the secular consensus. (I have *no* respect for the defining feature of fundamentalism—the belief about the date and duration of the Creation stated above—but this belief is only one belief among many held by fundamentalists, and, taking their world-view as a whole, I find much in it that is worthy of the deepest respect.)

Now I will say something that will appear to be a nonsequitur, although those who are outside the secular consensus will see where I am going well before I get there.

One of the most striking features of our civilization is that it contains experts, people possessing real knowledge about this or that subject matter, and that the lay person who disputes the pronouncements of the experts (concerning those matters in which they are expert) risks not only being wrong but being—rightly—perceived as a fool. But if experts of one sort or another are ubiquitous in our civilization, so are those who claim to be experts and are not. This fact raises a question whose philosophical interest is exceeded only by its practical urgency: How are we nonexperts to judge which are which? How are we to distinguish the chemists from the alchemists, the astronomers from the astrologers, the real physicians from the quacks? There is, of course, such a thing as having the proper credentials. Our society places a high value on credentials, and hands them out with what sometimes amounts to abandon. (If I were not a professor of philosophy, you would not be reading these words; if I did not have a Ph.D. in philosophy, I should not be a professor of philosophy; if the Regents of the State of New York had, in 1968, withdrawn the right they had granted to the University of Rochester to confer doctorates, I should probably not have a Ph.D. . . . .) Shall we then simply decide that a person is an expert if (and only if) he or she has the right pieces of paper in hand? No, indeed, for many of those who are experts by that criterion have talked the most awful nonsense about the matters on which society has proclaimed them experts. Examples of this would be controversial, but most of the readers of this book will probably be able to find some examples of nonsense in the following list: eugenics, parapsychology, psychoanalysis, "literary theory," economics accompanied by a suitable adjective like 'supply-side' or 'Marxist', critical legal theory. (Richard Feynman, the second-greatest physicist of this century, would have added philosophy—not this or that philosophy, but the subject itself—to this list.) And all these things have, or have had within living memory, advocates whose credentials as experts are impeccable. Nevertheless, simply to ignore the credentials that our culture passes out would be worse than a mistake; people who do that are called cranks, and they fully deserve the opprobrium that attaches to the word. In the end, lay people who want to know who the "real" experts are have no alternative to trying to figure it out for themselves, paying respectful attention to credentials but maintaining all the while a critical attitude toward them. Our opinions, like our salvation, must be worked out with fear and trembling. If one's opinions go contrary to those of the experts, the danger, the object of the fear and trembling, is that one will be thought—perhaps that one will actually be—a fool or a crank.

In the essays in the present section, I take issue with experts—or at least with those who have credentials that proclaim them experts—in fields in which I can claim no competence whatever. My considered opinion is that either the people I have taken issue with are not experts at all or, in some cases, they are experts who have reached conclusions in their own areas of expertise that are false or without support. In cases of the former sort, I believe that their status as acknowledged experts is an artifact of a climate of opinion, an artifact of the great secular consensus. In cases of the latter sort, I believe that the arguments that the (real) experts offer in support of the positions I say are false or unsupported depend on premises that could seem plausible only to someone who belonged to that climate of opinion. The reader must judge whether I am a crank or am on to something.

5

Genesis and Evolution

I am neither a theologian nor a biblical scholar nor a scientist. Indeed, I cannot even claim to know much about Old Testament studies or evolutionary biology. Nevertheless, I am going to discuss the book of Genesis and the evolution of life. I offer three excuses for presuming to pronounce on matters of which I am largely ignorant. First, war is too important to be left to the generals. Other people than those whose professional training most obviously qualifies them to speak on these topics have something invested in the conduct of debates about science and the Bible, and often these other people feel—I do at any rate—that it would do the professionals no harm to hear from *them* for a change. Secondly, the blunders of beginners can sometimes help the experts to see that they have failed adequately to communicate some aspect of their subject to the public and can suggest ways in which in this communication might be better done. Quite often there is some technical idea or thesis or argument that could be explained to the lay public in a much more useful way than it has been—and it *would* be, if only the specialists were aware of prevalent misconceptions. If nothing else, perhaps what I say can help the clerks to see what it is that needs to be better explained to the laity. Thirdly, if I can claim little knowledge of what the experts have said about the book of Genesis or the history of terrestrial life, I do claim, as a philosopher, to be something of an expert at tracing the relations between disparate things, and perhaps I can bring some of my expertise to bear in this essay.

I begin with two terminological points about my title. In that title,

Reprinted from *Reasoned Faith*, edited by Eleonore Stump. Copyright (©) 1993 by Cornell University. Used by permission of the publisher, Cornell University Press.

and in the remainder of this essay, I mean by *Genesis* the first three chapters of the book of Genesis: that is, the book of Genesis from "In the beginning . . ." to the expulsion of Adam and Eve from the Garden. Secondly, the word 'evolution', at least as it occurs in phrases like 'the theory of evolution', has a strictly biological meaning. It is a vulgar error to suppose that the word 'evolution' designates a sort of "force" which has been in operation from the very beginning of the universe and which has been responsible for the formation and development of the stars and the planets and everything else, and which, as a special case of this general activity, is engaged in pushing living organisms toward ever higher levels of complexity. Despite this fact about the meaning of the word 'evolution', however, and despite the fact that I shall have a lot to say about evolution in this strict sense, I have used the word in my title as a sort of catchall for a very diverse set of scientific considerations—cosmological and geological as well as biological—relating to various questions about how the earth and the cosmos got into their present forms.

Now as to the issue of the relation between these scientific considerations and the book of Genesis, a very wide range of positions is possible. But two positions stand out as extremes and have got the most publicity. The popular or journalistic names for these extreme positions are 'fundamentalism' and 'secular humanism'. But each of these names has been objected to on various grounds, and, rather than become embroiled in terminological disputes, I shall invent my own names for them. More exactly, I shall describe, and invent names for, two positions that I believe correspond to *some* of the things said by people who are popularly called 'fundamentalists' and *some* of the things said by people who are popularly called 'secular humanists'. I shall call the one 'Genesiac literalism' (or literalism for short) and the other 'saganism'—after one of its most illustrious and talkative ornaments.

I begin with a statement of Genesiac literalism. (I say Genesiac rather than *biblical* literalism, because I believe that the early chapters of the book of Genesis are a very special part of the Bible, and I mean to talk about them only. Nothing I say should be regarded as having any implications whatever for questions about how to read, say, Job or the Gospels or Revelation.)

"The planet earth came into existence about six thousand years ago, when God created it in a series of six twenty-four hour days. On the third, fifth, and sixth of these days, God created all the various species of living things, concluding with a single pair of human beings, the first man and the first woman. Any appearance to the contrary in the geological record is due to a worldwide flood that occurred about forty-five hundred years ago; the geological distortions caused by that vast deluge created phenomena that the clever and perverse have—like someone finding internal evidence of Baconian authorship in *Hamlet*—interpreted as showing that the earth is not thousands but thousands of *millions* of years old, its present geological features supposedly being due to the effects of various natural processes that have been at work over this immense stretch of time.

"We know the facts I have outlined concerning the beginning of the earth and life and man because God revealed them to Moses thousands of years later and Moses wrote them down in the book we call Genesis, a book that God has ensured is historically accurate in every respect because it is a part of His Holy Scripture. It is true that Scripture contains metaphor and hyperbole—as, for example, when it tells us that the soldiers of the kings of Canaan were as numerous as the grains of sand on the shore of the sea—but any reasonably intelligent and well-intentioned reader can tell when metaphor or hyperbole are intended by Scriptural writers, and the main historical statements of Genesis are clearly intended to be taken literally."

So says the literalist.

The saganist tells another story: "The cosmos, the totality of the distribution of matter and radiation in space-time, is 'all that is or was or ever will be.' Ten thousand million years ago or more, it was concentrated in a very tiny volume of space, which was, nevertheless, all the space there was. This tiny volume expanded very rapidly, and certain processes, which we are beginning to understand, led, after a few minutes, to the three-to-one ratio of hydrogen to helium nuclei that we observe today. A few hundred thousand years later, the density of the expanding universe had fallen to a point at which electrons could arrange themselves around the hydrogen and helium nuclei, and the space between the atoms thus formed was suddenly filled with free radiation, radiation that, vastly attenuated, is still detectable. Gravitational effects caused matter to be concentrated in stars and stars to be collected into galaxies. In the stars, new elements like carbon and oxygen were formed and were dispersed when these stars came to the ends of their lives and exploded. The scattered atoms of these elements eventually became parts of new stars and of solid planets circling them.

"On at least one planet, but presumably on many, natural processes led to the formation of a complex molecule capable of replicating itself with variations. Owing entirely to the operation of natural selection, the descendants of this molecule achieved a sufficient level of internal organization for us to feel comfortable about thinking of them as living organisms. The blind but, in appearance, creative processes of natural selection continued to operate, and produced the cell, the multicellular organism, sexual dimorphism, and, eventually, representatives of all the phyla we see today (and some that we don't). In due course, owing to the interplay of variation and selection over hundreds of millions of years, intelligence appeared. (The broad outlines of the latter part of this narrative, the part dealing with biological evolution, have been accepted by every serious scientist since about 1870. Opposition to it is due entirely to theological obscurantism.) A short time later, perhaps through a social analogue of natural selection, intelligence developed *science,* a powerful, self-correcting mechanism for understanding the cosmos. Various older and much less efficient competitors with science—notably religion—survive, but, having tried and failed to destroy their new and dangerous rival in its infancy, they are steadily losing ground to it and will soon go the way of the saber-toothed tiger. Perhaps the final nail in their coffin will be the discovery of intelligent life elsewhere in the universe, a shock they are too narrow-minded and parochial to survive.

"As to the book of Genesis [here the saganists in the sciences are aided by their colleagues in the other culture], it was not written by Moses or by any single author. It is easy to see that it contains two incompatible accounts of the creation of humanity. One account, which roughly coincides with the second chapter, the detailed story of the creation of the first man and woman, is thought to have been put into its present form in something like the ninth century B.C., hundreds of years after the death of Moses. The first chapter of Genesis (and a bit more), the 'seven days" story, was written by priests about three hundred years later, probably during the Babylonian captivity of Judah. What both sets of authors were doing was editing and rewriting traditional material (ultimately derived from primordial Semitic creation myths) to bring this material into line with their own theologies, and with an eye toward the polemical requirements of the contemporary religious and political situations."

Well, here are two extreme positions. Probably every position one could take on the relation between the book of Genesis and the scientific study of the origins of the universe, the earth, and humanity lies on the continuum between them. One possible position, for example, is *deism,* which accepts most of the saganists' story but rejects its contention that there is nothing besides the cosmos. Deism postulates an intelligent Creator who set the universe in motion and then sat back to watch the show. (Like the typical Hollywood producer, this Creator seems to have rather a taste for shows that involve sex and violence—especially violence. It is, however, doubtful whether he shares Hollywood's taste for happy endings.)

What I mean to do in the rest of this essay is, first, to set forth a position on the relation between Genesis and scientific accounts of the history of the universe that is radically different from literalism and saganism (and from deism). I shall then offer critiques of both literalism and saganism from the point of view afforded by this position. I pick these two positions to criticize because, first, they have been getting the lion's share of the publicity, and, secondly, as a consequence of the fact that they are extremes between which most if not all the other possible positions on this issue lie, what I would say about other positions may perhaps be gleaned from what I say about the extremes.

Now a word as to my own religious beliefs. I am a Christian. More exactly, I am an Episcopalian, and I fully accept the teaching of my denomination that "the Holy Scriptures of the Old and New Testaments are the revealed Word of God"; that they "contain all things necessary to salvation and are the rule and ultimate standard of faith"; that "God inspired their human authors and still speaks to us through the Bible."[1] But I am not constructing a position that I recommend only to Episcopalians. I recommend this position to any Christian—and to any Jew—who regards the book of Genesis as divinely inspired and who, nevertheless, rejects, as I do, Genesiac literalism. I will add that a Christian is not logically committed, by the very fact of being a Christian, to regarding the bible as being divinely inspired throughout. There are only two glancing references to Scripture in the creeds—"on the third day he rose again, in accordance with the Scriptures" and "he [the Holy Spirit] spoke through the prophets." One would suppose, therefore, that, as regards the Bible, a Christian is absolutely obliged to believe only that the Hebrew prophets were divinely inspired, and that the Resurrection is in some sense "in accordance with" *(secundum)* the Hebrew Bible. But such scriptural minimalism has not been the mind of the Church. While one might want to qualify this statement in various ways, in the light of such things as Martin Luther's remarks about the Letter of James, it seems roughly correct to say that all Christians whose witness on the matter has survived have regarded the

---

1. *The Book of Common Prayer: According to the Use of the Episcopal Church* (New York: Seabury Press, 1979). The first statement (p. 526) is from the Form for the Ordination of a Priest; the second (p. 877) is from Resolution II of the Lambeth Conference of 1888; the third (p. 853) is from the Catechism.

Bible as being divinely inspired throughout, and I have no intention of separating myself from this cloud of witnesses. How, then, shall those who agree with me and the literalists that Genesis is the inspired Word of God and who also agree with me and the saganists that life and the earth and the cosmos have histories that are measured in thousands of millions of years explain themselves? This question is not, in its essentials, a new one. A lot of people seem to think that all Christians were literalists before the geological discoveries of the early nineteenth century. Under the impact of these discoveries and the Darwinian account of evolution that was built upon them (the story goes) some Christians began desperately to scramble about to try to devise some way of reconciling science and the Bible.

This is historically false. Let us consider the greatest of all Christian theologians, St. Augustine (whose death in the year 430 places him at a comfortable remove from the impact of nineteenth-century science). Augustine argued that the "six days" account of creation in Genesis could hardly be literally correct, since (among other reasons he gives) it asserts that day and night existed before the sun was made. (Let me assure you parenthetically that if the author of Genesis 1 did not know much about geology, he certainly did know that daylight was due to the sun.) Now if Genesis is not a literally correct account of the Creation—Augustine reasoned—then it must belong to one of the many nonliteral modes of presentation recognized by the science of rhetoric (which, as we should say today, was Augustine's area of professional competence). But I do not propose to discuss Augustine's hermeneutical theories; I am more interested in the account he gave of what he took to be the literal reality behind the nonliteral presentation.[2] Augustine held that

2. Augustine's views on Genesis are found in his *De genesi ad litteram* ("On Genesis according to the Letter"). The standard English translation by J. H. Taylor (New York: Newman, 1982) is titled *On the Literal Meaning of Genesis.* The "literal meaning" of the English title refers not to what we would today call "the literal meaning of the text" but to what I have called 'the literal reality behind the nonliteral mode of presentation'. To read an inspired text *ad litteram,* for Augustine, is to read it with an eye toward discovering what its human author intended to convey; one could also read an inspired text *allegorically,* with an eye toward discovering types or foreshadowings of persons or events of later sacred history (which, if they are objectively present in the inspired text, were presumably unknown to its human author). In the discussion of Augustine in the text of this essay, I use the word 'literal' in its customary present-day sense. In this discussion, I have drawn heavily on Ernan McMullin's introduction to the collection *Evolution and Creation* (South Bend, Ind.: University of Notre Dame Press, 1985). In this account of Augustine's views, I have glossed over several important matters—such as the relation of the timeless reality of God to the unfolding temporal processes of the created world—that are irrelevant to our purposes.

God had created the universe all at once, and that, at the moment of its creation, the universe was, by present standards, without form, and was empty of things of the kinds it now contains. But there was *latent* form and there were things in which that form was latent. He calls these things *seed-principles,* using a botanical trope, as we use a political trope when we speak of the laws of nature. The newly created universe subsequently, by its own inner necessity, evolved into its present highly differentiated state, this present state having been implicit in its original state much as a field of grain is implicit in a mixture of seed and water and earth. (Or, at any rate, many aspects of the present state of the world were in this strong sense implicit in the initial state. Others may have been due to miraculous actions by God subsequent to the beginning of things. But if miracles did play a part in the development of the world, these miracles were not local acts of creation ex nihilo; they rather consisted in the miraculous activation of potentialities that had existed from the beginning.) This is not to say that Augustine believed in anything like what *we* call "evolution." He did not believe that elephants were remotely descended from fish. The idea of the mutability of species would have been quite foreign to his Platonism. Rather, elephants arose from one seed-principle and mackerel from another. The "days" of Genesis, Augustine says, represent *aspects* of the development of the world; perhaps—he is rather tentative about this—what is represented is six successive stages of the angelic understanding of creation. Augustine's science may strike us as quaint, but it is evident that his account of the origin and development of the universe is no more consistent with Genesiac literalism than is an article covering the same ground in last month's *Scientific American.* Nor is Augustine an isolated example of a nonliteralist in the ancient world: the Alexandrian theologians, Gregory of Nyssa, and St. Jerome (who produced the Latin translation of the Bible that was the Church's standard for fourteen hundred years) were nonliteralists. Jerome once remarked that, in his opinion, the author of Genesis had described the Creation mythically—"after the manner of a popular poet."[3] Genesiac nonliteralism is, therefore, both ancient and fully orthodox: it would be a bold literalist who called the Bishop of Hippo a wishy-washy theological liberal. Nonliteralism was, of course, *rejected* by many important authorities in the Western Church. St. Thomas Aquinas, for example, was a literalist who explicitly stated that the Creation took

3. Attributed, without citation, by C. S. Lewis, *Reflections on the Psalms* (London: Godfrey Bles, 1958), p. 92.

place over a period of six successive twenty-four-hour days. What it is important to note about Aquinas, however, is that, in his discussion of Augustine's "opinion that all the days that are called seven are one day represented in a sevenfold aspect," Augustine is, in the words of Jaroslav Pelikan, "criticized but not hereticized." Pelikan goes on to say, "It took the Reformation to change that."[4]

I agree, although perhaps my "agreeing" on a point of church history with one of our greatest church historians has its comic aspect. Literalism before the Reformation was no doubt the majority opinion. The theory that the Bible is literally and in every sentence and in every respect inerrant is, after all, the simplest and most natural theory of the "reliability" of the Bible that must in some sense be a consequence of the doctrinal statement that the Bible is the revealed Word of God— just as geocentrism is the simplest and most natural theory of the causes of observed celestial motions. But *militant* literalism, the literalism that makes the denial of plenary verbal inerrancy a heresy to be destroyed before any other, is a child of the Reformation. (And not of the Counter-Reformation. To say that Galileo was condemned for contradicting the Bible on astronomical matters is, at best, a vast oversimplification of an extremely complex episode.) It is not hard to see why this should be, for one of the most important offspring of the Reformation is biblical individualism, the doctrine that individual Christians are perfectly capable of reading the Bible for themselves with no help from anyone but the Holy Spirit—or at the very most with no human assistance but that of their pastors. Now no one but an extreme theological liberal would be happy with the prospect of widespread radically diverse interpretations of Scripture. This prospect is avoided (in theory) in the Roman church by the concept of a *magisterium,* or teaching authority, that God has granted to His One, Holy, Catholic, and Apostolic Church, an authority that of course extends to matters of biblical interpretation, the Bible being one of many important things the Church has in her care. A denomination that espouses biblical individualism, however, must avoid by some other means the danger of ubiquitous conflicting interpretations of the Bible, and it will find a theory about the Bible that minimizes the opportunities for diverse interpretations of a given text—as biblical literalism of course does— to be very useful. *Militant* biblical literalism, then, is not simply a

4. Jaroslav Pelikan, "Darwin's Legacy: Emanation, Evolution, and Development," in *Darwin's Legacy: Nobel Conference XVIII,* ed. Charles L. Hamrum (San Francisco: Harper & Row, 1983), p. 81. No citation of the words attributed to Aquinas is given.

product of the doctrine that the Bible is the revealed Word of God; its other parent is biblical individualism, a johnny-come-lately in the history of the Christian Church. Having said this, I must add that I do not mean to imply that all the great Reformers were themselves literalists. John Calvin, I understand, questioned the historicity of the book of Job.[5] But this qualification strengthens rather than weakens the credentials of nonliteralism.

To establish the credentials of nonliteralism, however, is not to establish its possibility. How can the Bible be the revealed Word of God if, to take one example among many, it says that birds and fish came into existence on the same day, when the plain truth is that there were fish for hundreds of millions of years before there were birds? Well, I don't *know* the answer to this question, but I will do what St. Augustine did: I will present an answer which I find plausible and which I am willing to recommend. To do this, I must discuss both the content of Genesis and its formation. These two matters are intimately related, but I shall begin by treating them separately.

First, as to content. Suppose that someone who had never heard of the Bible and had never so much as thought about the beginning of the world were one day to read the book of Genesis and were to take everything it contained in a pretty literal sense and were to believe every word of it. This person would thereby come to believe many true things and many false things. Among the false things there would be two that we have already mentioned: the proposition that the alternation of day and night existed before the sun, and the proposition that Aves and Pisces are coevals. We could make quite a list of such false propositions. Here are some of the true ones. That the world is finite in space and time—at least time past. That it has not always been as it is now but has changed from a primal chaos into its present form. That it owes its existence and its features to an immeasurably powerful being who made it to serve His purposes. That it was originally not evil and not neutral as between good and evil and not a mixture of good and evil but simply good. That human beings are part of this world are formed from its elements—that they were not separately created and then placed in it like figurines in a China cabinet. That the stars and the moon are inanimate objects and are without any religious significance—that, at least in relation to human beings, their main purpose is to mark the hours and the seasons. That it is not only kings but all men and women who are images of the divine. That human

5. Lewis, *Reflections on the Psalms,* p. 92. Again, no citation is given.

beings have been granted a special sort of authority over the rest of nature. That these divine images, the stewards of all nature, have, almost from their creation, disobeyed God, and have thereby marred the primal goodness of the world and have separated themselves from God and now wander as exiles in a realm of sin and death.

So our imaginary credulous reader of Genesis comes to believe some true things and some false things. The first (but not the last) point to note about the credulous reader's situation is that the true things are much more important than the false things. In fact, the true things are among the most important there are, and the false things are not very important at all. Someone who believes that the world began six thousand years ago is wrong; so is someone who believes that Columbus was the first European to reach North America. For the life of me, however, I can't see that it is much more important to get the age of the earth right than it is to get the identity of the first European voyager to reach North America right. I can expect a protest at this point from both the literalists and the saganists. Each will tell me that the question of the age of the earth is of very great importance. The literalist will say that it is important because a mistake about the age of the earth could lead one to reject the Word of God, and the saganist will say that it is important because a mistake about the age of the earth could lead one to reject science and reason. But these protests rest on a misunderstanding. I am talking about the *intrinsic* importance of a mistake in this area, not about its *extrinsic* importance. Clearly any false belief whatever, however trivial its subject matter, *could* have disastrous consequences in special circumstances. We could easily imagine circumstances in which a woman's mistaken belief that her husband had stopped to buy a newspaper on his way home from work led her to suspect that he was lying to her about his movements and eventually destroyed their marriage. And, of course, a false belief about the age of the earth could lead to a disastrous repudiation of the reliability of something that *is* reliable and whose reliability is important. It could, in fact, lead one to devote a large portion of one's life to defending the indefensible—as, no doubt, false beliefs about Columbus have done. What I am saying is that the matter of the age of the earth is of little importance in itself. This is far from an empty platitude. The last few hundred years have seen thinkers who overestimate the intrinsic value of scientific knowledge as absurdly as Matthew Arnold and F. R. Leavis overestimated the intrinsic value of a well-honed literary sensibility. Here is a quotation from the Nobel Prize–winning physicist Steven Weinberg that illustrates the evaluation I am deprecating:

The more the universe seems comprehensible, the more it also seems pointless.

But if there is no solace in the fruits of our research, there is at least some consolation in the research itself. Men and women are not content to comfort themselves with tales of gods and giants, or to confine their thoughts to the daily affairs of life; they also build telescopes and satellites and accelerators, and sit at their desks for endless hours working out the meaning of the data they gather. The effort to understand the universe is one of the very few things that lifts human life a little above the level of farce, and gives it some of the grace of tragedy.[6]

Against this, I would set the following statements of the "great champion of the obvious," Dr. Johnson:

We are perpetually moralists, but we are geometricians only by chance. . . . Our speculations upon matter are voluntary and at leisure.

[Scientific knowledge] is of such rare emergence that one man may know another half of his life without being able to estimate his skill in hydrostatics or astronomy; but his moral and prudential character immediately appears.

The innovators whom I oppose are turning off attention from life to nature. They seem to think that we are placed here to watch the growth of plants, or the motions of the stars.[7]

Well, I have set before you a choice of values. If you think that the evaluation of scientific knowledge that is implicit in my quotation from Weinberg is the right one and that Johnson's belongs to the rubbish of history and good riddance to it, you will not believe a word of anything I am going to say. But at least don't mistake my position: I am not saying that science is unimportant; I am only denying scientific knowledge the central place in the proper scheme of human values that Weinberg gives it. I also deny this central place to a knowledge and appreciation of history or music or literature, each of which is neither more nor less important than scientific knowledge.

My first step in reconciling the thesis that Genesis is the revealed Word of God with the findings of science is, therefore, to contend that

6. Steven Weinberg, *The First Three Minutes: A Modern View of the Origin of the Universe* (London: André Deutsch, 1977), p. 155.

7. Quoted by Michael D. Aeschliman, *The Restitution of Man* (Grand Rapids, Mich.: Wm. B. Eerdman's, 1983), pp. 25–26. The quotations are from Johnson's essay "Milton," in his *Lives of the English Poets*.

what Genesis is right about is of great intrinsic importance and that what it is wrong about is of little intrinsic importance. This contention, however, raises the question why Genesis, if it is the Word of God, is wrong about *anything*. I said that I should discuss questions both of content and of formation. I have said something about content. To discuss the question I have now raised I introduce some points having to do with the formation of the Genesis narrative—the genesis of Genesis, as it were.

What is the purpose of the first chapters of Genesis? What is their purpose in relation to the Hebrew Bible as a whole? The Hebrew Bible is mainly the narrative of God's covenant relationship with His people Israel. The opening chapters of Genesis are intended to set the stage for the story of that covenant. They are intended to describe and explain the relations between God and humanity as they stood when God made a covenant with Abraham. Thus, Genesis begins with an account of the creation of the world and of human beings, an account which displays God as the maker and sovereign of the world and the ordainer of the place of humanity in the world, and which does that in a way that militates against various disastrous theological misconceptions current among Israel's neighbors and conquerors—as that divinity is divided among many beings whose wills are often in conflict; or that the lights in the sky are objects of worship; or that the image of divinity is present in a few human beings—kings—but not in ordinary people. But then why doesn't Genesis get it right? I say that Genesis does get it right— in essence. W. J. Bryan may have been a fool in many respects,[8] but he had a more accurate picture of the cosmos than Carl Sagan (who, if we may trust the Fourteenth Psalm, is also a fool). Bryan believed that the world had been created by God, and that by itself is enough to outweigh all the matters of detail in which Sagan is right and Bryan wrong. But why doesn't Genesis get it right not only in essence but in detail? Why doesn't Genesis get it wholly right? After all, we expect a reliable source to get even relatively unimportant details right, insofar as it is able, and God knows all the details. The beginning, but not the end, of the answer to this question is that if Genesis did get it right in every detail, most people couldn't understand it. Never mind the fact

---

8. But not nearly so big a fool as the character who bears his name in the almost wholly fictional movie *Inherit the Wind*. The popular account of the Scopes trial is one of the two great legends of the saganist history of Darwinism, the other being the story (as it is usually told) of the confrontation between T. H. Huxley and Bishop Wilberforce in 1860. Of course, each of these legends, like Piltdown Man, was put together from pieces of real things.

that only a person with years of rigorous formal training in mathematics can fully understand the current theories about the first three minutes of the existence of the cosmos. Consider only the *age* of the cosmos: more than ten thousand million years. You and I can in a sense grasp numbers like 10^{10}: we know how to do arithmetic with them. But how could the age of the universe be conveyed to most people at most times? Suppose the Bible began, "Ten thousand million years ago, God created . . . " Suppose you are a missionary trying to explain the Genesis narrative to a tribe of Amazonian Indians. How shall you explain these words to them? Shall you leave off teaching them about important things like the sovereignty of God till you have taught them about unimportant things like the decimal system? (Do not suppose that teaching them the decimal system will be the work of an afternoon, for there is no basis in their culture for using the kinds of numbers it gives access to.) And most cultures have been like our imaginary Amazonian culture in that respect. A scientifically accurate rewriting of Genesis, therefore, would turn it into something all but useless, for the result would be inaccessible to most people at most places and times. Only a few people like you and me—who are simply freaks from the historical and anthropological point of view—could penetrate even its surface. I wonder how many of us believe, at some level, that God—if there is a God—regards scientifically educated people as being somehow the human norm and therefore regards Amazonian Indians or elementary-school dropouts as being less worthy of His attention than we; I wonder whether many of us aren't disposed to think that if the Bible were divinely inspired it would be written with the preoccupations of the scientifically educated in mind? I will not bother to quote the very clear dominical and Pauline repudiations of the values that underlie this judgment. Everyone is of equal value to God and the Bible is addressed to everyone. A Bible that was made easy for kings to understand at the cost of making it hard for peasants to understand would be in violation of this principle—if only because there are a lot more peasants than kings. And, of course, there are a lot more people who could not understand a scientifically accurate rewriting of Genesis than there are people who could.

To this I can expect the skeptic to reply along the following lines: "That's beside the point. Of course the universe is so complex—no doubt any *possible* universe would *have* to be so complex—that only a few highly trained people in a few very special cultures could understand a *detailed* account of its origin and development. But the writer of Genesis could have described the early history of the cosmos very *abstractly.* He could have included all of the theses that you regard as 'important truths', and, nevertheless, everything he said about the development of the physical universe could have been true as far as it went. When God inspired the author of Genesis. why didn't He inspire him to write it that way?" The answer to this question is threefold. One of the three parts I am not going to explore. I will simply mention it and leave it. I do this because I think it is very important, but that it could not be adequately discussed within the scope of this essay. It is this: not all the truths that are revealed in Genesis can be said; some (to employ a distinction of the early Wittgenstein) can only be shown. These truths, I believe, truths relating to sin and knowledge, can be shown only by telling a very concrete story. I believe that as a result of knowing the story of the fruit of the knowledge of good and evil, I know something important that I cannot articulate; something which could not have been conveyed in discursive prose and which perhaps did not have to be conveyed by a story about trees and a serpent but which certainly had to be conveyed parabolically—that is, by means of *some* story about the actions of concrete, picturable beings.

I pass with relief to the two more straightforward points I want to make. First, that an abstract version of Genesis would have little pedagogical value for most people at most times. Even if it contained all the correct lessons, the lessons would not be learned—or would be learned only by rote, as "lessons" in the schoolroom sense. Secondly, the idea of God's inspiring Moses (or whomever) to write an "abstract" Genesis purged of all harmless error seems either to presuppose a primitive "dictation" model of inspiration or else to imagine God as purging His revelation of harmless error at a very high cost to the recipients of that revelation. I will illustrate these points with a parable.

Imagine that a doctor visits our Amazonian Indians with the intention of teaching them some useful medicine—say, some elementary principles of first aid and hygiene and antisepsis, and such pharmacological lore and simple surgical procedures as they can be trusted with in the absence of continuing supervision. What would be the best way to teach such things? One might give one's pupils a précis of a medical encyclopedia, deleting whatever material was not applicable to their condition. But this précis, because it was presented in a form that was without model or precedent in their culture, might well be forgotten or ignored or even be sung as a chant to accompany the application of traditional tribal medical procedures. Another, and perhaps more effective technique, would be to revise and purify and extend the existing medical lore of one's pupils, making use of literary and mnemonic devices indigenous to their culture. In applying this technique, one might simply not bother to correct parts of the existing medical lore that were harmlessly wrong. If one's pupils believed that childbirth fever was caused by demons, why should one not teach them that the demons must make their way into the bodies of new mothers via the hands of midwives, and that this path could be blocked by a scrupulous ritual washing before the delivery? If this teaching would lead to the same behavior on the part of midwives as a much longer lesson that involved an introduction to the germ theory of disease, and if the extra time required by the longer lesson were time that could be devoted to a lesson about making effective splints—well, one would have to ascribe a very high value indeed to truth in the abstract to recommend the longer lesson.

This parable has, I hope, presented an analogical case for the pedagogical ineffectiveness of an "abstract" Genesis. It also shows, by analogy, some of the difficulties God would encounter in getting an abstract Genesis into our hands, even granted that it would be advisable to do so. He might, of course, have dictated it, Hebrew word by Hebrew word, to a shining-faced Moses or to some terrified priest in the time of the Captivity. I do not want to say that revelation never occurs in that mode: perhaps the Name of God and the Ten Commandments were delivered to Moses in that way. But it is certainly clear that little, if any, of the Bible has been simply dictated by God: God's usual procedure has been to use as His instrument of revelation the whole person of an inspired author and not simply the hand that held the pen. If God has simply dictated Genesis, then He might as easily have dictated a "pure" abstract version of Genesis as any other. If, however, He proceeded, as He seems usually to have done, by inspiring modifications of the kind of story that it was natural to the author—who must be the concrete product of a particular culture, even as you and I are—to tell, then it would have been a very difficult business to produce an abstract Genesis. Not that anything is too hard for God, but, if God chooses to work with human tools, He subjects Himself to limitations inherent in the nature of the tools.

The human author or authors of Genesis, whatever their historical period may have been, would have had no natural disposition to tell a story like our imaginary abstract Genesis, a story utterly at variance with every model provided by their own culture and every other culture I know of. People are not naturally inclined to divest a story they want to tell of the concrete details that give that story its character, and the ancient Hebrews had very concrete minds indeed—as did all their contemporaries. No doubt the continued influence of the Holy Spirit could *eventually* have produced an abstract Genesis. I have no idea how long this would have taken, but certainly longer than it took to produce the concrete, suggestive, effective Genesis that we have. And what would have been the value of this costly thing? Only this: that a few saganists in our own time would have had to find some other excuse to reject the Word of God than its disagreement with the fossil record. I do not see why God, who values any six holders of endowed chairs neither more nor less than He values any six agricultural laborers in ancient Palestine, should have thought the price worth paying.

This completes my outline of the position that I oppose both to Genesiac literalism and to saganism. I shall now, as I have promised, offer critiques of literalism and saganism from the point of view afforded by this position.

To the literalists, I have little to say. Anything I said to them would be based on a premise that no literalist could accept: that "creation science" is pretty much nonsense. It's not that it's not science at all, as the rather silly—and certainly politically motivated—Arkansas decision would have it. It's that—in my view, at least—it's very bad science, consisting of contrived, ad hoc arguments and selective appeal to evidence.[9]

As to the saganists, I can happily accept a good deal of the story they tell about how the world got into its present state. The universe of modern cosmology is a cozy, tightly knit affair, entirely unlike the rather frightening infinite and amorphous universe of nineteenth-century popular science, a universe which, in my view, was not based on the actual content of nineteenth-century science but which was rather an ideological construct put together for the express purpose of making theism seem implausible. The nineteenth-century cosmos was made infinite and amorphous so that anything might happen in it given sufficient time. It was made eternal to ensure sufficient time—and, of course, to avoid awkward questions about where it came from. But the lovely universe the late-twentieth-century cosmologists have given us is as tidy and peculiar and homely as the medieval *mundus* of crystalline spheres.

I cannot, of course, accept the saganists' statement that the cosmos is all that is or was or ever will be. (Nor can I accept the fatuous

9. This is well documented in many publications. Howard J. Van Till, Davis A. Young, and Clarence Menninga, *Science Held Hostage: What's Wrong with Creation Science and Evolutionism* (Downers's Grove, Ill.: InterVarsity Press, 1988), is as good as any.

attempt of the deists to append a Creator and Voyeur to the saganists' cosmos.) From my point of view, the cosmos depends from moment to moment on the sovereign power of God who is infinitely greater than it, and it would vanish, all in a moment, like a candle flame in a high wind, if He were to stop supplying it with the power to continue to be. And I believe that the Lord and sustainer of the cosmos, the only helmsman of the wide and single stars, the faithful guarantor of the laws of nature, has become locally involved in His creation in a special way, and that, as a result, a man has risen from the dead and many other miracles have occurred.

So I differ from the saganists on two points at least: the cosmos does not exist on its own, and the power that sustains it sometimes manifests its sustaining presence in ways radically different from the norm (that is, there are miracles). Now if I differed from the saganists on only these two points (and on such closely related points as the imminent end of the Church), they and I could accept pretty much the same science. Whether the world depends on a power outside itself, and whether there are miracles are not questions to be decided by science. (I do not of course deny that if science can provide a convincing natural explanation for a hitherto mysterious event, then that is an important piece of evidence that must be taken into account by anyone who is trying to determine whether *that event* is a miracle. But this point has nothing to do with the question whether there are miracles.) Thus it would seem that on one point at least the saganists and I agree against the literalists: we accept the same science, or, at least, they and I are no more likely to disagree about science than are any two saganists.

As a matter of fact, however, this is very far from being true. If the saganists' science were entirely correct, this would not trouble me a bit. Nevertheless, I'm very skeptical about some of it. It's just not clear to me that it all *works*. There are three points about which I am doubtful. The first of them has to do with the beginning of the cosmos. When it began to emerge that the cosmos had a beginning in time, or, at least, that the cosmos did not have an infinite past in which it was pretty much the same as it is now, saganists began to try to come to terms with this awkward fact—producing in the process such philosophically motivated theories as the now discredited steady-state theory, the pretty much discredited "oscillating universe" theory, and the currently rather fashionable theory that the cosmos began as a quantum fluctuation. All these theories are addressed to the same sort of questions as the cosmological argument. I will not discuss them. I want instead to raise some questions in the general vicinity of the argument from design. (But I am not going to discuss those very general features of the cosmos and the laws it obeys that have led some to observe that it appears to have been "fine-tuned" to permit the existence of life—the features that led Fred Hoyle to say, one might almost say to *complain*, that it looked as if a superintellect had been monkeying with the laws of physics.) The two theses which are important components of the saganists' science and about which I am doubtful are their theses concerning macroevolution and human origins. (To these two theses a third might be added: that life arose as the result of a purely natural process. But it would be hard to have a profitable discussion of this question, because, owing to the fact that the origin of life is at present wholly mysterious, wise saganists will probably want to say only that life arose by *some* natural process, and, while I am not as sure of this as they are, I see no particular reason to dispute it. I will remark only that if all life on earth is, as someone facetiously suggested, descended from bacterium-like organisms negligently deposited by extraterrestrial picnickers on the recently cooled surface of the earth, this would account perfectly for the earliest fossil evidences of life.)

Let us turn to the topic of macroevolution, the evolutionary differentiation of very broad taxa, such as phyla. Macroevolution, according to saganism, is microevolution writ large. The same principles of random variation and natural selection that have caused a pair of fruit flies blown by chance to the Hawaiian Islands to have descendants that belong to many different species have brought it about that that first self-replicating molecule has as descendants arthropods and vertebrates and the members of every other phylum.

There is, I think, no reason to believe this, beyond the bare fact that phylogenesis has in fact occurred. This is not to say that there is no reason to believe that all living organisms have a common ancestry. No doubt the fact that penguins and spiders and algae share at least one apparently arbitrary characteristic—the code by which nucleic acid specifies the structures of proteins—is best explained by the same hypothesis that explains the common features of the Hawaiian fruit flies: common ancestry. The common-ancestry thesis cannot be regarded as a fact that is known simply on the basis of induction on many observations since (I believe) no two known species, living or extinct, are such that it is universally agreed by the experts that one is ancestral to the other; even cases in which, of two known species, one is believed by some experts to be ancestral to the other (e.g., *Homo sapiens* and *Homo erectus*) are rare.[10] But the indirect arguments are persuasive. It

10. The logical structure of this thesis could easily be misunderstood. Compare the following similar statement: No living human being is known to be descended from any

is not that there are no difficulties with the common-ancestry hypothesis, but, as Cardinal Newman said in another connection, a thousand difficulties do not add up to a single doubt, and it seems reasonable to believe that these difficulties will someday be resolved. So I am not saying that the common-ancestry thesis is supported by no evidence beyond the bare fact that phylogenesis has occurred. What seems to me to have only that much evidential support is that the interplay of random variation and natural selection—I shall hereafter refer to this interplay as simply 'natural selection'—is the sole mechanism responsible for the genesis of phyla and other broad taxa. Or, since we are not disputing the common-ancestry thesis, we may say: for the *differentiation* of phyla and other broad taxa—that is, for macroevolution.

One of the strongest reasons for being skeptical about the hypothesis that natural selection is the only mechanism driving macroevolution is the absence of intermediate forms. This absence is striking, even at the level of the biological class. Amphibians, for example, are supposed to have evolved from lobe-finned fish in a sequence that involved no radical difference between one generation and the next. A few fish of some species, or so the story goes, got into some environmental situation in which, owing to natural selection, their descendants in due course formed a new species; a population of fish belong to *that* species suffered a similar fate, and, eventually, across a bridge of many, many species, the original population of fish produced descendants with pentadactyl limbs and all the other taxonomic characteristics of amphibians. The trouble with this scenario is that the fossil record reveals none of these intermediate species. Full-blown amphibia simply *appear* at a certain point in the fossil record with no visible not-quite-amphibian antecedents. And this is not an isolated example: there are few, if any, even remotely plausible fossil candidates for intermediates between reptiles and amphibians or between any class and the class out of which, by general agreement, it is supposed to have evolved. And yet the theory of evolution by natural selection seems to predict that, if the members of class *A* are descended from a population belonging to class *B*, then there must once have existed a vast number of "transitional" organisms, organisms intermediate between the two classes. The theory seems to make this prediction because the members of any two classes are radically different in anatomy and physiology

----

known human being who lived before the fall of Rome. Indeed, it is possible (although unlikely) that no person known to history who lived prior to A.D. 400 has any currently living descendants.

and because the effects of natural selection on a population accumulate very gradually.

Darwin was deeply troubled by the fact that no trace had been discovered of forms intermediate between broad taxa. His solution to the problem was to ascribe the absence of known intermediates to the inherent imperfection of the fossil record and to the fact that "only a small portion of the surface of the earth has been geologically explored and no part with sufficient care."[11] In Darwin's day, fewer than 1 percent of the fossils that have today been discovered and catalogued were known. My impression is that today few if any paleontologists accept his solution. If my amateurish researches have not led me astray, the current judgment of most paleontologists is that if, for example, amphibians had evolved from some population of fish as gradually as Darwin believed they must have, then the fossils of some forms intermediate between fish and amphibians would almost certainly have been discovered. The obvious move to make in the face of this judgment, if one wants to save the hypothesis that natural selection is the sole mechanism behind macroevolution, is to say that the evolutionary differentiation of the amphibia proceeded not gradually but explosively and that the number of generations separating true fish and true amphibian was consequently very small. ('Gradual', 'explosive', and 'small' are, of course, relative terms. Any evolution by natural selection must be "gradual" by some standards, since any generation of the most rapidly evolving population must be practically indistinguishable from its predecessor. The idea is that, contrary to what Darwin thought, the time required for a species to become distinct is small in comparison with the average "lifetime" of a species of that sort.) In that case, the intermediate organisms would not have been numerous or widespread. If they were few and were confined to a small geographical area, then the discovery of even one fossilized intermediate could be highly improbable. And, of course, the same story can be told about all macroevolutionary transitions. It goes like this: *all* taxa at whatever level tend to be stable—particularly as regards the gross anatomical properties evidence of which is preserved in fossils—for long periods and then, under special environmental conditions, to differentiate locally and all but instantaneously. Now by the timetable of the geological record, "instantaneously" could comfortably encompass many thousands of generations of evolving organisms. The trick is to suppose that differen-

11. Charles Darwin, *The Origin of Species*, 6th ed. (1872; New York: Collier Books, 1962), p. 327.

tiation occurs slowly enough to be explained by natural selection and fast enough to account for the absence of intermediate forms from the fossil record.[12] Well, maybe this will work. But the skeptic will wonder whether such a rate exists, even as an abstract possibility. Despite my very real awareness of my ignorance of these matters, I make bold to confess that I find it difficult to believe that some fish was separated from some amphibian by only—to pick a figure that must be right within a factor of two or three—ten thousand generations, each of which differed from is predecessor only to the extent allowed by the operation of natural selection. Most biologists, apparently, find this easy enough to believe. The ignorant skeptic like myself, the village atheist, will wonder whether their ability to believe this is rooted in their nuts-and-bolts anatomical, physiological, and biochemical expertise, or whether it is a product of their belief that things could easily have happened this way because this is how things did in fact happen.

And then there is a statistical problem. Even if there were few enough intermediates between fish and amphibian for it to be highly improbable that we should have found any of their fossils, it could nevertheless be highly probable that we should have found fossils of intermediates between *some* two classes.[13] The statistical principle I am appealing to is illustrated by the following fact: If I am a member of a randomly selected group of twenty-three people, the odds are just short of 17 to 1 against any of the others having the same birthday as I, but the odds are better than even that *some* two people in the group of twenty-three will have the same birthday.

One can also raise the question whether the missing intermediates are even logically possible, given that evolution proceeds by natural selection alone. Let us ask the question this way. If you took the genotype of a given lobe-finned fish, could you change it into the genotype of a given primitive amphibian by a sequence of gradual steps of the kind that evolution—even explosive evolution—by natural section requires? (Here we think of natural selection as operating at the genetic

12. These words are my own attempt to give a brief statement of the "theory of punctuated equilibria" in such a way that this theory is clearly represented as a Darwinian theory. For a description of the theory of punctuated equilibria by its most eloquent exponent, see Stephen Jay Gould, "The Episodic Nature of Evolutionary Change," in his *The Panda's Thumb* (New York: Norton, 1980).

13. But what about *Archaeopterix*? Is it not an intermediate between reptiles and birds? This is possible. There are, nevertheless, powerful arguments for the conclusion that *Archaeopterix* was simply a bird. See chap. 8 of Michael Denton, *Evolution: A Theory in Crisis* (Bethesda, Md.: Adler & Adler, 1986), for a discussion of *Archaeopterix* and the coelacanth and other candidate "intermediates."

level; we think of selection pressure changing the relative frequencies of the genes that make up a population's gene pool.)

It might be argued that it is easy to see that this would be possible. Suppose that the fish and the amphibian genomes each contain one hundred thousand loci and that, in our two selected organisms, the same genes are present at ninety thousand of them and different ones at the other ten thousand. Then to change the genotype of the fish into the genotype of the amphibian in a sequence of one thousand steps, we simply make the necessary gene replacements ten at a time. The problem with this argument is that there is no guarantee that such a procedure would produce at each step a genotype that corresponds to a viable organism. In fact, I find it hard to believe that it would. Let me try to make my difficulties with this notion clear by means of an analogy.

Suppose we own a very sophisticated automated factory. Properly programmed, our factory is capable of turning suitable raw materials into just about any sort of finished product. At present, a stream of steel ingots is flowing into the factory and a stream of meat grinders of identical design is flowing out. Another program, which we have in our files, would cause the factory to produce meat grinders of a more advanced design. (No single part of the "advanced" meat grinder, not even the smallest nut or bolt, would be exactly like any part of the current, "primitive" meat grinder.) Now let us examine printouts of the two programs. Each program consists of one hundred thousand lines, each line being a complex string of characters. Ninety thousand lines are the same in the two programs, and the rest different. Could you change one program into the other by a sequence of one thousand ten-line-at-a-time changes? Obviously you could. But would all the "intermediate" programs produce some sort of meat grinder—or anything at all? It is hard to see how this could be. The new instruction that you insert at line 27 tells a bolt-making machine to produce bolts of a size slightly larger than the bolts it contributed to the original meat grinder. In order to accommodate that change, you have to change the size of 24 holes to be bored in 16 pieces of metal produced by four stamping machines and two milling machines; you have to change the instructions that determine the sizes of the nuts intended to fit those bolts; you have to reprogram the devices that pick up and manipulate the nuts and bolts; it will now take only 960 bolts instead of 1,000 to fill a standard bolt-bin, so the bins will have to be emptied every 88 seconds instead of every 92 seconds or they will overflow, and so the rate at which the bolt-collecting machine moves among the bins will have to be increased by an appropriate amount—and so on and so on. Unless all of these modifications in the factory's behavior can be embodied in nine other one-line changes in the program—changes that do not themselves necessitate yet further changes—*any* ten-line change in the program that includes the change we have introduced at line 27 will produce not meat grinders but a lot of jammed milling machines and conveyors belts.

It seems to me that the genotypes that underlie the physiology and anatomy of a given fish and a given amphibian are probably in this respect a lot like the programs that underlie our two styles of meat grinder. That is, I doubt whether there is any path in logical space from one to another that proceeds by changing a small number of genes at each step: every path you try will (I suspect) eventually run up against organs and systems that are no longer coordinated—perhaps even against proteins that don't fold properly. You can only look from one to the other and shake your head sadly and say, "You can't get there from here." At least not by the mode of transport envisaged. Not by a sequence of steps the size that selection pressure can effect in a given gene pool in one generation. That is *local* transport. It can take you from light peppered moths to dark ones and—a much longer ride— from one species of fruit fly to another. These are in different parts of the same town. It's no good if you want to go from Europe to Australia—that is, from the fish to the amphibia. I should also point out that even if there *are* possible"small-step" paths from fish to amphibia, these paths might compose only an infinitesimal region within the space of all the possible paths that confront the ancestral population of fish, and thus the evolution by natural selection of amphibia from fish might be so vastly improbable as not to be worth considering.[14] And—to return to our previous theme—it might be that all or most of the possible paths are too long to be consistent with the absence of intermediate forms from the fossil record.

Nevertheless—or so I believe—the amphibia did evolve from some population of fish. If this is right, there are two possibilities. There is

14. We should remember, however, that vastly improbable events are not necessarily surprising events: the conception and birth of a human being with any *particular* genetic makeup is a vastly improbable event. It might be that the number of possible biological classes that could evolve out of *some* population of fish is so huge that it is not surprising that one such class did evolve, despite the fact that the prior probability of *its* evolving was all but infinitesimal. I cannot myself believe that logical space contains a suitably enormous number of possible classes that could evolve from some population of fish, but one's intuitions in this area are probably not of much value.

the possibility that an intelligent being has been guiding evolution by a series of actions that directly affect the genes of the evolving organisms. If we think in terms of our "meat-grinder" analogy, such a being would correspond to a computer programmer who turns one program into the other in a series of steps each of which involves a very large number of carefully coordinated changes. And there is the possibility that there is some yet undiscovered mechanism that does the same thing—perhaps not as efficiently as an intelligent being, but efficiently enough. The second possibility is the one that should be investigated, if only because the first cannot be *investigated*.

Remember the cautionary tale of Lord Kelvin. Assuming that the mechanisms underlying solar radiation must be explainable in terms of the physics he knew, the great physicist calculated—correctly, I understand, given his assumptions—that the sun could not have been shining for more than about twenty million years. When the paleontologists told him that there had been life on earth for much longer than that, he contemptuously replied, "There are two sciences, physics and stamp collecting," meaning that a paleontologist's *estimate* of a period of time must fall before a physicist's *calculation* of a period of time. But if he had had an open mind, he might have looked at the paleontological data and said something like, "It may be only an estimate, but it's a damned good one. It begins to look as if solar radiation may be produced by some mechanism other than heating due to gravitational compression, though I can't imagine what it might be." And, of course, there *was* such a mechanism, one that Lord Kelvin couldn't imagine because it was conceptually inaccessible to a physicist at the turn of the twentieth century.

Many areas of science present us with examples of cases in which long-term effects are produced by different mechanisms from those that produce short-term effects. Michael Denton has pointed out that this is true in the case of meteorology and geology: the mechanisms that underlie changes in climate are not those that underlie changes in the weather; mountain building is explained by mechanisms other than those that account for short-term, superficial geological change.[15] Nevertheless, it may be, for all I have said, that natural selection *can* account for macroevolution. Against the cautionary tale of Lord Kelvin should be set the cautionary tale of Sir Isaac Newton. Newton thought he saw that planetary orbits must be unstable, and he speculated that they were subject to periodic divine correction. Laplace, however, was

15. Denton, *Evolution*, pp. 87–88.

able to show that Newton's own mechanisms—the laws of motion and the law of universal gravitation—entail that planetary orbits are stable enough to account for our observations. The point of this tale would be unaffected if Newton had postulated not supernatural interference with planetary dynamics but an unknown natural mechanism that supplemented the mechanisms he had discovered. The totality of the implications of the theory of evolution by natural selection, like the totality of the implications of Newtonian mechanics, cannot be grasped by the mind in a single flash of insight. But I say this: our understanding of macroevolution is either in the position of our understanding of orbital mechanics before Laplace or else in the position of our understanding of solar radiation before the advent of nuclear physics. If the former— well, the theory of evolution by natural selection has had in Darwin its Newton, but it has not yet had its Laplace. I think that our tentative conclusion should be that the theory of evolution by natural selection alone is doubtful in a way that many scientific theories are not. We may be confident that we understand, at least in very broad outline, where the stars get the energy to shine and what the forces are that cause mountains to rise. It is premature to believe that we have even in broad outline a satisfactory theory of macroevolution. If we temporarily suspend our belief in the theory that macroevolution is microevolution writ large, I cannot see that we shall thereby come to any harm. The theory does not *do* anything for us that I know of, beyond just sitting there and providing an explanation for the diversity of life. In this respect it is like the theory that the diversity of life is the work of an intelligent designer. There are many beautiful and satisfying explanations of microevolutionary phenomena in terms of natural selection. (My favorite is the explanation of the showy plumage of male dabbling ducks.) But I know of no explanation of any macroevolutionary phenomenon—sexual dimorphism, say—in terms of natural selection.

Let us now turn to the evolution of humanity, or, more exactly, to the evolution of those cognitive capacities that make humanity so strikingly different from all other species: I mean the capacities that allow us to do fantastic things like theoretical physics or evolutionary biology or drawing in perspective or, for that matter, making a promise or deciding not to plant wheat if there's a dry winter—things absolutely without analogues in any other species.[16] The evolution of these capaci-

16. When I wrote the pages that follow in the text, I was aware that they were inspired by a wonderful lecture of Hilary Putnam's, "The Place of Facts in a World of Values"—in *The Nature of the Physical Universe: The 1976 Nobel Conference,* ed. Douglas Huff and Omer Prewett (New York: John Wiley & Sons, 1979)—that I had read

ties, unique in the history of life, is a phenomenon of microevolution, and, therefore, even if macroevolution involves other mechanisms than natural selection, it may be that our special cognitive capacities are entirely a product of natural selection. It must be understood that by "cognitive capacities" I mean capacities determined by the physiology of the brain: not capacities that are conferred on one by one's culture and education, but capacities that are written on one's chromosomes. I think that no one doubts that our paleolithic ancestors—our ancestors of, say, thirty thousand years ago—had more or less the same cognitive capacities as we. A paleolithic infant, transported to our era by a time machine and raised in our culture, would be as likely to grow into a normal and useful member of our culture as an infant brought here by airplane from Tibet. Moreover, an immigrant paleolithic baby would be as likely to become a brilliant high-energy physicist or evolutionary biologist as an immigrant Tibetan baby. If this is true, then the cognitive capacities needed to master—and to excel at—any modern scientific discipline were already present, in more or less their present statistical distribution, among our paleolithic ancestors. (A race of mute, inglorious Miltons indeed!) And this means, according to the saganists, that these capacities evolved by the operation of natural selection among the ancestors of our paleolithic ancestors. And this, in its turn, implies that there was some character, or set of characters, such that (a) possession of those characters by some of its members conferred a reproductive advantage upon some population composed of our remote ancestors and (b) the presence of those characters within the present human population constitutes the biological basis of the human capacity for theoretical physics and evolutionary biology.

Have we any reason to think that there exists any set of characters having both these features? (Let us arbitrarily call a set of characters having both features *special;* I choose an arbitrary designation because an arbitrary designation is at least not tendentious.) If we have indeed evolved by natural selection from ancestors lacking the biological capacity to do physics and biology, then the answer to this question must be Yes; after all, we're here, and we are as we are. But if we set aside any conviction we may have that our cognitive capacities were produced by

---

several years before. When I recently reread that lecture, in connection with preparing the present essay for publication, I discovered that I had remembered it better than I knew, and that in some places I had come close to reproducing Putnam's exact words. I have let these passages stand, on the principle that imitation is the sincerest form of flattery. (But Professor Putnam should not be held responsible for the ways in which I have used the materials he has provided.)

natural selection, can we discover any reason to believe that there exists—even as an abstract possibility—a "special" set of characters? It might be said that we know that a special set exists because we can point to it: our collective name for it is "intelligence." Now "intelligence" is a pretty vague concept, but not so vague that we can't see that this suggestion is wrong. I expect that no one would care to maintain that if (say) Albert Einstein and Thomas Mann had been switched in their cradles,[17] Mann would have made fundamental contributions to physics—or even that he would have become a physicist. It is very doubtful whether Mann possessed (in however latent a form) the quality that Einstein's biographers call "physical intuition," a quality which Einsein possessed in an extraordinary degree and which even a run-of-the-mill physicist must possess in some degree. And yet it would be simply silly to say that Einstein was more *intelligent* than his fellow Nobel Prize winner. Einstein did not discover the general theory of relativity because he was so very bright—though doubtless high intelligence was a necessary condition for his achievement—but, insofar as a "cause" can be named at all, because of his superb faculty of physical intuition. Couldn't we easily imagine a population whose members were as *intelligent* as we—if they were dispersed among us, we should hear them commended for their "intelligence" with about the same frequency as we should hear the members of any randomly chosen group of our fellows commended—but who were as lacking in "physical intuition" as the average accountant or philosopher or pure mathematician? (I mean, of course, to imagine a population that is *biologically* incapable of displaying any appreciable degree of physical intuition. No doubt certain genes must be present in an individual who possesses that enviable quality; what I want to imagine is a population of human beings within which some of these genes are so rare that the chance of the requisite combination of genes occurring in any of its members is negligible.) Couldn't such a population develop quite an impressive civilization—as impressive, say, as classical Chinese civilization or the civilization of ancient Egypt? The point raised by this question would seem to apply a fortiori to the reproductive success of such a population in a "state of nature." Why should a population with the gene frequencies I have imagined fare any worse in the forests or on the savannas than a population in which the genes that, in the right combination, yield the capacity for physical intuition are relatively numerous?

17. Actually, Mann was born in 1875 and Einstein in 1879.

The saganists' answer to this question will, I think, go more or less as follows. "You are making mysteries where none exist. You might as well make a mystery of my contention—and I do contend it—that the ability to play the cello is a product of natural selection. Isn't that mysterious, the mystery-monger asks, when there were no cellos, not even primitive cellos, on the primeval savannas? But the capacity to play the cello—that is, the biological capacity to be taught to play the cello in the right cultural circumstances, a biological capacity that was presumably about as frequent among our paleolithic ancestors as it is among us—is an aggregate of a lot of generally useful capacities. Two obvious ones are manual dexterity and the ability to discriminate pitches. Each was advantageous to our primitive ancestors, since they needed to chip flints and to interpret subtle changes in the chorus of insect noises in the forest night. We should also not neglect the fact that most, if not all, genes have many different effects on the constitution of the whole organism. It may therefore be that some of the genes whose co-presence in Einstein was responsible for his remarkable physical intuition were selected for in the remote past because of advantageous effects functionally unrelated to physical intuition. In sum, while we perhaps don't understand physical intuition all that well, there is no reason to doubt that its presence in a given present-day individual is due to a combination of genes that were, individually if not collectively, advantageous to our primitive ancestors."

Well, if there is no reason to doubt this, is there any reason to believe it? If I wanted to pick someone to learn to chip flints or to interpret insect noises, I should certainly pick a cello player over someone who was all thumbs or someone who was tone-deaf. But if you know nothing about a certain person except that he or she is a first-rate theoretical physicist, what can you predict that that person will be good at—other than theoretical physics? You know that the physicist will be of high general intelligence, but you don't need to look for a physicist if you want intelligence. You know that the physicist will have a certain flair for thinking in terms of differential equations, though not necessarily a degree of mathematical ability that would excite the admiration of a mathematician. And that's about it. I don't suppose that you can predict that the physicist will have much in the way of spatial intuition (in the sense in which spatial intuition is required by an architectural draftsman). Nor is the physicist particularly likely to be a good mechanic or an accomplished inventor of mechanical devices or especially good at balancing a checkbook or counting cattle.

Quite possibly the first person to have the idea of the bow and arrow or to conceive the idea of making fire from the heat produced by friction would have to have had the qualities that would make a good physicist. Nevertheless, the intellectual conception of the great prehistoric inventions must have been a pretty rare occurrence; I can't see the great, but very rarely operative, advantages to a population of having in its gene pool the capacities for making such inventions as exerting much selection pressure on the population's gene pool. But let us concede that a population of modern human beings transported to some vastly ancient time (and divested of modern knowledge) would have had a distinct reproductive edge on otherwise similar populations that lacked the biological basis of physical intuition, owing to its capacity to invent the bow and arrow and fire-by-friction. This concession simply raises a further question: How did the gene frequencies that ground this capacity get established before—it must have been *before*—there was a relatively advanced technology to confer on them the opportunity to be advantageous? I find this question puzzling, but it may well have a plausible answer, and I don't want to let my case rest very heavily on the assumption that it has no plausible answer. I rest my case primarily on two further points.

First, *is* it all that clear that the idea of making fire by friction and the idea of understanding gravitation as a function of the curvature of space-time were arrived at by the exercise of the same cognitive capacity? "This causes heat; greater heat than this causes fire; therefore doing this longer and harder may produce enough heat to cause fire" is a splendid piece of abstract reasoning. But is there any reason to believe that a population a few of whose members are capable of such reasoning must also contain a few people who are, genetically speaking, Newtons and Einsteins? I can see no reason to be confident about the answer to this question, one way or the other.

Secondly, the "cello" analogy is deeply flawed. Cellos are human artifacts and are constructed to be playable by organisms that have such abilities as human beings happen to have. The structure of the science of physics is certainly not arbitrary in the way that the structure of a cello is. A race of intelligent beings descended from pigs rather than from primates might have invented stringed instruments radically different in structure from cellos and quite unplayable by human beings. And music itself is rather an arbitrary thing compared with science. If there are intelligent extraterrestrials who, like us, derive pleasure from listening to rhythmic sequences of sounds among which there are certain definite relations of pitch, it does not seem to be very reasonable to expect that we could make much of their sounds. To adapt an aphorism of Wittgenstein's, if a lion could sing, we shouldn't want to listen. But if extraterrestrials have invented physics, their physics will have to be a lot like ours. Extraterrestrial physics must resemble terrestrial physics because physical theories are about the real world, and the same real world confronts pig, primate, and extraterrestrial. And yet (to take one example of the sort of thing physicists look into) the structures of the various families of elementary particles, and the forces by which they interact, can hardly have had any sort of effect on the evolution of the cognitive capacities of our remote ancestors. There is no reason for the paleoanthropologist to learn about the decay modes of the Z^0 boson in order to learn about how the brains of our ancestors evolved toward the possession of a capacity that is (among other things) a capacity to theorize about the decay modes of the Z^0 boson. Our ability to do elementary-particle physics seems to me, therefore, to be as puzzling as our ability to play the cello would be if cellos were not artifacts but naturally occurring objects, objects whose occurrence in nature was wholly independent of the economy of *Homo habilis*. Suppose, for example, that cellos grew on trees and only in a part of the world never inhabited by our evolving ancestors. Wouldn't it be a striking coincidence that some of us could learn to play them so well? Isn't it a striking coincidence that we can theorize about elementary particles so well?

I once heard Noam Chomsky say that our ability to do physical science depends on a very specific set of cognitive capacities, and that, quite possibly, the reason that there are no real social sciences may be that we just happen to lack a certain equally specific set of cognitive capacities. He went on to speculate that we might one day discover among the stars a species as good at social science as we are at physical science and as bad at physical science as we are at social science. He did not raise the question why natural selection would bother to confer either of these highly specific sets of capacities on a species. (Presumably the answer would have to be that the right gene combinations for success in physical science were just part of the luck of our remote ancestors' draw and that, having arisen by chance, these gene combinations endured because they were in some way advantageous to our ancestors. But we have already been over this ground.) Einstein once remarked that the only thing that was unintelligible about the world was that it was intelligible. He was calling attention to the (or so it seemed to him) unreasonable simplicity of the laws of nature, and he supposed, I think, that the world was intelligible because it was simple. That does not seem to me to be quite right. The ultimate laws of nature may be simple, but that does not make them intelligible to highly intelligent people—Thomas Mann, say, or Virgil, or J. S. Mill, or Nietzsche—who lack the very specific set of cognitive capacities that enables physicists to pick their way through the flux of the phenomena to the deep simplicities. What is "unintelligible" if anything in this area is, is that some of us should possess those capacities.

Saganists, therefore, owing to their adherence to natural selection as the sole engine of evolution, believe in what I have dubbed a "special" set of characters—a set of characters that *both* conferred a reproduction advantage on some population of our remote ancestors *and* underlies our ability to do science. I, for reasons that I have tried to explain, am a skeptic about this. It seems to me that there is no very convincing argument a priori for the existence of a special set of characters and that the only argument a posteriori for its existence is that our scientific abilities could not be a consequence of natural selection unless such a set existed. For my part, however, I am going to suspend judgment about whether our scientific abilities are a consequence of natural selection till I see some reason to believe that there exists a special set of characters. Belief in a special set of characters, indeed, seems to me to be, in its epistemic features, very strongly analogous to belief in a Creator. More exactly, it is analogous to the type of belief in a Creator that is held by its adherents to rest on rational argument and public evidence—as opposed to private religious experience and historical revelation. There are, in my view, no *compelling* arguments for the existence or for the nonexistence of a Creator, no arguments that would force anyone who understood their premises to assent to their conclusion or else be irrational or perverse. There are compelling arguments for *some* conclusions: that the world is more than six thousand years old, for example, or that astrology is nonsense, but there are no compelling arguments for any conclusion of philosophical interest, whether its subject matter be God or free will or universals or the nature of morality or anything else that philosophers have argued about. Nevertheless, there are some very *good* philosophical arguments: serious arguments which are worth the attention of serious thinkers and which lend a certain amount of support to their conclusions. Among these, there are certain arguments having to do with God. The cosmological argument and the design argument, for example, appear to me to be arguments that are as good as any philosophical argument that has ever been adduced in support of any conclusion whatever. And yet the conclusions of these arguments (they are not quite the same) can be rejected by a perfectly rational person who understands perfectly all the issues involved in evaluating them.

I very much doubt whether there is any argument for the existence of a special set of characters that is any better in this respect than the design argument or the cosmological argument. It may nevertheless be that certain people—paleoanthropologists, perhaps—know that a special set of characters exists. It may be that they know this because of their mastery of a vast range of data too complex to be summarized in anything so simple as a single argument. By the same token, however, it may be that there are certain people who know that a Creator exists and know this because of their mystery of a vast range of data too complex to be summarized in anything so simple as a single argument.

My own guess is that neither sort of knowledge exists. If there are people who *know* that there is a Creator, this must be due to factors other than (or, perhaps, in addition to) the inferences they have drawn from their observations of the natural world; and no one knows whether there is a special set of characters. Belief in a special set of characters is based on nothing more than a conviction that natural selection must be the ultimate basis of all evolutionary episodes (except those so minor that, if no explanation in terms of natural selection is apparent, they may plausibly be assigned to genetic drift). And that conviction, like nineteenth-century conviction that the universe has always been much as it is at present, is one that is held mainly because of its supposed antitheistic implications. (Actually, it has no antitheistic implications, but it is widely believed that it does.) Atheists often preach on the emotional attractiveness of theism. It needs to be pointed out that atheism is also a very attractive thesis. Very few people are atheists against their will. Atheism is attractive for at least two reasons. First, it is an attractive idea to suppose that one may well be one of the higher links in the Great Chain of Being—perhaps even the highest. (This idea is attractive for several reasons, not the least of which is that most people cannot quite rid themselves of the very well justified conviction that a being who knew all their motives and inmost thoughts might not entirely approve of them.) Secondly, there are very few atheists who do not admire themselves for possessing that combination of mental acuity and intellectual honesty that is, by their own grudging admission, the hallmark of atheists everywhere. The theist, however, is in a position to be an agnostic about the existence of a special set of characters, just as someone who accepts the saganists' science is in a position to be an agnostic about the existence of a Creator. Each is in a position to say, "Well, I don't know. There may be such a thing. What are the arguments?"

Confident and logically acute theists are not going to be impressed by arguments for the nonexistence of God. Because they are logically acute, they will see that, while some of these arguments may be worthy of serious attention, they are not compelling in the very strong sense I spelled out above. Because they are confident, they will not abandon a world-view of which that belief is an integral part for anything less than a compelling argument. Similarly, confident and logically acute saganists are not going to be impressed by arguments for the nonexistence of a special set of characters. Because they are logically acute, they will see that, while some of these arguments may be worthy of serious attention, none of them is compelling. Because they are confident, they will not abandon a world-view of which that belief is an integral part for anything less than a compelling argument.

In the past, theism has made important contributions to science. It has, in fact, been very plausibly argued that modern science did not (as the saganists suggest) arise in the teeth of clerical opposition but is rather a *product* of Western Latin Christianity, as closely connected with it (causally and historically, not logically) as is Gothic architecture. Those who accept this thesis, however, sometimes say that the umbilical cord connecting science to Mother Church has long since been cut, and that science now proceeds quite independently of the religious or antireligious convictions of its practitioners. I wonder if the case of evolutionary biology doesn't show that this is at least a partial falsehood. Suppose I am right in suggesting that there are grave difficulties with the idea that natural selection is the only mechanism behind macroevolution and the evolution of certain specifically human cognitive capacities. Suppose that the allegiance of saganists—and saganism is certainly widespread among evolutionary biologists—to these two evolutionary theses is due not to scientific considerations but to the atheism that is a central component of saganism. Consider, finally, the following two evaluations of the situation in evolutionary biology. The first quotation, rather a famous one, is from the *Encyclopédie française* (1965). Its author is the naturalist Paul Lemoine, professor at the Museum of Paris:

> The result of this exposé is that the theory of evolution is impossible. Basically, despite appearances, no one believes it anymore, and one says—without attaching any other importance to it—"evolution" in order to signify "a series of events in time"; or "more evolved" or "less evolved," in the sense of "more perfected," "less perfected" because such is the language of convention, accepted and almost obligatory in the scientific world. Evolution is a sort of dogma which the priests do not believe in anymore, but which they keep up for the sake of their flocks.

> It is necessary to have the courage to say this in order that the men of the next generation may direct their research in another way.[18]

Now taken as a sober sociological thesis about the beliefs of scientists, this must be regarded as Gallic overstatement. Many of the priests, perhaps a large majority, really do believe sincerely in their dogma. But there is an important truth behind the overstatement—or so it seems to me in my ignorance. The truth is that the theory of macroevolution by natural selection alone is doing no scientific work, and that adherence to it consists mainly in talking in a certain way. This quotation, by the way, gives the lie to the saganist thesis that the only resistance to the theory of evolution by natural selection is provided by theological obscurantists. As a matter of fact, there has been, ever since Darwin, a respectable body of scientific opinion opposed to the Darwinian account of evolution. For some reason, such opposition has been more prominent on the continent of Europe than in the English-speaking countries.

My second quotation is from the Australian biochemist Michael Denton:

> The overriding supremacy of the myth [sc., that natural selection accounts for all evolutionary phenomena] has created a widespread illusion that the theory of evolution was all but proved one hundred years ago and that all subsequent biological research—paleontological, zoological and in the newer branches of genetics and molecular biology—has provided ever-increasing evidence for Darwinian ideas. Nothing could be further from the truth. The fact is that the evidence was so patchy one hundred years ago that even Darwin himself had increasing doubts as to the validity of his views, and the only aspect of his theory which has received any support over the past century is where it applies to microevolutionary phenomena. His general theory, that all life on earth had originated and evolved in the gradual successive accumulation of fortuitous mutations, is still, as it was in Darwin's day, a highly speculative hypothesis entirely without direct factual support and very far from that self-evident axiom some of its more aggressive advocates would have us believe.[19]

18. Paul Lemoine, quoted by Etienne Gilson in *From Aristotle to Darwin and Back Again* [a translation by John Lyon of Gilson's 1971 *D'Aristote à Darwin et retour*] (South Bend, Ind.: University of Notre Dame Press, 1984), pp. 88–89.

19. Denton, *Evolution*, p. 77. Denton's book is indispensable reading for anyone interested in the scientific difficulties faced by the Darwinian theory of evolution. Since this essay was written, another indispensable book has appeared: Phillip E. Johnson, *Darwin on Trial* (Washington, D.C.: Regnery Gateway, 1991).

May we not speculate that atheism is impeding progress in evolutionary biology? If there are actually other mechanisms at work in evolution than natural selection, and if atheism is emotionally (though not, of course, logically) wedded to the idea that natural selection is the only mechanism of evolution, perhaps a leaven of theists among evolutionary biologists would make a genuine search for such a mechanism possible. Perhaps, in fact, a more general allegiance among its practitioners to the important truths contained in the book of Genesis could be of real service to science. If that is possible, however, it is not probable. Owing to the general perversity of human beings—a feature of our species whose explanation can be found in St. Paul's reading of the third chapter of Genesis—there is likely to continue to be only one kind of interaction between the book of Genesis and science: silly squabbles between Genesiac literalists and saganists.[20]

20. Parts of this essay were delivered as the Kraemer Lecture at the University of Arkansas, Fayettesville, Arkansas, in March 1989.

6

Critical Studies
of the New Testament and
The User of the New Testament

BY *users* of the New Testament, I mean, first, ordinary churchgoers who read the New Testament and hear it read in church and hear it preached on, and, secondly, the pastors who minister to the ordinary churchgoers, and, thirdly, theologians who regard the New Testament as an authoritative divine revelation.

By *critical studies of the New Testament* (hereinafter "Critical Studies"), I mean those historical studies which either deny the authority of the New Testament or else maintain a methodological neutrality on the question of its authority, and which attempt, by methods that presuppose either a denial of or neutrality about its authority, to investigate such matters as the authorship, dates, histories of composition, historical reliability, and mutual dependency of the various books of the New Testament.[1] Source criticism, form criticism, and redaction criticism provide many central examples of Critical Studies as I mean to use the term, but I do not mean to restrict its application to Gospel studies. An author who argues that Paul did not write the letter to the Ephesians or that 2 Peter was composed well into the second century is engaged in what I am calling Critical Studies. For that matter, so are

Selection taken from *Hermes and Athena: Biblical Exegesis and Philosophical Theology,* edited by Thomas Flint and Eleonore Stump; PCR 1993 by University of Notre Dame Press. Reprinted by permission of the publisher.

1. This is a purely stipulatory definition. My conclusions about "Critical Studies" apply only to those studies that meet the strict terms of this definition.

authors who argue that Paul *did* write Ephesians, or who (like the late J. A. T. Robinson) argue that 2 Peter was probably composed about A.D. 61, provided that they do not argue for those conclusions from premises concerning the authority or inspiration of the New Testament.

I exclude from "Critical Studies" all purely textual studies, studies that attempt to determine the original wording of the New Testament books by the comparative study of ancient manuscripts. Thus, the well-known arguments purporting to show that the last chapter of John was not a part of the original composition (arguments based mainly on a supposed discontinuity of sense in the text) belong to Critical Studies, while the well-known arguments purporting to show that the last twelve verses of Mark were not a part of the original composition (arguments based mainly on the fact that important early manuscripts do not contain those verses) do not belong to Critical Studies.

Again, a close study of a New Testament book or group of books or idea may not be an instance of what I am calling Critical Studies, for it may be that it does not raise questions of dates, authorship, historical reliability, and so on, but, so to speak, takes the texts at face value. An example of such a study would be Oscar Cullmann's famous Ingersol Lecture, "Immortality of the Soul or Resurrection of the Dead?"[2] But it is unusual for a book or article or lecture about the New Testament to be a "pure" example of the genre Critical Studies, and it is even more unusual for a book or article or lecture on the New Testament to contain no material that belongs to the genre. Most recent works on the New Testament (to judge from the very small sample of them that I have read) are mixtures of Critical Studies with many other things. My term 'Critical Studies' should therefore be regarded as a name for an aspect of New Testament scholarship, rather than for something that is a subject or discipline in its own right.

It is taken for granted in many circles that pastors and theologians must know a great deal about Critical Studies if they are to be responsible members of their professions, and it has been said that even ordinary churchgoers should know a lot more about Critical Studies than they usually do. My purpose in this essay is to present an argument against this evaluation of the importance of Critical Studies to users of the New Testament. I present this argument first in the form of a schematic outline, and proceed to fill in the detail of the argument by commentary on and defense of the premises.

2. Oscar Cullmann, *Immortality of the Soul or Resurrection of the Dead?* (London: Epworth Press, 1958).

Premise 1. If a user of the New Testament has grounds for believing that the New Testament is historically and theologically reliable, grounds that are independent of Critical Studies, and if he has good reason to believe that Critical Studies do not undermine these grounds, then he need not attend further to Critical Studies. (That is, once he has satisfied himself that Critical Studies do not undermine his reasons for believing in the historical and theological reliability of the New Testament, he need not attend further to Critical Studies.)

Comment on Premise 1

The famous Rylands Papyrus, a fragment of the Fourth Gospel, has been dated to around A.D. 130 on paleographic grounds. Clearly the methods by which this date was arrived at are *independent of* radiocarbon dating. But if radiocarbon dating of the fragment assigned it to the fourth century, this result would *undermine*—if it were incontrovertible, it would refute—the paleographic arguments for the second-century date. (The radiocarbon dating would not, of course, show where the paleographic arguments went wrong, but, if it were correct, it would show that they went wrong somewhere.)

Premise 2. The liturgical, homiletic, and pastoral use the Church has made of the New Testament, and the Church's attitude toward the proper use of the New Testament by theologians, presuppose that the New Testament is historically and theologically reliable.

Premise 3. These presuppositions of reliability do not depend on accidents of history, in the sense that if history had been different, the Church might have held different presuppositions and yet have been recognizably the same institution. If the Church's use of the New Testament had not presupposed the historical and theological reliability of the New Testament, the Church would have been a radically different sort of institution—or perhaps *it* would not have existed at all; perhaps what was called 'the Christian Church' or 'the Catholic Church' would have been a numerically distinct institution.

First Comment on Premise 3

If the Constitutional Convention of 1787 had established a political entity called 'the United States of America' by uniting the thirteen former colonies under a hereditary monarchy and an established church, the United States would have been a radically different sort of political entity; perhaps, indeed, the nation that was called 'the United States' would not have been the nation that is called that in fact.

If the New Testament books had never been collected into a canon and portions of this canon read at Mass and as part of the Divine Office, if preachers had not been assigned the task of preaching on New Testament texts, if Christians had not generally believed that the New Testament narratives presented a reasonably accurate account of Jesus' ministry, death, and Resurrection, and of the beginnings of the Church, if they had not believed that God speaks to us in the pages of the New Testament on particular occasions (as in the story of Augustine's conversion), if theologians had not generally believed that their speculations must be grounded in the spirit of, and subject to correction by the letter of, the New Testament—then the Church would have been a radically different institution. We might in fact wonder whether an institution that regarded what we call the New Testament as nothing more than twenty-seven venerable but nonauthoritative books would really be the institution that is referred to in the Nicene Creed as the one, holy, Catholic, and Apostolic Church. I think that we should have to say that if it *was* the same institution, it was that institution in a radically different form.

Second Comment on Premise 3

One might wonder why I am conducting my argument in terms of what the Church has presupposed about the New Testament, rather than in terms of what the Church has *taught* about the New Testament. The answer is that it is much clearer what the practice of the Church presupposes about the New Testament than it is what the Church has taught about the New Testament, the main reason for this being that the Church's practice as regards the New Testament has been much more uniform than its teaching. I grant that there can be disputes about just what it is that a given practice presupposes, but I prefer dealing with disputes of that sort to dealing with the disputes that would attend any very specific attempt to define the Church's teaching about the New Testament.

> Premise 4. There are grounds, grounds independent of Critical Studies, for believing that whatever the Church has presupposed is true—provided that presupposition is understood in the strong or "essential" sense described above.

Comment on Premises 3 and 4

There are things the Church has pretty uniformly presupposed in certain periods that are false. I would say, for example, that Paul, and probably all first-century Christians, presupposed that Christians would never be able to do much to change the large-scale features of what they called the World and people today call 'society'. This was doubtless partly because they expected that the World was not going to last long enough to be changed by *anything,* but they seem also to have thought of Christians as necessarily held in contempt (if not actively persecuted) by those on whom the World has conferred power and prestige. Today we know that, for good or ill, it is possible for there to be a formally Christian society, and that even in a society that is not formally Christian, or is formally anti-Christian, it is possible for Christians to exert significant influence on society as a whole.

No doubt there are false presuppositions that the Church has held uniformly from the day of Pentecost to the present, though it is not for me, who do not claim to be a prophet, to say what they might be. The combined force of premises 3 and 4 is this: Any such universally held but false presupposition of the Church is not essential to the Church's being what it is. And (the two premises imply) any presupposition of the Church that is essential to the Church's being what it is is true— or, more exactly, there are grounds for believing that it is true.

Premise 5. Critical Studies do not undermine these grounds, and there are good reasons for believing that they do not, reasons whose discovery requires no immersion in the minutiae of Critical Studies, but which can be grasped by anyone who attends to the most obvious features of Critical Studies.

These five premises entail the following conclusion:

Once users of the New Testament have satisfied themselves that Critical Studies do not undermine their independent grounds for believing in the historical and theological reliability of the New Testament, they need not attend further to Critical Studies.

First Comment on the Argument

I have already said that by Critical Studies I do not mean just any historical studies of or related to the New Testament. I have explicitly excluded from the category of Critical Studies purely textual studies and studies of aspects of the New Testament that, as I said, take the texts at face value. Many other historical studies related to the New Testament are obviously essential to pastors and theologians, and advisable for ordinary churchgoers who have the education and leisure to be able to profit from them.

Pastors and theologians should obviously know something about the history and geography of the ancient Mediterranean world. They should know something about who the Pharisees, Sadducees, and Zealots were, what the legal status of the Sanhedrin was, what the powers and responsibilities of a procurator were, what it meant to be a Roman citizen, and how an appeal to the emperor worked. They should know something about the Jewish religion and the other religions of the Roman world. They should know something about second-century Gnosticism and something about its probable first-century roots. They should know something about the social, agricultural, and legal facts and customs, knowledge of which is presupposed in the parables of Jesus. (I have found facts about fig trees to be enlightening.) All of this is obvious, and a lot more that could be said in the same vein is obvious. I mention it only to show that I do not mean to deny the obvious.

It is worth mentioning that there are historical studies that users of the New Testament need know little if anything about, but on which things that they must know something about are based. (The painstaking comparisons of manuscripts by which our present New Testament texts have been established would be an example, but far from the only example, of what I mean.) It is my position not only that users of the New Testament need know little about Critical Studies, but that nothing that they need to know much about is so much as based upon Critical Studies.[3]

Second Comment on the Argument

The conclusion of the argument applies to users of the New Testament qua users of the New Testament. Consider, for example, theologians. The conclusion is consistent with the thesis that *some* theologians, in

---

3. Many studies of the New Testament presuppose the results, or the alleged results, of Critical Studies. The conclusion of our argument applies to such studies to the extent that these presuppositions are essential to them. Consider, for example, the following quotation from Professor Adams's paper in the volume from which this essay was taken (p. 258): "Luke's Gospel was written in the 80s C.E. and arguably reflects the conflict between Christian and non-Christian Jews over who is to blame for the destruction of Jerusalem." The thesis that Luke's Gospel was written in the eighties is an alleged result of Critical Studies. To the extent, therefore, that this thesis is essential to her paper (I do not claim that this extent is very great; it seems to me that most of what Professor Adams says in her paper could be true even if Luke's Gospel was, as I myself believe it to have been, written in the early sixties), the conclusion of our argument applies to her paper. Any study of Luke that is *wholly* dependent on the thesis that Luke was written well after the destruction of Jerusalem is, if our argument is sound, a study that users of the New Testament may, if they wish, ignore with a clear intellectual conscience.

virtue of the particular theological vineyard in which they labor, may need to be well versed in Critical Studies. For example, a theologian trying to reconstruct Luke's theology from clues provided by the way Luke used his sources would obviously need to have an expert's knowledge of Critical Studies. This qualification is strictly parallel with the following statement: A physicist qua physicist need have scant knowledge of biology, but a *bio*physicist has to know a great deal about biology.

Third Comment on the Argument

The conclusion of the argument is not that users of the New Testament must not or should not have an extensive acquaintance with Critical Studies, but that they need not. Biophysicists need to know a lot of biology, but it is not generally supposed that physicists working in the more abstract and general areas of physics need know much about biology. Erwin Schrödinger, however, set out to educate himself in biology because he thought that the observed stability of the gene was inexplicable in terms of known physics, and that the study of living systems therefore held important clues for the theoretical physicist. Well, he was wrong about the gene, but he was no fool, and the matter was certainly worth looking into. I want to say that something like that should be the case in respect of theology and Critical Studies: that Critical Studies are not, in general, particularly relevant to the theologian's task (except in the case in which the task is to reconstruct the theology of the writer of a New Testament book, or something of that sort); but a theologian may conclude at a certain point in his or her investigations that those investigations require a deep knowledge of Critical Studies. But this is no more than a special case of what I would suppose to be a wholly uncontroversial thesis: A theologian may conclude at a certain point in his or her investigations that those investigations require a deep knowledge of just about anything—physics, say, or formal logic, or evolutionary biology. I am arguing that Critical Studies cannot be said a priori to be of any greater relevance to the concerns of the theologian (or the pastor or the ordinary churchgoer) than physics or formal logic or evolutionary biology.

Fourth Comment on the Argument

Users of any very recent edition or translation of the Bible are going to be exposed to the judgments of those engaged in Critical Studies and the corresponding historical studies of the Old Testament. I mention the Old Testament because my favorite example of the way in which one can be exposed to such a judgement is Genesis 1:2. If one's translation says, "and a mighty wind swept over the face of the waters," instead of, "and the Spirit of God moved over the face of the waters," one may want to know what the arguments in favor of the former reading are. Or if in one's Bible the twenty-first chapter of John has some such heading as "An Ancient Appendix," one may want to know what the arguments are upon which this editorial comment rests. No such example as these is individually of any very great importance, but a large number of such translations and editorial comments may combine to produce an impression of the nature of the biblical texts, an impression which may be correct, but which certainly reflects views of editors and translators that are at least partly conditioned by Critical Studies. If one wants to make up one's own mind about the views that have shaped modern editions and translations of Scripture, one may have to devote more time to Critical Studies than the conclusion of my argument suggests—in self-defense, as it were. An analogy: in ideal circumstances, a student of Plato would not need to know much about nineteenth-century British Idealism; but if the only available edition of Plato were Jowett, such knowledge would be prudent.

Fifth Comment on the Argument

The argument refers to Critical Studies as they actually are. For example, the thesis of premise 5, that Critical Studies do not undermine the user's grounds for believing in the historical and theological reliability of the New Testament (the grounds alleged to exist in premise 4), does not imply that Critical Studies could not possibly undermine these grounds, but only that they have not in fact done so.

Even when the qualifications contained in these five comments have been taken into account, the argument is unlikely to win immediate and unanimous approval. The place of Critical Studies in theological education is more eloquent testimony to the strength of the convictions opposing the conclusion of the argument than any chorus of dissent could be. In the seminaries maintained by my own denomination, for example, seminarians spend more time reading works that fall in the area I am calling Critical Studies, or works that are deeply influenced by the supposed results of Critical Studies, than they do reading the Fathers of the Church. I doubt whether things are much different in typical Roman Catholic and "mainline" Protestant seminaries. And, no doubt, any suggestion that Critical Studies should have at most a marginal role in doctoral programs in theology would be greeted with the same sort of incredulity that would attend a suggestion of a marginal role for the study of anatomy in the training of physicians. As to the laity (as opposed to both the ordained clergy and the theologically learned), probably no small number of diocesan vicars of education, and their Protestant counterparts, would agree with the proposal of Ellen Fleeseman-van Leer that the Bible be taught to the laity "in such a way that the question of its authority is for the time being left to one side and that modern biblical scholarship is taken into account at every step."[4]

The remainder of this essay will be devoted to further clarification of some of the ideas contained in the argument and to a defense of its premises. Unfortunately, I haven't the space to perform either of these tasks adequately. I must either touch on all of the points that deserve consideration in a very sketchy way or else be selective. I choose the latter course.

The ideas that figure in the argument that are most in need of clarification are the ideas of "historical reliability" and "theological reliability." The premises most in need of defense are the fourth and the fifth.

Despite the fact that the idea of theological reliability is badly in need of clarification, I am not going to attempt to clarify it, because that would be too large a task. I could not even begin to explain what I mean by the words 'The New Testament is theologically reliable' in the one or two pages I could devote to the topic here. I shall, therefore, attempt to clarify only the idea of *historical* reliability. It is certainly true that the idea of historical reliability is more directly related to the topic of Critical Studies than is the idea of theological reliability. There are plenty of people who believe that Critical Studies have shown that the New Testament cannot be, in any sense that could reasonably be given to these words, theologically reliable. But the primary argument for this thesis would, surely, have to be that Critical Studies have shown that the New Testament is not theologically reliable *by* showing that it is not historically reliable. (After all, if we cannot believe the New Testament when it tells us of earthly things, how can we believe it when it tells us of heavenly things?)

But what thesis do I mean to express by the words 'The New Testament is historically reliable'? What is meant by historical reliability?

The concept of historical reliability, although it is much simpler than

4. The quotation is taken from a sort of open letter written by Dr. Fleeseman-van Leer to the New Testament scholar Christopher Evans, and included, under the title "Dear Christopher," in a Festschrift for the latter. See Morna Hooker and Colin Hickling, eds., *What about the New Testament? Essays in Honour of Christopher Evans* (London: SCM Press, 1975), p. 240.

the concept of theological reliability, is sufficiently complex that I am going to have to impose two restrictions on my discussion of it. I hope that what I say within the scope of these restrictions will indicate to the reader what I would say about other aspects of the topic of historical reliability.

First, I am going to restrict my attention to the narrative passages of the New Testament: passages written in the past tenses or the historical present, in which the author represents himself as narrating the course of past events (one typical sign of this being the frequent use of connecting and introductory phrases like 'in those days' and 'about that time'), passages in which what is presented is not represented as a dream or a vision, and in which the references to persons and places are in the main concrete and specific. Secondly, I am going to restrict my attention to descriptions of the words and actions of Jesus. I do this because there are certain stylistic and expository advantages to my focusing my discussion on a strictly delimited class of events, and this class of events has attracted more attention from those engaged in Critical Studies than any other strictly delimited class. I will attempt to explain what I mean by saying that the descriptions of the words and actions of Jesus in the narrative passages of the New Testament are historically reliable. It should be kept in mind that in what immediately follows, I am explaining what I mean by this thesis and not defending it. I give three explanations of historical reliability, which I believe are consistent and, in fact, mutually illuminating.

I begin with a formal explanation—roughly, an explanation in terms of how much of what is said in the texts is historically accurate—for obviously the notion of historical reliability must be closely related to the notion of historical accuracy. I mean by saying that the New Testament narratives are historically reliable (as regards the words and acts of Jesus) that (i) Jesus said and did at least most of the things ascribed to Him in those narratives, and (ii) any false statements about what Jesus said and did that the narratives may contain will do no harm to those users of the New Testament who accept them as true because they occur in the New Testament. But clause (ii) of this explanation is itself in need of an explanation.

I will explain the idea of "doing no harm" by analogy. Suppose that a general who is fighting a campaign in, say, Italy is separated by some misadventure of battle from all of his military maps and reference materials. Suppose he finds a prewar guidebook to Italy with which he makes do. Suppose that this guidebook is in some respects very accurate: its maps, tables of distances between towns, statements about the width of roads, and so on are all without error. On the other hand, it has wrong dates for lots of churches, contains much purely legendary material about Italian saints, and it has Garibaldi's mother's maiden name wrong. If the general, so to speak, treats the guidebook as gospel, and as a consequence, believes all of the legends and wrong dates and mistakenly concludes that he is related to Garibaldi, it will probably do him no harm. At any rate, it will do him no military harm, and that is the kind of harm that is relevant in the present context. And if he later comes to believe that God providentially put the guidebook into his hands in his moment of greatest need, it is unlikely that he will be argued out of this belief by a skeptic who shows him that it contains a lot of misinformation about churches and saints and Italian patriots.

The false statements in our imaginary guidebook were militarily irrelevant. So it may be that there are false statements about the words and acts of Jesus in the New Testament that are irrelevant to the spiritual warfare. Let us examine this possibility.

Suppose that Jesus never said, "Blessed are the peacemakers, for they shall be called sons of God."[5] Suppose, however, that this is something He might very well have said. Suppose that it in no way misrepresents His teaching, and is in fact an excellent expression of something He believed. If these things are so, it is hard to see how anyone would be worse off for believing that He said these words. We may contrast this case with the following one: If the early Church had twisted the story of the widow's mite into an injunction to the poor to give to the Church, even to the point of starvation, the changed version of the story would have done grave harm to those who believed it.

My explanation of the notion of historical reliability, therefore, is consistent with the supposition that Jesus did not say all of the things ascribed to Him in the Gospel narratives. But this statement naturally raises the question, How much? Is it possible that these narratives ascribe to Him *lots* of things He never said or did, all of them being nevertheless things He might well have said or done? I think that there is no contradiction in the idea that the narratives are perfect guides to what Jesus might well have said and done, even though they are most imperfect guides to what, in point of historical fact, He did say and do. I do not, however, regard their having this feature as a real possibility. I

5. I learn from reports in the press that the seventh Beatitude has been established as inauthentic by the majority vote of a group of biblical scholars, and will be so marked in the group's forthcoming edition of the New Testament, in which the words the evangelists ascribe to Jesus are to be printed in four colors, signifying "certainly said," "probably said," "probably didn't say," and "certainly didn't say."

believe that if very *many* of the ascriptions of words and acts to Jesus in the New Testament narratives are historically false, then it is very unlikely that any significant *proportion* of those ascriptions attribute to Him things He might well have said or done. I shall presently touch on my reasons for believing this.

We can see a second kind of "harmless" historical inaccuracy if we consider the order in which events are narrated. Suppose that, as most scholars apparently believe, the things Jesus is represented as saying in Matthew 5, 6, and 7 (the Sermon on the Mount) are things that—assuming that Jesus said all of them—He did not say on any single occasion. But it has certainly never done anyone any harm to believe that He did; not, at least, if He did say all of them, and said them in contexts that give them the same significance that the "Sermon on the Mount" narrative framework gives them. It is not an altogether implausible thesis that the order in which many of the sayings and acts of Jesus are recorded is of no great importance to anyone but New Testament scholars trying to work out the relations among the Synoptic Gospels. If Mark, as Eusebius said Papias said, "wrote down accurately all that [Peter] mentioned, whether sayings or doings of Christ; not however in order," [6] and if a simple reader of Mark believes that *X* happened before *Y* because that is what it says in Mark, when in fact *Y* happened before *X*, it is hard to see how this could have done the simple reader any harm.[7]

6. *Ecclesiastical History*, iii, 39.

7. In correspondence, Harold W. Attridge has suggested that the various New Testament texts that have been used to justify persecution of the Jews pose a difficult problem for my thesis about historical reliability. In connection with this question, it is important to realize—I don't mean to imply that Professor Attridge is confused on this point—that my thesis does not entail that these texts, or any texts, have done no harm; it entails only that, if any of these texts is not historical, no one has come to any harm by believing that it was historical. Nevertheless, I am willing to defend the strong thesis that Matthew 27:25, John 8:44, 1 Thessalonians 2:14, and Revelation 2:9 have done no harm. These texts have indeed been used as proof-texts by persecutors of the Jews, but it seems wholly obvious to me that only people who were already dead to both reason and the Gospel could use them for such a purpose. As to the masses who may have been swayed by such texts—well, they must have been pretty easy to sway. ("There are in England this day a hundred thousand men ready to die in battle against Popery, without knowing whether Popery be a man or a horse.") I doubt whether the Devil needs to quote Scripture to get people to murder Jews or any other harmless and inoffensive people. At any rate, I'd need a strong argument to believe that any New Testament text has been anything more than a sort of theological ornament tacked on the racks and gas chambers, like a cross on a Crusader's shield. The only harm involving these texts I'm willing to concede is this: to attempt to use Scripture to justify murder and oppression is blasphemy, and those who have done this may have been damned for six reasons rather than five.

This completes my formal explanation of what I mean by historical reliability. I now give a *functional* explanation of this notion.

As I have said, the Church has made very extensive liturgical, homiletic, and pastoral use of the New Testament, including the narrative portions thereof. These texts have been read to congregations and preached on for getting on toward a hundred thousand Sundays. My functional explanation of what is meant by the historical reliability of the New Testament narratives is this: the narratives are historically reliable if they are historically accurate to a degree consonant with the use the Church has made of them. Again, the explanation needs to be explained. Let us consider a rather extreme suggestion. Suppose that most of the New Testament stories about the sayings and actions of Jesus were made up in various communities of the early Church in response to certain contemporary and local needs. (We suppose that when the Evangelists eventually came to hear these stories, they took them for historical fact and incorporated them into their Gospels, adding, perhaps, various fictions of their own composition.) This suggestion is, I believe, *not* consonant with the use the Church has made of the New Testament historical narratives. The Church has caused these stories, these past-tense narratives bursting with concrete and specific historical reference, to be read, without any hint that they should not be taken at face value, to fifty generations of people the Church knew full well *would* take them at face value. If these narratives were indeed largely a product of the imaginations of various people in the early Church, then the Church has, albeit unwittingly, been guilty of perpetrating a fraud. (We might compare the position of the Church—if this suggestion is right—with the position of the paleoanthropological community in the thirties and forties in respect of Piltdown Man. The comparison is not an idle one: it would be hard to find a better case of a fraud that was accepted because it met the needs created by the *Sitz im Leben* of a community.)

What, then, is the degree of historical accuracy that is required of the New Testament narratives (as regards the words and actions of Jesus) if they are to satisfy the present functional characterization of historical reliability? Not surprisingly, I would identify it with the degree of accuracy that figured in our formal explanation of historical reliability. Last Sunday,[8] for example, many churchgoers heard a reading from the gospel according to John that began, "There was a man

---

8. That is, the Sunday preceding the conference at the University of Notre Dame for which this essay was composed: the second Sunday in Lent, 1990.

of the Pharisees named Nicodemus, . . . this man came to Jesus by night. . . ." The degree of historical accuracy exhibited by this passage is consonant with the use the Church has made of it only if (i) there was a Pharisee named Nicodemus who came to Jesus by night and had a certain conversation with Him about being born again, or (ii) the passage falls short of historical accuracy in ways that will do no harm to those who hear it read and accept it as a historically accurate narrative. As to the latter possibility—well, perhaps it isn't very important whether Jesus said those things to *Nicodemus*. Perhaps (despite Jesus' characteristic depreciation of the knowledge of "the teachers of Israel") the passage has its historical roots in a conversation Jesus had with some wholly unimportant person, although He might well have said the same things to a distinguished Pharisee if the occasion had arisen. Perhaps the passage is woven together from things Jesus said on several different occasions, or perhaps it records a set speech that He delivered many times with only minor variations. Perhaps the "voice" Jesus is represented as using is to some degree a literary device of the Fourth Evangelist, or displays a way of speaking that Jesus sometimes used in the presence of a few people like the Apostle John, but rarely if ever used in conversations with strangers. All of this, and a great deal more in the same line, would be consonant with the Church's use of John 3:1–17. If historical inaccuracies of all these kinds were present in that passage, and if someone heard or read the story and took it as unadorned historical fact, it would be a hard critic of the Church indeed who accused her of deceiving that person.[9] If, on the other hand, Jesus never talked about being "born again" at all, the charge of ecclesiastical deception would have considerable merit.

The third explanation I shall give of the notion of historical reliability is *ontological,* an explanation that proceeds by describing the basis in reality of the fact (supposing it to be a fact) that the New Testament narratives possess the degree of historical accuracy that I have characterized formally and functionally. In giving this explanation, I adapt to the New Testament narratives what I have said elsewhere about a very different part of the Bible, the creation narrative in Genesis.[10] What I said there had to do with the work of the Holy Spirit in the transforma-

---

9. I am myself inclined to take this passage as at least very close to unadorned historical fact. (This is, of course, merely one of my opinions—like my opinion that Anglican orders are valid—and not a part of my Christian faith.) If, on another shore, in a greater light, it should transpire that this opinion of mine had been incorrect, I should not regard the Church as having deceived me.

10. See Essay 5 in this volume.

tion of myth. What I say here pertains to the work of the Holy Spirit in the preservation of tradition.

It was natural for primitive Christian communities to tell stories about what Jesus had said and done. (I continue to restrict my discussion to this class of events. But what I shall say is applicable with no important modification to those parts of the Gospel narratives that are about people other than Jesus, and to the Acts of the Apostles.) Every reporter, lawyer, and historian knows that the stories people tell about past events are not always entirely consistent with one another—and therefore not entirely true. Intelligent, observant, and wholly disinterested witnesses to a traffic accident will shortly afterward give wildly different descriptions of the accident. The four ancient writers who provide our primary documentation of the life of Tiberius Caesar give accounts of his reign that are at least as hard to "harmonize" as the four gospels.[11]

Now let us assume that God was interested in Christians' having an account of the things Jesus said and did during the years of His public ministry, an account that conforms to the standard of "historical reliability" described above; let us in fact assume that He was sufficiently interested in there being such an account that He was willing to take some positive action to ensure its existence. (But let us put to one side the question why God would have this interest.) Given the facts about the unreliability of witnesses briefly touched on in the last paragraph, and the many mischances that a piece of information is subject to in the course of its oral transmission, what might God do to ensure the existence of such an accurate account?

I suppose that no one seriously thinks that God might have chosen to achieve this end by dictating narratives of Jesus' ministry, Greek word by Greek word, to some terrified or ecstatic scribe. (People are often accused of believing that God did this, but I have never seen a case of anyone who admits to it.) Though I firmly believe in miracles, I do not believe—I expect no one believes—that God's governance of the world is entirely, or even largely, a matter of signs, wonders, and powers. God created the natural processes whose activity constitutes the world. They are all expressions of His being, and He is continuously present in them. The natural process of story formation and transmission among human beings is as much an expression of God's being as is any other natural process, and there is no reason to suppose that He

11. See A. N. Sherwin-White, *Roman Society and Roman Law in the New Testament* (Oxford: Clarendon Press, 1963), pp. 187–189.

would choose, or need, to circumvent this process to ensure the historical reliability of the New Testament narratives. Nevertheless, I believe that His presence in the formation of the New Testament—and, more generally, Scriptural—narratives was different from His presence in the formation of all other narratives, just as His presence in the formation of Israel and the Church was different from His presence in the formation of all other nations and institutions.

I suppose that the New Testament writers and their communities were chosen by God and were rather special people. I suppose that if, say, St. Luke was told one of the bizarre stories about Jesus' boyhood that survive in the apocryphal infancy gospels, the Holy Spirit took care that his critical faculties, and, indeed, his sense of humor, were not asleep at the time. I suppose that if an elder of the Christian community at Ephesus in A.D. 64 was tempted by want of funds to twist the story of the widow's mite into an injunction to the poor to buy their way into the Kingdom of God, the Holy Spirit saw to it that his conscience was pricked, or that no one believed his version of the story, or that the changed story never got out of Ephesus and soon died out. I suppose that the Holy Spirit was engaged in work like this on many occasions in many places during the formation of the New Testament books. I suppose that the Holy Spirit was at work in the Church in similar modes during the process of canonization and during the formation of the opinion that the canonical books were the inspired Word of God. I suppose that (although no good book is written apart from the work of the Holy Spirit) the Holy Spirit is present in just *this* way only in the formation of Holy Scripture, and that this mode of presence is part of what we mean by inspiration. (I say 'part of' because we are touching here only on the narrative aspect of Scripture.)

If I am right, God has guided the formation of the New Testament historical narratives by acting on the memories and consciences and critical faculties of those involved in their formation. His employment of this "method" is certainly consistent with there being historically false statements in the New Testament. A false saying of Jesus might have arisen and gained currency without dishonesty or conscious fabrication on anyone's part. (No doubt many did.) And if it were in His "voice," and if its content were consistent with His teaching, then it would not be of a sort to be "filtered out" by the critical faculties of those who transmitted and recorded it, however perfect the operation of those faculties might be. The inclusion in the New Testament of such a false saying would, as I have said, do no one any harm, for it would by definition be consistent with His teaching. (There are many other, if less important, ways in which historically false but harmless ascriptions of words to Jesus might arise: the attribution to Him of an apposite quotation of a well-known proverb in a situation in which He said something less memorable; the substitution of one arbitrary place-name for another in a parable. . . .) But if this method is consistent with there being some inauthentic sayings of Jesus in the New Testament (the same point, of course, applies to actions), it does not seem to allow any real possibility of a very high proportion of inauthentic sayings. One's critical faculties need something to work on: one cannot judge that an alleged saying of Jesus is not the sort of thing He would have said unless one has at one's disposal a large body of sayings characteristic of Jesus. And the only real possibility of having at one's disposal a large body of sayings characteristic of Jesus is this: having at one's disposal a large body of actual sayings of Jesus.

If the Holy Spirit has indeed been at work in the formation of the New Testament narratives in the way I have described, what would the results be? I think we could expect two results. First, we could expect the narratives to be historically reliable in the formal sense. Secondly, I think that we could expect them to look pretty much the way they do—or at least we can say that the way they look is consistent with their formation having been guided by the Holy Spirit in the way I have described. In one sense, the New Testament narratives are far from coherent. That is, while "harmonization" of the narratives is no doubt logically possible, any attempt at harmonization is going to look rather contrived. (The same could be said of the Tiberius sources.) But these incoherencies are of little consequence to the people I have called users of the New Testament, however important they may be to those engaged in Critical Studies. Let us grant for the sake of argument—I am in fact very doubtful about this—that it is impossible to reconcile Jesus' representation of Himself in John with His representation of Himself in, say, Mark. How Jesus represented Himself to his audiences and to the authorities and to His disciples at various points in his ministry is no doubt of great interest to certain scholars, but what has it got to do with the Christian life, or with Christian ministry, or even with Christian theology? Or does this incoherency (supposing always that it exists) show that the Holy Spirit cannot have guided the formation of the New Testament narratives in the way I have supposed? How, exactly, would an argument for this conclusion go?

This completes my tripartite explanation of the meaning of 'historically reliable'. I now turn to my promised defense of premises 4 and 5. This was premise 4:

There are grounds, grounds independent of Critical Studies, for believing that whatever the Church has presupposed is true.

I am a convert. For the first forty years of my life, I was outside the Church. For much of my life, what I believed about the Church was a mixture of fact and hostile invention, some of it asinine and some of it quite clever. Eventually, I entered the Church, an act that involved assenting to certain propositions. I believe that I had, and still have, good reasons for assenting to those propositions, although I am not sure what those reasons are. Does that sound odd? It should not. I mean this. I am inclined to think that my reasons for assenting to those propositions could be written down in a few pages—that I could actually do this. But I know that if I did, there would be many non-Christians, people just as intelligent as I am, who would be willing to accept without reservation everything I had written down, and who would yet remain what they had been: untroubled agnostics, aggressive atheists, pious Muslims, or whatever. And there are many who would say that this shows that what I had written down could not really constitute good reasons for assenting to those propositions. If it did (so the objection would run), reading what I had written on those pages would convert intelligent agnostics, atheists, and Muslims to Christianity—or would at least force them into a state of doublethink or intellectual crisis or cognitive dissonance. Perhaps that's right. If it is, then among my reasons there must be some that can't be communicated—or *I* lack the skill to communicate them—like my reasons for believing that Jane is angry: something about the corners of her mouth and the pitch of her voice, which I can't put into words.

Philosophers are coming to realize that the fact that one cannot articulate a set of reasons that support one's assent to a certain proposition, reasons that are felt as having great power to compel assent to that proposition by everyone who grasps them, does not mean that one does not have good reasons for assenting to that proposition. And they are coming to realize that being in this sort of epistemic situation is not the peculiar affliction of the religious believer. Let me give an example of this that is rather less abstract than the examples that philosophers usually give, a political example. When I was a graduate student, in the Vietnam era, it was widely believed among my friends and acquaintances that there was something called "the socialist world" which was at the forefront of history and which was soon (within ten or fifteen years) to extend over the entire surface of the globe through the agency of something called "the Revolution." Now

I believed at the time that all of this was sheer illusion. In fact, I didn't just believe it was sheer illusion, I *knew* it was sheer illusion. Nevertheless, although I knew this, if you had asked me why I thought it was true, I could not have cited anything that was not well known to, and which would not have been cheerfully conceded by, any reasonably alert campus Maoist: that such-and-such a story had appeared in the *New York Times,* that George Orwell had once said this, or that Leopold Tyman was currently saying that.

A second illustration of this philosophical point is provided by philosophy itself. A philosopher I deeply respect once told me that he could not accept any religion because there were many religions and they disagreed about important matters. I pointed out to him that he himself accepted many philosophical positions that other, equally able philosophers rejected, philosophers who knew all the arguments *he* knew. (He resisted the parallel, but on grounds that are still opaque to me.) And his situation is not unique. Every philosopher, or so it seems to me, accepts at least some philosophical theses that are rejected by some equally able and equally well informed philosopher. But I am not willing to say that no philosopher knows anything philosophical.

Such examples can be multiplied indefinitely. What do you think of psychoanalysis, the theory of evolution by natural selection, or the Documentary Hypothesis? Someone as intelligent and as knowledgeable as you rejects your position. Are you willing to say that this shows that you lack reasons that support your opinions on these matters? If so, why do you continue to hold them? (Why, in fact, did you hold them in the first place, since you were perfectly well aware of the disagreements I have alluded to?) If not, then it would seem to follow that you should agree that it is possible for one to have reasons that support a belief, even if one is unable to give an account of those reasons that has the power to compel belief in others.

In my view, I have such reasons with respect to the propositions assent to which is essential to membership in the Church—although, as is typical in such cases, many will dispute this claim. One of these propositions is the proposition that Jesus Christ (who, in addition to being the Way and the Life, is the Truth) is the head and cornerstone of the Church. I cannot reconcile assent to this proposition with assent to the proposition that falsehoods are presupposed in the essential operations of the Church. I have argued that the historical reliability of the New Testament is presupposed in the essential operations of the Church. I therefore claim to have good reasons for believing that the New Testament is historically reliable—they are just my reasons for accepting the whole set of propositions essential to membership in the Church. And those reasons are independent of the findings of Critical Studies.

Or so I say. But are they really, *can* they really be, independent of the findings of Critical Studies? Some would perhaps argue as follows. Among the propositions essential to Christianity are certain historical propositions; for example, that Jesus was at one time dead and was later alive. Therefore (the argument proceeds), if the believer has reasons for accepting the propositions essential to Christianity, reasons that actually warrant assent to those propositions, they must be partly historical reasons, reasons of the kind that historians recognize as supporting a thesis about the past. (And it is in Critical Studies that we see the methods of objective historical inquiry applied to the task of sifting historical fact from myth, legend, and fancy in the New Testament narratives.) I have said "some would perhaps argue..."; I concede, however, that the only people I can remember actually arguing this way are avowed enemies of Christianity like Antony Flew. And they of course believe that it is impossible to demonstrate, on historical grounds, certain of the historical propositions essential to Christianity. While I would agree with them that it is impossible to demonstrate on historical grounds that, for example, Jesus was at one time dead and was later alive, I see no merit in the thesis that the only grounds that could warrant assent to that proposition are grounds of the kinds that historians recognize. If I have, as I believe I have, good grounds for accepting what the Church teaches, and if the Church teaches certain things about the past, and if some of those things cannot be established by the methods recognized by historians, why should I cut myself off from those truths about the past by believing only those statements about the past that are endorsed by the methods recognized by historians?

I think it is worth noting that, whether the thesis that propositions about the past should be accepted only if they can be established by the methods recognized by historians is true or false, it is certainly incompatible with Christianity. A more careful statement of the thesis would be this: a proposition about the past should be accepted *by a given person only if that person knows* (or at least *has good reason to believe*) *that* it can be established by the methods employed by historians. Now it is obvious that many of the historical propositions essential to Christianity are rejected by large numbers of historians. I do not know whether it is possible for there to be a historical proposition that is (i) rejected by large numbers of historians, and (ii) such that some people know, or have good reason to believe, that its truth can be established by the methods recognized by historians. But if this is possible, it can hardly be doubted that only a very well educated person could know, with respect to a proposition that is rejected by large numbers of historians, that its truth could be established by the methods recognized by historians. It follows that some of the propositions essential to Christianity have the following feature: only a very well educated person—if anyone—should accept them. This conclusion is, of course, radically inconsistent with the Gospel. It is, in fact, very close to Gnosticism, for it entails that a form of knowledge accessible only to an elite is necessary for salvation.

I conclude that I do have grounds for accepting the historical reliability of the New Testament that are independent of Critical Studies. As we have seen, however, it is still possible that my grounds may be *undermined* by Critical Studies. Let us therefore see what can be said in defense of premise 5:

> Critical Studies do not undermine these grounds, and there are good reasons for believing that they do not, reasons whose discovery requires no immersion in the minutiae of Critical Studies, but which can be grasped by anyone who attends to the most obvious features of Critical Studies.

That discoveries by those engaged in Critical Studies have undermined whatever grounds anyone may ever have had for accepting the historical reliability of the New Testament is not an unknown opinion. The late Norman Perrin, for example says:

> In revealing the extent to which the theological viewpoint of the evangelist or transmitter of the tradition has played a part in the formation of the Gospel material, [redaction criticism] is forcing us to recognize that a Gospel does not portray the history of the ministry of Jesus from A.D. 27–30, or whatever the dates may actually have been, but the history of Christian experience in any and every age. At the same time this history of Christian experience is cast in the form of a chronicle of the ministry of Jesus, and some parts of it—whether large or small is irrelevant at this point—are actually based on reminiscence of that ministry. The Gospel of Mark is the prototype which the others follow and it is a mixture of historical reminiscence, interpreted tradition, and the free creativity of prophets and the evangelist. It is, in other words, a strange mixture of history, legend, and myth. It is this fact which redaction criticism makes unmistakably clear.[12]

12. Norman Perrin, *What Is Redaction Criticism?* (Philadelphia: Fortress Press, 1969), p. 75.

It is obviously a consequence of the point of view expressed in this quotation that whatever grounds I may have for believing in the historical reliability of the New Testament have been undermined by Critical Studies—just as F. C. Baur's grounds for believing that the Fourth Gospel was a product of the late second century (whatever they may have been) have been undermined by the discovery of the Rylands Papyrus.

How shall I, who possess none of the tools of the New Testament critic, decide whether this evaluation (or other less extreme but still highly skeptical evaluations) of the historical reliability of the New Testament is to be believed? Someone might well ask why reasoning parallel to my earlier reasoning does not show that I need not raise this question. Why not argue that if one needed to decide that the findings of Critical Studies did not undermine one's grounds for believing in the historical reliability of the New Testament before accepting the historical reliability of the New Testament, this would entail the false conclusion that only highly educated people—if anyone—could accept the historical reliability of the New Testament? The answer is that there are good reasons for thinking that Critical Studies do not cast any doubt on the historical reliability of the New Testament, and that one does not have to be a highly educated person to understand these reasons.[13]

This is not surprising. In general, it is much harder to find reasonable grounds for deciding whether a certain proposition is true than it is to find reasonable grounds for deciding whether so-and-so's arguments for the truth (or for the falsity) of that proposition are cogent. If the proposition under consideration is one whose subject matter is the "property" of some special field of study (like 'The continents are in motion' and unlike 'Mario Cuomo is the governor of New York'), and if the "reasonable grounds" are those that can properly be appealed to by specialists in that field of study, then it is almost certain that only those specialists can find reasonable grounds for deciding whether it is true. (I suppose it is reasonable for me to decide that the continents are in motion on the basis of the fact that it says so in all the geology

13. At any rate, one does not have to have the tools of a trained New Testament scholar at one's disposal. It is certainly true that the reasons I shall give for believing that Critical Studies do not cast any doubt on the historical reliability of the New Testament could be understood only by someone who had enjoyed educational opportunities that have not been available to everyone to whom the Gospel has been preached. I would say, however, that these reasons could be understood by anyone who could understand the passage that I have quoted from Perrin's book.

textbooks. But this is not the sort of fact that geologists can properly appeal to when they are asked to explain why they believe that the continents are in motion.) But if the "reasonable grounds" are ones that it is appropriate for the laity to appeal to, then it is almost always possible for the laity to find reasonable grounds for deciding whether the arguments employed by some group of specialists are cogent.

Suppose, for example, that the director of the Six Mile Island Nuclear Facility delivers to Governor Cuomo a long, highly technical case for the conclusion that the facility's reactor could never possibly present a radiation hazard. The governor, of course, doesn't understand a word of it. So he selects ten professors of nuclear engineering at what he recognizes as leading universities to evaluate the case he has been presented with. Eight say the reasoning on which the case is based is pretty shaky, one says it's abominable, and one—who turns out to be married to the director of Six Mile Island—says it's irrefutable. It seems to me that the governor has found reasonable grounds on which to decide whether the director's arguments in support of the proposition *Six Mile Island is safe* are cogent. And this is true despite the fact that he is absolutely unable to judge the case "on its merits"—that is, unable to judge it using the criteria employed by nuclear engineers.

It is not impossible, therefore, that it turn out to be a comparatively easy matter for me to decide whether the findings of Critical Studies undermine my grounds for believing in the historical reliability of the New Testament. I say this in full knowledge of the fact that the field of New Testament scholarship is as opaque to me as nuclear engineering is (I suppose) to Governor Cuomo. I am aware that an academic field is an enormously complex thing, and that it takes years of formal study and independent research to be in a position to find one's way about in one of them. (Independent research in a field is absolutely essential for understanding it. This fact leads me to take with a grain of salt what some of my fellow philosophers who have had some seminary or university training in New Testament studies tell me about the field. I think of new Ph.D.'s in philosophy from Berkeley or Harvard or Pittsburgh, whose mental maps of academic philosophy are like the famous Steinberg *New Yorker* cover—the world as two-thirds midtown Manhattan—the philosophical world as two-thirds Berkeley or two-thirds Harvard or two-thirds Pittsburgh.)

Nevertheless, some facts about New Testament studies are accessible even to me. One of them is that many specialists in the field think— in fact, hold it to have been demonstrated—that the New Testament narratives are, in large part, narratives of events that never happened.

I have quoted Perrin to this effect. On the other hand, one can easily find respectable workers in the field who take precisely the opposite view. In this camp I would place F. F. Bruce, John Drane, and (to my astonishment, given *Honest to God*) John A. T. Robinson. Could it be that these people are *not* respectable? Well, their paper or "*Who's Who*" qualifications are excellent, and how else shall *I* judge them? That, after all, was how I judged Perrin: if he had not had impressive paper qualifications, I should have picked someone else to quote.

How can one expert in a field say what I have quoted Perrin as saying, when two other experts—as nearly simultaneously as makes no matter—write books called *The New Testament Documents: Are They Reliable?*[14] and *Can We Trust the New Testament?*[15] and answer their title questions Yes? (Drane's *Introducing the New Testament*[16] is if anything more trusting of the New Testament than the writings of Bruce and Robinson are.) A philosopher, at any rate, will not be at a loss for a possible answer to this question. A philosopher will suspect that such radical disagreement means that New Testament scholarship is a lot like philosophy: Either there is little *knowledge* available in the field, or, if there is, a significant proportion of the experts in the field perversely resist acquiring it.[17]

Is New Testament scholarship a source of knowledge? Or, more exactly, is what I have been calling Critical Studies a source of knowledge? Well, of course, the *data* of Critical Studies constitute knowledge; we know, thanks to the labors of those engaged in Critical Studies, that about ninety percent of Mark appears in closely parallel form in Matthew, and that the phrase *en tois epouraniois* appears several times in Ephesians but in none of the other letters that purport to be by Paul,

14. F. F. Bruce, *The New Testament Documents: Are They Reliable?* 6th rev. ed. (London: Inter-Varsity Press, 1981). Bruce was Rylands Professor of Biblical Criticism and Exegesis in the University of Manchester.

15. John A. T. Robinson, *Can We Trust the New Testament?* (Oxford: A. R. Mowbray, 1977). Robinson was the Bishop of Woolwich and the Dean of Trinity College, Cambridge.

16. John Drane, *Introducing the New Testament* (New York: Harper & Row, 1986). Drane is Lecturer in Religious Studies at Stirling University.

17. In the case of philosophy, my own view is that, while certain people know certain philosophical propositions to be true, it would be very misleading to say that the field of academic philosophy has any knowledge to offer. I consider cases of philosophical knowledge—a particular person's knowledge that human beings have free will, say—to be something on the order of individual attainments. A philosopher who knows that human beings have free will is not able to pass the grounds of his or her knowledge on to other persons in the reliable way in which a geologist who knows that the continents are in motion is able to pass the grounds of his or her knowledge on to other persons.

and many things of a like nature. But such facts are only as interesting as the conclusions that can be drawn from them. Do any of the conclusions that have been reached on the basis of these data constitute knowledge? Or, if you don't like the word *knowledge*, can any of these conclusions be described, in Perrin's words, as a "fact" that Critical Studies "make unmistakably clear"? (We know, thanks to the geologists, that the continents are in motion. This is a fact, which their investigations make unmistakably clear. Is there any thesis that we know in this sense that we can credit to the practitioners of Critical Studies?) I suppose that if any of the conclusions of Critical Studies is known to be true, or even known to be highly probable, it is this: Mark's Gospel was composed before Luke's or Matthew's, and both Luke and Matthew used Mark as a source. But this thesis, while it is almost universally accepted (at least everyone I have read says it is), has periodically been controverted by competent scholars, most recently by C. S. Mann in his Anchor commentary on Mark.[18] One might well wonder whether this thesis is indeed known to be true. If it is, how can it be that Mann, who is perfectly familiar with all the arguments, denies it? If it is unmistakably clear, why isn't it unmistakably clear to *him*? And if the *priority* of Mark has not been made unmistakably clear, can it really be plausible to suppose that the much more controversial thesis that Mark is "a strange mixture of history, legend, and myth" has been made unmistakably clear?

My suspicion that Critical Studies have made nothing of any great importance unmistakably clear, or even very clear at all, is reinforced when I examine the methods of some of the acknowledged experts in that field. Here I will mention only the methods of Perrin and his fellow redaction critics, for it is they and their predecessors, the form critics, who are the source of the most widely accepted arguments for the conclusion that the New Testament is historically unreliable; if someone supposes that Critical Studies undermine my supposed grounds for believing in the historical reliability of the New Testament, he will most likely refer me to the redaction critics for my refutation. (No doubt there are highly skeptical New Testament critics who reject the methods of redaction criticism. I can only say that I am very ignorant and don't know about them. I suppose them to exist only because it has been my experience that in the world of scholarship every possibly position is occupied. I shall have to cross their bridge when I come to it.)

I have few of the skills and little of the knowledge that New Testa-

18. C. S. Mann, *Mark* (Garden City, N.J.: Doubleday, 1986).

ment criticism requires. I know only enough Greek to be able painfully to work my way through a few sentences that interest me, using an interlinear crib, a dictionary, and the tables at the back of the grammar book. I have more than once wasted time looking for a famous passage of Paul's in the wrong letter. But I do know something about reasoning, and I have been simply amazed by some of the arguments employed by redaction critics. My first reaction to these arguments, written up a bit, could be put in these words: "I'm missing something here. These *appear* to be glaringly invalid arguments, employing methods transparently engineered to produce negative judgments of authenticity. But no one, however badly he might want to produce a given set of conclusions, would 'cook' his methods to produce the desired results quite so transparently. These arguments must depend on tacit premises, premises that redaction critics regard as so obvious that they don't bother to mention them." But this now seems to me to have been the wrong reaction, for when I turn to commentaries on the methods of the redaction critics by New Testament scholars, I often find more or less my own criticisms of them—although, naturally enough, unmixed with my naive incredulity.

I could cite more than one such commentary. The one I like best is an article by Morna Hooker, now Lady Margaret Professor of Divinity in Cambridge University. The article is called "On Using the Wrong Tool,"[19] and it articulates perfectly the criticisms I would have made of the methods of redaction criticism if I had been as knowledgeable as she and had not been hamstrung by my outsider's fear that there had to be something I was missing. If Professor Hooker, as she is now, is right, I have certainly not missed anything: All of the premises of the redaction critics are right out in the open. If she is wrong—well, how can *I*, an outsider, be expected to pay any attention to redaction criticism? If its methods are so unclear that the future Lady Margaret Professor couldn't find out what they were, what hope is there for me? I might add that Professor Hooker's witness is especially impressive to an outsider like me because she does not criticize the methods of the redaction critics in order to advance the case of a rival method of her own; rather, their methods are the very methods she herself accepts. She differs from a committed and confident redaction critic like Perrin mainly in her belief that these methods can't establish very much— perhaps that certain *logia* are a bit more likely on historical grounds to be authentic than certain others—and she adheres to these methods

---

19. Morna Hooker, "On Using the Wrong Tool," *Theology* 75 (1972): 570–581.

only because (in her view) these methods are the only methods there are. (But if she accepts Perrin's methods, she would appear to dissent from one of his premises: that, owing to the pervasive influence in the formation of the Gospels of the theological viewpoints of the transmitters and evangelists, the Gospel narratives are intrinsically so unreliable as historical sources that, in the absence of a very strong argument for the authenticity of a given saying, one should conclude that that saying is not authentic. If I understand Hooker, however, she would say in such a case that nothing can be said about its authenticity; she would conclude that a saying was inauthentic only if there were good arguments—arguments relating to the content and Gospel setting of the particular saying—for its inauthenticity.)

I conclude that there is no reason for me to think that Critical Studies have established that the New Testament narratives are historically unreliable. In fact, there is no reason for me to think that they have established *any* important thesis about the New Testament. I might, of course, change my mind if I knew more. But how much time shall I devote to coming to know more? My own theological writings, insofar as they draw on contemporary knowledge, draw on formal logic, cosmology, and evolutionary biology. I need to know a great deal more about these subjects than I do. How much time shall I take away from my study of them to devote to New Testament studies (as opposed to the study of the New Testament)? The answer seems to me to be: very little. I would suggest that various seminaries and divinity schools might consider devoting a portion of their curricula to these subjects (not to mention the systematic study of the Fathers!), even if this had to be done at the expense of some of the time currently devoted to Critical Studies.

Let me close by considering a *tu quoque*. Is not philosophy open to many of the charges I have brought against Critical Studies? Is not philosophy argument without end? Is not what philosophers agree about just precisely nothing? Are not the methods and arguments of many philosophers (especially those who reach extreme conclusions) so bad that an outsider encountering them for the first time might well charitably conclude that he must be missing something? Must one not devote years of systematic study to philosophy before one is competent to think philosophically about whether we have free will or whether there is an objective morality or whether knowledge is possible?—and yet, is one not entitled to believe in free will and knowledge and morality even if one has never read a single page of philosophy?

Ego quoque. If you are not a philosopher, you would be crazy to go to the philosophers to find anything out—other than what it is that the philosophers say. If a philosopher tells you that you must, on methodological grounds, since he is the expert, take his word for something—that there is free will, say, or that morality is only convention—you should tell him that philosophy has not earned the right to make such demands. Philosophy is, I think, valuable. It is a good thing for the study of philosophy to be pursued, both by experts and by amateurs. But from the premise that it is a good thing for a certain field of study to be pursued by experts, the conclusion does not follow that that field of study comprises experts who can tell you things you need to attend to before you can practice a religion or join a political party or become a conscientious objector. And from the premise that it is a good thing for a certain field of study to be pursued by amateurs, the conclusion does not follow that anyone is under an obligation to *become* an amateur in that field.

This is very close to some of the depreciatory statements I have made about the authority of Critical Studies. Since I regard philosophy as a Good Thing, it should be clear that I do not suppose that my arguments lend any support to the conclusion that the critical study of the New Testament is not a Good Thing. Whether it is, I have no idea. I don't know enough about it to know whether it is. I have argued only that the very little I do know about Critical Studies is sufficient to establish that users of the New Testament need not—but I have said nothing against their doing so—attend very carefully to it.[20]

20. I am grateful to Ronald Feenstra for his generous and careful comments on this essay, which were included in the volume in which this essay was originally published. I am also grateful to Harold W. Attridge, who sent me a long and thoughtful letter about various of the points raised in the essay. I have tried to address one of his concerns in note 7. I should also like to express my indebtedness to the writings of Professor E. L. Mascall, particularly his *Theology and the Gospel of Christ: An Essay in Reorientation* (London: SPCK, 1977), which directed me to many of the authors I have cited.

7

Non Est Hick

MOST of us probably remember from our childhoods a kind of puzzle called "What is wrong with this picture?" The child confronting one of these puzzles would be presented with a picture that contained details like a dog smoking a pipe or a woman writing a letter with a carrot instead of a pen. It would be announced that there were, say, ten such "mistakes" in the picture and the object was to find all ten.

There is a currently very popular picture of what are called "the World Religions" that looks to me a lot like those puzzle pictures from my childhood. The picture is done in prose, rather than in pen and ink outline. I shall have to provide you with a copy of it if I am to proceed with this essay, but it will not be easy for me to do this, for I am constitutionally unable to write the kind of prose suited to the task. Nonetheless, here goes.

There are a number of entities called "religions"; the most important among them are called the "World Religions," with or without capitals. The world religions are the religions that appear in the history books, and appear not merely as footnotes or as clues to "what the Assyrians were like" or evidences of "the beginnings of cosmological speculation." The world religions are important topics of historical inquiry in their own right. Each of them, in fact, has a history of its own; the majority of them have founders and can be said to have begun at fairly definite dates. The list of world religions must include at least the following: Buddhism, Christianity, Confucianism, Hinduism, Islam, Judaism, and Taoism. But other religions are plausible candidates for

Reprinted from *Rationality of Belief and the Plurality of Faith*, edited by Thomas D. Senor. Copyright (©) 1995 by Cornell University. Forthcoming. Used by permission of the publisher, Cornell University Press.

inclusion in the list, and some might want to split some of the items in the list into two or more religions. It is the division of humanity into the adherents of the various world religions (of course, many people practice a tribal religion or belong to some syncretistic cult or have no religion at all) that is the primary datum of all responsible thinking about religion. Comparative studies of the world religions have shown that each of these religions is a species of a genus and that they have important common characteristics that belong to no other human social institutions. There are, of course, differences as well as similarities among the world religions, and some might think that there were *grave* differences, or even outright inconsistencies. It might be thought, for example, that the Middle Eastern or "Abrahamic" religions required their adherents to believe in a God who was a person and that other religions denied the existence of a divine person or subjected this thesis to "the death of a thousand qualifications" or even deprecated as a sign of spiritual immaturity any interest in a transcendent reality, whether personal or impersonal. It might be thought that Christianity taught that if your country was occupied by foreigners who despised you and your countrymen, and if a soldier of the occupying forces ordered you to carry his pack for a mile (which he was allowed by his own law to do), you should carry his pack for an extra mile; and it might be thought that Islam most definitely did not teach this. It might be thought that most forms of Buddhism taught that desire was intrinsically a bad thing, whereas Christianity taught that desire was made by God and that the Buddhist doctrine was therefore a blasphemous inveighing against the Creation. It might be thought, moreover, that these apparent inconsistencies among the world religions were not matters of the surface. It might be thought that each of them pertained to the very root and essence of the religions involved.

It cannot be denied that the apparent inconsistencies exist. What can be denied is that they have anything to do with "the root and essence" of the world religions. Each of the world religions is a response to a single divine reality. The responses are *different*, of course; no one could dispute that. The world religions are different because they arose and developed under different climatic, geographical, cultural, economic, historical, and social circumstances. The God of the Abrahamic religions, for example, is male—that is, He is described almost exclusively in terms of male imagery. This is because He represents the response to the divine of a people who in their beginnings were nomads and herdsmen, and who therefore were little concerned with the craft of growing things in the soil. Growth in the soil is particularly associated in the human imagination with the female, and religions that have their roots in a community whose economy is based on sowing and reaping tend to incorporate a strong female element. It is because the ancestors of the Jews were herdsmen and not farmers that the God of the Jews and their spiritual children is, whatever refinements may have crept into His nature over the course of the millennia, at root an exclusively male sky-god—in fact, the Lord of Battles.

The divine reality that each of the world religions responds to is in an important sense beyond the reach of human thought and language. Therefore, any attempt to conceptualize this reality, to describe it in words, to reduce it to formulas, must be woefully inadequate. And when we reflect on the fact that all our religious conceptualizations, descriptions, and formulations are reflections of local and temporary conditions of human social and economic organization, we are led irresistibly to the conclusion that the letter of the creed of any particular religion cannot possibly be an expression of the essence of the divine reality toward which that religion is directed. What we can hope to see over the next couple of hundred years—as each of the great world religions becomes more and more separated from the conditions and the geographical area in which it arose, and as the earth becomes more and more a single "global village"—is a sloughing off of many of the inessential elements of the world religions. And we may hope that among these discarded inessentials will be those particular elements that at present divide the world religions. It may be that each will retain much of its own characteristic language and sacred narrative and imagery. Indeed, one hopes that this will happen, for diversity that does not produce division is a good thing. But it is to be hoped that the great religions will "converge" to the point at which the differences between them are not incompatibilities—not even apparent incompatibilities. We may look forward to the day when a sincere seeker after the divine may (depending on the momentary circumstances of his or her life) move back and forth among the world religions as easily and consistently as the late-twentieth-century American Protestant who attends a Presbyterian church in California and a Methodist church after moving to North Carolina.

This is as much of the picture as I can bear to paint. There is a lot more that I might have included. I might, for example, have said something more about the sense in which each of the great world religions is supposed to be a response to the divine. (I might have included the idea that the aim of each of the world religions is to lead humanity to salvation, and that the real essence of salvation is a move from self-centeredness to "reality-centeredness.") I might have said something about the "credentials" that each of the world religions can produce to support its claim to be a response to the divine reality. (I might have included the idea that the hallmark of a religion that is truly a response to a divine reality is its capacity for "saint production," its capacity to produce people who have left self-centeredness behind and become reality-centered.) But one must make an end somewhere.

Now what am I to do with this picture? I might treat it as the child is supposed to treat the puzzle picture, and point out the dog smoking the pipe and the woman writing with the carrot. I will not do this. For one thing, there is (in my view) so much wrong with the picture that I hardly know where to begin. For another, the whole topic of "religious pluralism"—which is the standard name for what might be called the doctrinal basis of the picture—is surrounded with a nimbus of rhetoric (the defense of religious pluralism has always been entirely rhetorical), and this rhetoric is designed to make any criticism of religious pluralism look like mean-spirited hair-splitting. To attempt actually to analyze the rhetoric of the religious pluralists is to be drawn into a game the main rule of which is that the other side gets to make the rules. Rather than be drawn into this game, I will strike out on my own. I will present a sort of model or theory of "religion" that is intended to provide a perspective from which the traditional, orthodox Christian can view such topics as "the world religions," "the scandal of particularity," and "religious pluralism." I do not expect this theory to recommend itself to anyone who is not a traditional, orthodox Christian.

There is, to begin with, a God. That is, there is an infinite, perfect, self-existent person, a unique and necessarily unique bearer of these attributes. It may be, as many great Christians have said, that the language of personality can be applied to this being only analogically. It may be that when we say things that imply that this being is conscious and has thoughts and is aware of other things than Himself and makes choices and has plans and acts to bring these plans to fruition, we are using language that is literally correct when we apply it to ourselves, and can be applied to God only in some way that is to be understood in terms of the concept of analogy—as we are using language that is literally correct when we say that Watson is following the suspect, and only "analogically correct" when we say that he is following Holmes's reasoning. And it may not be. It may be, as William P. Alston has suggested, that there is available a plausible functional account of personal language that has the consequence that the meanings of terms like 'conscious' and 'thought' and 'plan' are so abstract that it is possible for them to apply univocally to God and to human beings.[1] But even if the language of personality can be applied to God only analogically, it is the only language we Christians have been given and the only language we have. It is not open to us to talk of God only in the impersonal terms appropriate to a discussion of Brahman or the Dialectic of History or the Absolute Idea or Being-as-Such or the *Elan vital* or the Force. (If it is the implication of "apophatic" or "negative" theology that it is improper to use personal language in speaking of God—I do not say that it is—then apophatic theology must be looked at as an assault by Athens on Jerusalem.) This is the meaning of Genesis 1:26–27. It is because we are made in the image of God and after His likeness that we can properly apply to Him terms that apply to human beings.

This God, although He is the only thing that is self-existent, is not the only thing that exists. But all other things that exist exist only because He has made them. If He had not, by an act of free will, brought other things into existence, there would be nothing besides Himself. When we say that He "made" other things than Himself, we do not mean that He formed them from some preexistent stuff that existed independently of His will. There could be no such stuff, for He is the Creator of all things, visible and invisible. Moreover, He did not produce the world of created things and then allow it to go its own way. Even He could not do that, for it is intrinsically impossible for anything to exist apart from Him—the *fons et origo* of being—even for the briefest moment. He sustains all other things in existence, and if He were to withdraw His sustaining power from any being—a soap bubble or a cosmos or an archangel—it would, of absolute, metaphysical necessity, immediately cease to exist. And He does not confine His interactions with the created beings to sustaining them in existence. He is, as we learn from St. John, love; He loves His creatures and, because of this love, governs the world they inhabit providentially.

Among His creatures are human beings, who were, as we have said, made in His image. They were made for a purpose. They have, as the Shorter Catechism of the Church of Scotland says, a "chief end": to glorify God and to enjoy Him forever. This end or purpose implies both free will and the ability to know God. Human beings have not been made merely to mouth words of praise or to be passively awash in a pleasant sensation of the presence of God. They have been made

---

1. William P. Alston, "Can We Speak Literally of God?" in *Divine Nature and Human Language: Essays in Philosophical Theology* (Ithaca: Cornell University Press, 1989).

to be intimately aware of God and capable of freely acting on this awareness; having seen God, they may either glorify and enjoy what they have seen—the glorification and the enjoyment are separable only by the intellect in an act of severe abstraction—or they may reject what they have seen and attempt to order their own lives and to create their own objects of enjoyment. The choice is theirs and it is a free choice: to choose either way is genuinely open to each human being.[2]

God wishes to be the object of human glorification and enjoyment not out of vanity but out of love: He is glorious and enjoyable to a degree infinitely greater than that of any other object. He has given us free will in this matter because it is only when a person, having contemplated the properties of something, freely assents to the proposition that that thing is worthy of glory, and then proceeds freely to offer glory to it, that a thing is truly glorified. And it is only when a person, having enjoyed a thing, freely chooses to continue in the enjoyment of that thing that true enjoyment occurs.

Unfortunately, the first human beings, having tasted and enjoyed God, did not persist in their original felicity. (Perhaps they chose to ignore some stricture on the course of their development that, in their pride, they thought they could bypass. We cannot say, for the form in which temptation could be present in the mind of an as yet unfallen creature is necessarily a mystery to us. The suggestion that it would be psychologically impossible for an Edenic human being to feel, or, at any rate, to succumb to, temptation to do wrong is, however, an assertion and not an argument. The idea that we are in a position to say what is psychologically possible for beings in circumstances that are literally unimaginable to us is nothing more than an illustration of the apriorism that is an endemic intellectual disease of philosophers and theologians.) They turned away from God—perhaps they did not describe what they were doing in that way, just as an alcoholic husband may not describe what he is doing as "turning away from his wife and children"—and ruined themselves. In fact, they ruined not only themselves but their posterity, for the separation from God that they achieved was somehow hereditary. This turning away from God and its consequences are known as the Fall.[3]

I find the following analogy helpful in thinking about the condition

2. It may sound as if I am preaching Pelagianism here, but it will become evident in a moment that this can hardly be my meaning. In my view, in the present age of the world, this freedom comes to us only by Grace.

3. For a discussion of the Fall that takes up some points that cannot be gone into here, see Essay 4 in this volume.

of fallen humanity. Imagine a great modern city—New York, say—that has been lifted several yards into the air by the hand of some vast giant and then simply let fall. The city is now a ruin. The mass of the buildings stand at crazy angles. Others have been totally destroyed or lie on their sides. Some few still stand more or less straight. The suitability of the buildings for human habitation varies. Most of the rooms in most of the buildings are now, in some measure, open to the wind and the rain, but a small proportion of them are still snug and dry. Water mains and gas mains and electrical cables have mostly been severed by the catastrophe, but here and there a building still has water or gas or electricity. How these remnants of function are distributed among the various buildings of the city is simply a matter of chance: the fact that a particular building is snug and dry and more or less upright and still has running water is a consequence of the way a vast network of forces redistributed themselves when the city was dropped. Certainly it does not reflect any particular credit on the design of the building: no building could be designed to withstand such a catastrophe, and that this one emerged relatively intact (but in normal circumstances it would be condemned) is due to the fact that a complex array of forces happened to come close to "canceling out" at this location.

I have said that this story provides a model for the fallen human race. We are all ruins, in a sense very closely analogous to the sense in which the Parthenon is a ruin. That is, we cannot be said without qualification to be the products either of chance or of design. Each of us is at birth the product of two factors: the original plan of a wise and providential Creator and the changes that chance—different in the case of every individual—has introduced into the original perfection that came from the Creator's hand. The effects of these changes are not grossly physical, of course, as they are in the buildings that are the other term of the analogy. They are moral and intellectual and aesthetic and spiritual. A particular human being may labor under a genetic predisposition to a vicious temper, or to an almost total lack of sensitivity to the needs of others, or even to a positive enjoyment of the sufferings of others. Another human being may be blessed with a genetic disposition to a sweet temper and great human sympathy and a horror of any human suffering. A particular human being may be born with almost no capacity for sustained rational thought, or with a tendency recklessly to disregard evidence, or with an inherent disposition to deprecate any use of the mind that is not directed toward what is immediately useful. Another human being may be genetically endowed with dispositions to intellectual virtue. Similar points may be made about our various genetic endowments as regards aesthetic matters. There is little more that needs to be said about our genetic endowments in these areas, except perhaps to stress the point that I have been talking about our *genetic* endowments, and that the bad dispositions we have been born with can no doubt be to some degree mitigated, and the good dispositions corrupted or rendered impotent, by social and other environmental factors.

What is more relevant to our present concerns is our "spiritual endowments"—that is, the degree to which the spiritual endowment that was a part of the Creator's plan for each individual has managed to survive the Fall. We have said that human beings were made to be intimately aware of God. It would not be profitable for me—whose spiritual life is devoid of the least tincture of mystical or religious experience—to speculate at any length on the nature of this awareness. I expect that this awareness was somehow connected with the subject's ordinary sensory awareness of physical objects (which endure and move and have their being in God). I expect that the way in which I am aware of the "invisible" thoughts and emotions of others through their faces and voices provides some sort of analogy.[4] I expect that the way the natural world looked to unfallen humanity and the way it looks to me are as similar and as different as the way a page of Chinese calligraphy looks to a literate Chinese and to me. But whatever the nature of our primordial awareness of God, we have largely lost it. Perhaps, however, none of us has lost it entirely, or only a very few of us have. And it may be that this awareness is present in various people in varying degrees. (The city is now a ruin. The mass of the buildings stand at crazy angles. Others have been totally destroyed or lie on their sides. Some few still stand more or less straight.) It is because some vestige of the capacity to be aware of God is present in all or most people that there is such a thing as religion. (We should note that an awareness of God does not necessarily seem to be an awareness of God to the person who has it: an awareness of a distant mountain range may seem to the person who has it to be an awareness of a bank of clouds.)[5]

4. Cf. Romans 1:20; Wisdom of Solomon 13:1–9.

5. This useful analogy has a defect: it suggests that "misperceptions" of God are invariably as innocent as ordinary perceptual mistakes. But this is not so. I will make my point by means of an extreme example, without meaning to imply that this point is confined to cases of the extreme sort that I shall consider. There have been and still are those who believe in dark gods, gods whose favor can be gained only by ritual sodomy or by the immolation of babies or by tearing the heart out of a living victim. I see no reason to suppose that the remnant of our original awareness of God is any less a causal

It is because a capacity to be aware of God is present in people in varying degrees that people are more religious or less religious—or at any rate this is one reason among others for the varying degrees of engagement with religion exhibited by various people. It is because there are people in whom the capacity to be aware of God is relatively intact (the buildings that stand almost straight and provide shelter from the elements and perhaps even a tickle of water from the taps) that there are great religious leaders and doctors and saints—or, again, this is one reason among others. And these people are not confined to any particular geographical area or to any historical period. This statement is, of course, consistent with the statement that it is only in certain social and cultural milieux that they will flourish spiritually or have any effect upon history.

In a way, what I have said in the preceding paragraph looks a great deal like the picture of the world religions that I have made it clear that I reject. Although I have talked about a personal Creator and a Fall, it might be argued that these are no more than details, and that the picture I have painted differs from the picture I have undertaken to attack in only a few background details. What difference does it make (someone might ask) what the exact nature of the relation between the great spiritual leaders and the divine reality is—as long as it is admitted that they are spread throughout the human race? In fact (the questioner might continue), don't your "details" undermine themselves? If you know about this "Fall," you know about it from certain great spiritual teachers: Augustine and Paul and the authors of the early books of Genesis. But their authority, if they have it, to pronounce on the relation of the human and the divine can be due only to their being in closer touch with the divine reality than most of us. And they are not in closer touch with the divine reality than, say, Lao Tzu or Gautama. (At least, you have not given us any reason to suppose so; and if it were so, how should *you*, who by your own admission are spiritually nothing out of the ordinary, know this?) If you are right, spiritual gifts are distributed more or less randomly in space and time, as randomly as intellectual and aesthetic gifts. Why, then, should a

---

factor in the life of the religions of ancient Mesopotamia or pre-Columbian Central America (or current Satanism) than in the life of what the nineteenth century called "the higher religions." I do not believe, however, that God would allow any of His creatures *innocently* to perceive Him as a dark god. The belief that there were divine powers that demanded the immolation of babies can no more have been an "honest mistake" than the belief of the Nazis that a cabal of Jewish plutocrats arranged the defeat of Germany in 1918 can have been an innocent misreading of history.

certain stream of stories told in the ancient Levant be normative for all of humanity? If things were as you say, if there has been a primordial catastrophe that has left us all, in varying degrees, spiritual ruins, then the details of our relation with the divine would have to be "blurry," too blurry to be read with confidence by such as you. Therefore, you can have no ground for your statement of the details, and when the details—which are of no great intrinsic importance in any case—have been erased, your picture is indistinguishable from the standard picture of the "world religions."

There is a great deal of merit in these pointed questions. Indeed, if I had no more to put into my "model" than this, they would be unanswerable. I do, however, have more to put into my model than this. The consequence of what I shall add is this: the standard picture of the world religions is not so much false as it is out of date. For God has not left us to deal as best we can with our state of spiritual ruin. If He had, then the picture of the world religions that I deprecate as false to the facts would have been true to the facts. But . . .

In many and various ways God spoke of old to our fathers by the prophets; but in these last days He has spoken to us by a Son, whom He appointed the heir of all things, through whom also He created the world. Let me expand on this theme, in rather a different vein from the author of Hebrews—or perhaps not so different.

The world religions, insofar as they have any reality at all (this qualification is an adumbration of a point I shall take up presently), are human creations. That is, they are the work of human beings, and their existence and properties are not a part of God's plan for the world. Other examples of human creations that are similar to religions in that they are in some sense composed of human beings would be: the Roman Empire, Scotland, the Children's Crusade, Aunt Lillian's sewing circle, the Comintern, the Vienna Circle, the Gestapo, the American Academy of Religion, Tokyo, fauvism, the Palestine Liberation Organization, the *New York Times,* and the National Aeronautics and Space Administration.

The existence and properties of the institutions in this list are due to chance and to the interplay of a wide variety of "climatic, geographical, cultural, economic, historical, and social circumstances" that it is the business of the social sciences to identify and map. When I say that they are "not a part of God's plan for the world," I am assuming that there *are* things in the world that are not a part of God's plan for the world.[6] As to the individual items in the list, I am assuming that—

6. For a defense of the thesis that there are many things in the world that are not a part of God's plan for the world, see Essay 2 in this volume.

given that there is *anything* that is not a part of God's plan for the world—it is fairly evident that none of these things is. Perhaps some will disagree with me about particular cases. And even if no one disagrees, it may be that we are all wrong. God's ways are mysterious, and I do not claim to be privy to them. I am proceeding only by such dim lights as I have. Nothing in the sequel really depends on whether the *New York Times* or the Vienna Circle is a part of God's plan for the world: the items listed are meant only to be suggestive examples. But I should make it clear that in saying that these institutions are not parts of God's plan for the world, I do not mean to deny that God may make use of them in carrying out His plan—as I may make pedagogical use of various physical objects that happen, independently of my plans and my will, to be among the fixtures of a lecture room in which I am giving a lecture on perception. Indeed, I would suppose that God makes *constant* use of human institutions, human individuals, animals, inanimate objects, and transient psychological phenomena in His moment-to-moment shepherding of His creatures toward the fulfillment of His plan.

Like the *New York Times* and the Vienna Circle, the world religions have arisen amid the turmoil of the fallen world by chance and have developed and grown and acquired their peculiar characteristics partly by chance and partly by the interplay of the factors that a completed social science would understand. In the case of the world religions, however, a third factor is present, one that can hardly be supposed to have been involved in the development of the *Times* and the Vienna Circle: their growth and properties are affected by the innate awareness of God (both within their "ordinary" members and within their founders and great teachers) that is still present, in varying degrees, throughout fallen humanity. It is also possible—and we might make the same point about any things that exist in this present darkness—that the world religions have been partly shaped by God so that they may be instruments of His purpose. (If this is so, it does not follow that there is some *common* purpose that they serve. For all I know, God may have shaped Islam partly to be a reproach to a complacent Christendom, and it may be that no other religion has this purpose.)

"But if God has created the world, and if the world religions are parts of the world, how can they not be His creations?" It is important to realize that the following argument is invalid: God is the creator of all things visible and invisible; *hence,* God is the creator of Taoism (or of the *New York Times* or of the Vienna Circle). St. Augustine pointed out that the premise that God is the creator of all things does not entail the conclusion that God is the creator of evil, owing to the fact that evil is not a "thing" in the requisite sense: evil is not a substance. And just as evil is, ontologically speaking, not a substance, so religions are not substances; when a particular religion comes into being, this does not imply the coming to be of a substance, but merely certain substances'—certain human beings'—coming to stand in a new set of relations. And it may well be that God has not ordained that any human beings should stand in the particular set of relations that is the only being that a religion has. It is, of course, *possible* for God to create a religion; for Him to do this would be for Him to bring it about that certain human beings came to stand in a certain set of relations. I maintain, however, that He has not in fact done so: no religion is a divine creation. (But this conviction of mine is not essential to my point. If I am wrong about this, if God has created Taoism or Islam, I am wrong about a peripheral matter—as I should be wrong about a peripheral matter if the *New York Times* or the Vienna Circle were a divine creation.)

There are, I suggest, two and only two things that are in any sense composed of human beings and are both God's creations and a part of His plan for the world.[7] These are His people Israel and the Catholic Church.

By Israel I mean a *people*. I mean those descendants of Jacob who are the heirs of the promises made to Abraham. It was to this people, and not to a religion called Judaism, that the Law was given ("I have set before you life and death, blessing and curse; therefore, choose life that you and your descendants may live, loving the Lord your God, obeying his voice, and cleaving to him, . . . that you may live in the land which the Lord swore to your fathers, to Abraham, to Isaac, and to Jacob, to give them").[8] It was not "Judaism" whom David ruled and who heard the prophets, but a people.

By the Catholic Church I mean a certain *thing*. (The word is Chesterton's, and I have no better. God's people Israel are a unique people, but they are not the only people. The Church is the only thing of its kind, and we have, therefore, no useful general term under which it may be classified.) It was this thing that was created by the Holy Spirit

7. From the premise that a certain thing has been created by God, the conclusion does not follow that it is a part of His plan for the world. It is possible—for all I know, it is true—that God has created the Red Cross, as a divine mitigation of the human invention of war. But if war is not a part of the divine plan for the world, then, even if the Red Cross has been created by God, it is not a part of His plan for the world.

8. Deut. 30:19–20.

on the day of Pentecost, of which Jesus Christ is the head and cornerstone, which has charge of the good news about Jesus Christ and the
sacraments of Baptism and the Eucharist, which is specifically mentioned in the Creeds. There are, we believe, both a visible and an invisible Church. I might say a great deal about the invisible Church and its
relation to the visible Church, but I will say nothing. As to the visible
Catholic Church, the right to pronounce on its boundaries is a bone of
contention among Christians. Roman Catholics, Anglicans, Orthodox
Christians, and Protestants will have different ideas about the boundaries of the visible Church. It is not my intention to say anything controversial about this matter, so I will say nothing. (Nor will I say
anything of consequence about the divisive question of the relation
between Israel and the Church.)

It will be noted that my characterization of Israel and the Catholic
Church has been in terms of God's action in history. If God has not
acted in history, these things do not exist. If God has not spoken of
old by the prophets, then Israel does not exist. If He has not spoken
in these last days by a Son, then the Catholic Church does not exist. (I
do not mean to deny what is self-evidently true: that there are perfectly
good senses of the words in which even an atheist can admit that there
are such things as "Israel" and "the Catholic Church.")

The question naturally arises, Suppose that these two things, these
two supernatural foundations, Israel and the Church, do exist; what is
their relation to the two "world religions" Judaism and Christianity?

I do not know how to answer this question because I do not know
what the words 'Judaism' and 'Christianity' mean. More exactly, although there are many contexts in which I understand these words (as,
for example, if it is said that someone is a convert to Judaism, or has
written a book that is critical of Christianity), there are many contexts
in which I do *not* understand them, and this question is an example of
one. Let me concentrate on the world 'Christianity'. Most of what I
say will be applicable, the appropriate changes being made, to my
difficulties with the word 'Judaism'. Many statements that contain the
word 'Christianity' can be easily rewritten as statements about Christians and their beliefs and their religious practices and their behavior
in secular matters.[9] In most cases, I have no difficulty understanding

9. My difficulties with 'Christianity' do not extend to the noun 'Christian'. Like
most English words, it has more than one meaning, but it has a "central" meaning that
is something like this: a Christian is a person who has accepted Jesus Christ as Lord and
Savior, who has assented to certain creedal statements, and who has received the sacra-
ment of Baptism. (There could, of course, be some dispute about what the creedal state-

statements of this kind. My difficulties are with statements that are not of this sort, with statements that imply, or appear to imply, that 'Christianity' is the name of a thing.

Is 'Christianity' really the name of a thing?—that is, is this word really a name, or is it simply a word that allows a speaker to take certain statements about "Christians and their beliefs and their religious practices and their behavior in secular matters" and compress them into statements about a feigned thing called 'Christianity'? Is the word like, say, 'the *New York Times*' or 'the Vienna Circle', which are names of real social entities? Or is it like the words 'morality' and 'violence', which (in many contexts, anyway) are no more than linguistic devices for compressing statements about moral or violent people and their behavior into statements about a feigned object ('The decline of morality in our time has reached serious proportions'; 'Violence never solves anything')?

I believe the latter. I think that a strong argument for this thesis is provided by the fact that one cannot "be a member of" or "belong to" Christianity. (Nor is there any more specific "membership word" like 'employee' or 'citizen' that can be used to describe the relation between an individual and Christianity.) One cannot say, "I am a member of Christianity," or "I belong to Christianity." A Christian is no more a member of Christianity than a violent person is a member of violence or a skeptic is a member of skepticism. (One can, of course, be a *convert* to Christianity, but conversion to Christianity does not imply membership in Christianity as conversion to Roman Catholicism implies membership in the Roman Catholic Church. To be a convert to Christianity is simply to become a Christian.) It should be evident from the way I have worded this discussion of 'Christianity' that its point

---

ments would have to contain, and about when Baptism has been validly administered.) I am aware that, human beings being the contentious lot they are, there are those who would say that this definition was fundamentally inadequate—because, for example, real Christians must be *good* Christians, or real Christians must display gifts of the Holy Spirit. My purpose in this note is not to resolve vexed questions about who is and who isn't a Christian, but simply to dissociate the question "What does 'Christianity' mean?" from the question "What does 'Christian' mean?"

The adjective 'Christian', unlike the noun, is very vague. Its vagueness, however, has nothing specifically to do with religion, but is rather typical of adjectives of its type. Compare, say, 'Italian' or 'Asian'. *An* Italian, in the central meaning of the word, is a citizen of Italy; *an* Asian, in the central meaning of the word, is an inhabitant of Asia. But a definition of the adjectives 'Italian' and 'Asian' will have to make use of such extremely vague terms as 'pertaining to' and 'typical of'. This fact has the consequence that the meaning of the adjective 'Christian'—like the meanings of 'Italian' and 'Asian'—is highly sensitive to context.

has nothing to do with nominalism or the reality of social entities or any other abstract question of logic or metaphysics. I am perfectly willing to say that there is such a thing as, for example, the class of all Christians, and I have said that the Catholic Church and Israel—and the *New York Times* and the Vienna Circle—are real things. There is no logical or conceptual barrier to there being a real social entity that is, as one might say, coextensive with Christianity, a thing that people belong to if and only if they are Christians, as people belong to the Roman Catholic Church if and only if they are Roman Catholics. (Indeed, there is no logical or conceptual barrier to there being *more* than one social entity that is coextensive with Christianity.) But—unfortunately—no such thing exists in the world as it is.

I hope it is also evident that in saying that 'Christianity' is not a name for a thing, I am not denying the existence or reality of Christianity—just as I do not deny the existence or reality of violence when I say that 'violence' is not a name for a thing. Here is an analogy: In saying, with St. Augustine, that evil is not a thing—that it is among neither the *visibilia* nor the *invisibilia* mentioned in the Nicene Creed— one does not express agreement with Mary Baker Eddy.

What has been said of 'Christianity', and by implication of 'Judaism', applies equally to 'Islam' and 'Buddhism' and the other words that occur in any list of the world religions. None of these words is a real name; if it were a real name, it would name a social entity of some sort, and people could belong to it. But (although there are Muslims) no one is "a member of Islam," and (although there are Buddhists) no one is "a member of Buddhism."

Let us return to our question: What is the relation of the Catholic Church to "the world religion Christianity"? I would say that insofar as this unclear question has an answer, it is contained in the following statement: All members of the Catholic Church are Christians, and some Christians are not members of the (visible) Catholic Church. In this answer, I have used the relatively clear word 'Christian' and have deliberately avoided the vague word (vague in this context, at any rate) 'Christianity'. If my suggestion that the word 'Christianity' is a "compression-word"—that it is a device for compressing statements about Christians into shorter statements about a feigned object—is correct, it should be possible to replace any meaningful statement in which the word 'Christianity' occurs with a statement in which this word does not occur. Therefore, if I am right, insofar as the question has an answer, it must have an answer in which the word 'Christianity' does not occur. There may be those who would wish to challenge my thesis. Perhaps not everyone will agree that my answer to this question is the correct answer; perhaps not everyone will agree that I have understood the question; perhaps not everyone will agree that all statements involving the word 'Christianity' can (insofar as they have any meaning at all) be replaced by statements containing no related word but 'Christian'.

I should have to see how a challenge to my thesis would be developed before I knew what to say in response to it. But I shall view any such challenge with suspicion. I think it is an important fact about compression-words that they are often used as devices of obfuscation. A notorious case is that of the statement 'Error has no rights', which in former days was used by some Roman Catholic apologists to defend the use of political coercion in religious matters. If we try to say what this statement says without using the compression-word 'error', we find that we must say either 'People who have erroneous beliefs have no rights' or 'If a thesis is erroneous, then those who sincerely believe it to be true have no right to defend it in public—or even publicly to express belief in it'. While 'Error has no rights' has an impressive and convincing ring to it, the same can hardly be said of these two statements.

The use of compression-words and the hypostatized abstractions they purport to denote may sometimes be harmless—I have no objection, for example, to the statement 'Violence never solves anything', although I believe I could think of more useful ways to express the thought behind these words. (It will be observed that in the sequel I allow myself to hypostatize "the Enlightenment.") But I am convinced that the practice often disguises a political or theological agenda, the advancement of an ideology.

Let me make a highly speculative suggestion (I put this forward as worthy of further reflection, rather than as a thesis whose truth I am convinced of): the list of world religions—indeed, the concept of a "religion"—is a piece of misdirection intended to advance what I shall call the "Enlightenment agenda."

The historical phenomenon that named itself "the Enlightenment" (it still exists, although it has abandoned the name) is, and always has been, an attack on the Catholic Church. Its social goal is the destruction of the Church. Its main intellectual goal is twofold: first to show that there is no God, or at least no providential God who acts in history (and hence that all that the Church teaches is false), and, secondly, that the Church not only is wrong about history and metaphysics and eschatology, but is a socially retrograde force. An important part of this intellectual goal is to exhibit those things that the Church sees as unique as very much of a piece with lots of other things.

The Church, for example, has taught that the human species is radically different from all other species. The Enlightenment has sought to show that the human species is not all that different from many other species. Since it is blindingly, boringly obvious that humanity *is* radically different from all other species—although it is far from obvious whether the Church is right about the nature of or the reasons for this difference—any opponent of this thesis must proceed by misdirection. Thus it is pointed out by the proponents of the Enlightenment agenda that human DNA differs from chimpanzee DNA in fewer base-pairs than the number by which the DNA of grizzly bears differs from that of Kodiak bears. Or it is confidently stated that modern science has delivered a succession of "nasty shocks to human pride" (by its discovery that the earth is not at the center of the universe, or by its discovery of the vast reaches of geological time, or by its discovery that human beings and the other primates are descended from a common ancestor). Well, the point about the base-pair count is certainly true, and the statement about the nasty shocks to human pride is probably not true, but, whether their premises are true or false, these arguments are mere smoke and mirrors, for the fact is that human beings *are* radically different from all other animals, and a scientific discovery can no more challenge this fact than the transition from Ptolemaic to Copernican astronomy could challenge the fact of the alternation of day and night.[10]

It is a part of the Enlightenment agenda to undermine the confidence of Christians in the thesis—from the earliest times an undisputed axiom of Christian theology—that the Catholic Church is radically different from everything else in the world.[11] Is it "blindingly, boringly obvious" that this thesis is right?

10. Another important example of this Enlightenment strategy is provided by the attempt of the Enlightenment to show that the creation-and-flood story in Genesis is really very much the same sort of thing as the Sumerian and Akkadian and Iranian and other creation-and-flood stories. All these stories are clearly historically related and share some structural features that are interesting to the student of comparative mythology. The strategy is to go on at great length about the historical relation and the structural similarities, while studiously ignoring the fact that in every respect that could matter to anyone who was not a scholar of comparative mythology, the Hebrew story is radically different from the Sumerian and Akkadian and Iranian stories (the average educated reader will find those three stories to be very similar)—and from all other creation-and-flood stories.

11. With the possible exception of Israel. According to Christians, the Church is the New Israel, in which the promises that God made to Abraham are fulfilled (but not superseded). What the "differences" are between the New and the Old Israel, and

Perhaps it is not so obvious that the Church is radically different from all other human institutions as it is that human beings are radically different from all other animals. But there is a closely connected fact that is just that obvious, and the connection is worth developing. Here is the fact: "Western Civilization" (that is, what used to be called Christendom) is radically different from all other civilizations and cultures. Modern Euro-American civilization has produced physical and biological science,[12] the rule of law, the independent judiciary, universal suffrage, the concept of human rights and its embodiment in working constitutions, and near-universal literacy. And it has a long list of "minor" innovations to its credit, such as drawing in perspective, scientific cartography and navigation, and anesthesia. (A good sense of the uniqueness of "Western Civilization" can be obtained by comparing the anatomical drawings of Leonardo with the best anatomical drawings from classical antiquity or the Islamic world or China or India.) It will no doubt be pointed out that "Western Civilization" also originated world wars, hydrogen bombs, and worldwide colonialism.[13] But I am not arguing that "Western Civilization" is morally superior to other civilizations and cultures; I am arguing only that it is radically different. Indeed, the horrible items in this second list simply go to prove my point, for no "non-Western" civilization has been in a position even to contemplate adding any of these things to the burden of humanity's ills. "Western Civilization" may or may not be morally superior to various other civilizations. That question could be argued interminably. What is certain beyond the shadow of a doubt is that it

whether they should be described as "radical," are delicate theological questions that do not fall within the scope of this essay.

12. "But what about ancient Greek science?" What we today call Greek "science"—the Greeks, of course, did not call it that, owing to the fact that they had no word meaning 'science'—is only a part of what we call science today. The achievements of Greek science, magnificent though they were, were entirely phenomenological, in the sense in which physicists use the term. That is, they pertained to such matters as size and motion and taxonomy. Modern astronomy is applied physics; Greek astronomy was applied geometry. There is no achievement of Greek science that can be in any way compared to Newton's derivation of Kepler's phenomenology of planetary motion from his laws of motion and universal gravitation. Greek science did not do that *kind* of thing, and it did not, therefore, *explain* things in the way in which modern science explains things. Greek science, having given what it regarded as an adequate description of all observed phenomena that it found of interest, had really nowhere to go, and, by the beginning of the Christian era, had ceased to make any significant advances. The scientific achievements of late antiquity were refinements, small increments of knowledge, and systematizations of what had already been discovered.

13. And industrial capitalism. I suppose it is controversial whether that invention should be listed with the rule of law or with the world wars.

is vastly more dangerous than any of them, owing simply to its vastly greater knowledge of the workings of the physical world. (Anyone who suggests that our list shows that "Western Civilization" is somehow morally *inferior* to some or all other civilizations should meditate on Nietzsche's pointed remark about those animals that call themselves good because they have no claws.)

Why was the continent of Europe the scene of the development of a civilization that was radically different from all other civilizations and cultures? Why did this thing happen then and there and not in classical antiquity or in India or China? I think that a very plausible answer is that the Church has made the difference. The Church was the single greatest influence in the formation of modern European civilization, and it would be odd if it had nothing to do with the unique character of that civilization. (The Enlightenment was forced by its presuppositions into the odd position of holding that the unique appearance on the world stage of science happened at just that place on earth at which—owing to the presence of the powerful, antirational, and superstitious Catholic Church—conditions were most hostile to its birth.) Is it not plausible that science and the rule of law and the rest were products of the Church in much the same sense as that in which Gothic architecture was a product of the Church?

The analogy is instructive. I am not saying that science et al. were inevitable products of the existence of the Catholic Church. If the whole Church had been as the Eastern Church was, then, quite possibly, none of these things would ever have come to be. And yet the Eastern Church is, and has always been, fully Catholic, in both its governance and its doctrine. To my mind, the Church did not *have to* produce the fruits (either the sweet or the bitter) that I have listed as the features that make "Western Civilization" unique; nevertheless, the Church *did* produce them, and nothing else that has ever existed could have. Whether or not this conviction of mine is true, it should be understood as strictly parallel with the following (presumably uncontroversial) thesis: the Church did not *have to* produce Gothic architecture; nevertheless, the Church *did* produce Gothic architecture, and nothing else could have.[14] If a tree bears unique fruit, then it is probably a unique tree, even if it might never have flowered.[15]

14. But this analogy is in a way misleading. Gothic architecture is unique, but it is not, so to speak, *uniquely* unique. There are other architectural styles, each of them, I suppose, "unique," that can claim to rival Gothic architecture in beauty and sublimity. But the items in the list in the text have no rivals. They are not only unique in the way that any great architectural style must be unique, but simply *without parallel.*

15. I will try to give some sense in this note of how it was in my view that the Church "produced" one of the things in our list, modern science. The Church taught

I do not mean to suggest that it was the purpose of the Church to produce these fruits, even the sweet fruits. To say that would make nonsense of the New Testament, where we are told that Christ's kingdom is not of this world. If we should "lose" science and representative government and the rule of law—as I am inclined to think we are in danger of doing—if these things should take their places among the "wrecks of time," the Cross will still be there. The purpose of the Church is that we should not lose the end for which we were made, a purpose beside which physical science and the rule of law are of literally infinitesimal significance. And yet it did produce these things. If, again, a tree bears unique fruit, then it is probably a unique tree, whether or not the fruit was a part of the central purpose of the planter of the tree.

If a thing is to be known by its fruits, then the Church is unique. But it does not follow that it is unique in every respect, and, in particular, it does not follow that the Church is spiritually unique. I have conceded that the fruits of the Church that have made "Western Civilization" radically different from all other civilizations and cultures are irrelevant to the purpose of the Church. (Logically and conceptually irrelevant:

---

that the material world was not an illusion. Hence it taught, in effect, that there was something for science to investigate. (All the "teachings" that I mention in this note are the denials of beliefs that have had a significant number of adherents. The combination of teachings is unique to the Church.) The Church taught that the material world was not evil, and hence that it could be investigated without moral contamination. The Church taught that no part of the material world was a divine being (as many of the ancients had thought the stars and planets to be) and thus that it could be investigated without impiety. The Church taught that the material world was the creation of a single perfectly rational mind, and thus that it was not simply a jumble of things that had no significant relation to one another; its teaching therefore implied that the material world made sense, and that croquet balls were not going to turn into hedgehogs. The Church taught that the material world was a finite, contingent object; its teaching therefore implied that the nature of the world could not be discovered by a priori reasoning (a lesson Descartes was to forget). The Church taught that humanity was made in the image and likeness of God, and thus encouraged the belief that the human mind, being a copy of the mind of the Creator, might be equal to the task of discovering the nature of the Creation. The Church taught that not only humanity but the whole physical universe was redeemed in Christ ("For God so loved the *kosmos* . . ."), and thus that the investigation of that universe could be a Christian vocation, a way of glorifying its Creator and Redeemer. Assent to these teachings was second nature to the general run of educated Christians in the High Middle Ages, although some of them were disputed in the Schools. This assent produced a climate of thought and attitude that made the birth of modern experimental science possible. It is probably also worth mentioning that the Church's consistent condemnation of magic and astrology can hardly have hindered the development of science. (There is, of course, another relevant factor: the physical world cooperated. That is, it turned out to be the sort of thing whose nature *could* be investigated by the methods devised in Medieval and Renaissance Christendom.)

it is very plausible indeed to suppose that these fruits are in another way all too relevant to the purpose of the Church. The power and leisure and personal security that modern Euro-American science and social organization have given to great numbers of people in the West are no doubt the main causes of the long and continuing apostasy of the West.) May it not be that some or all of the world religions are the spiritual equals of the Church, even if they lack the Church's power to produce a wholly new kind of civilization? The Eastern Church apparently lacks the power of radically transforming the temporal aspects of civilization that the Western Church has displayed, and is nevertheless the spiritual equal of the Western Church.

May it not be that all the world's religions are instruments of God's salvation? May it not be that Islam and Buddhism are not merely accidental instruments of salvation, as literally anything under the sun may be, but intended instruments, spiritual equals of the Catholic Church?

I have no way to prove that this is false. If I had, I should be living not by faith but by sight. I can say only this: if that suggestion were true, then the Bible and the Creeds and all of Jewish and Christian history (as Jews and Christians tell the story) are illusions. The teachings of the Church are quite plain on the point that the Church is a unique instrument by which Christ and the Holy Spirit are working (and the Father is working through them) to bring us to the Father. And the teachings of the Church are quite plain on a second point: While the genesis and purpose of the Church belong to eternity, it has been given to us temporal creatures in time. (How else could it be given to us?) It was given to us through events that happened in Palestine in the first century of our era, and all possibility of our salvation depends on those events and on the Church's bringing us into the right relation with them. The Church is a thing that operates in history, and no hypostatized abstraction called Buddhism or Islam—or Christianity— is even in competition with the Church. These hypostatized abstractions, I speculate, are devices in the service of the Enlightenment agenda, and their purpose is to direct the attention of people away from the Church and to focus it on the abstraction "Christianity," which is the sort of thing that can be compared and contrasted with other abstractions like Buddhism and Islam. The comparisons, incidentally, are often extremely instructive. In reading or hearing them, the Christian is continually reminded of Chesterton's remark that, according to the students of comparative religion, Christianity and Buddhism are very much alike, especially Buddhism. (But nowadays Hinduism is the world religion that stands *prima inter pares;* it owes this preeminence to its proclivity for syncretism, to its ability to absorb what the proponents of the view of the world religions I have been discussing would regard as the essential features of all other religions.) But the nature of the comparisons is not central to my point. My point is that even if the comparisons were invariably honest and just, they would still be a piece of misdirection, a device to draw our attention away from the concrete reality of the Catholic Church and direct it toward the abstraction "Christianity."

I want to turn our attention away from this abstraction and back to the Church. I can hope to do no more than to attempt to convince a few people that this is where the attention of Christians who are interested in the question of their relation as Christians to the non-Christian religions of the world should be directed. I am certainly not particularly qualified to say anything in detail about the Church and Buddhism or the Church and Islam. It is not my business to tell Christians what they ought to think about Buddhism or Islam. If that is the business of any individuals (as opposed to, say, ecumenical councils), it is the business of Christian historians and Christian students of Buddhism and Islam and Christian theologians. I have been concerned only to argue that Christians should think not in terms of, for example, "Christianity and Buddhism," but rather in terms of "the Church and Buddhism"—or, better still, "the Church and the Buddhists."

I will devote the remainder of this essay to an investigation of a difficulty that people sometimes feel in connection with the idea of the uniqueness of the Church. If I understand the phrase, this difficulty is what is sometimes referred to as "the scandal of particularity." Is there not something arrogant about the Church's claim to be unique? The odd thing is, the idea of there being such a scandal seems to make no sense at all.

Most of us have probably heard the old anti-Semitic quatrain, "How odd / Of God / To choose / The Jews." In addition to being morally rather nasty, this verse makes no sense at all. It presupposes that the Jews are "the chosen people" in the following sense: They were *about* somewhere, and God examined the various peoples of the world and, from among them, chose the Jews. But that is not how things went. The only thing that God chose in that sense was Abraham and his household—who were not yet "the Jews." God's people are a *product* of that choice. In a very straightforward sense, God did not choose, but made, or, one might even say, *forged,* Israel. The Hebrew scriptures are the story of that terrible forging ("for it is a terrible thing I will do with you").

If the Jews claim the distinction of being the one people among all the peoples of the world that God has made, do they call down a charge of scandal upon themselves? No, indeed. One can understand why it would be scandalous if the Jews claimed that God had chosen them from among all the peoples of the earth because of their excellent qualities, if they claimed to have bested all the other peoples of the earth in a contest for God's favor. (That is the claim that is ascribed to them in the nasty little verse I have quoted—together with the implication that they of all people are the most unlikely to be the winners of such a contest.) But that is not the story the Jews tell.

In a similar way, if the Catholic Church claims to be the unique instrument of salvation, there is no scandal. The United States and the Soviet Union and many other things have invented themselves, but the Church did not invent herself. The Church is God's creation, and what makes her the unique instrument of His salvation is no more the achievement of her members than the splendor and bounty of the earth are the achievements of her inhabitants. Those features of the Church that are the work of human beings (like those features of the earth that are the work of human beings) are mere details added to God's design. And those details, like all the other works of human hands, contain good, bad, and indifferent things, hopelessly intermingled.

"Well, isn't it fortunate for you that you just happen to be a member of this 'unique instrument of salvation.' I suppose you realize that if you had been raised among Muslims, you would make similar claims for Islam?" Yes, it is fortunate for me, very fortunate indeed. And I concede that if I and some child born in Cairo or Mecca had been exchanged in our cradles, very likely I should be a devout Muslim. (I'm not so sure about the other child, however. I was not raised a Christian.) But what is supposed to follow from this observation? If certain people claim to be the members of a body that is the unique instrument of God's salvation, who is supposed to defend their claim? Those who are *not* members of that body? It should be noted, moreover, that this style of argument (whatever its merits) can hardly be confined to religion. Consider politics. As is the case with religious options, a multitude of political options faces the citizens of any modern nation. And which of us can say that his political allegiances are coded into his DNA? Tell the Marxist or the liberal or the Burkean conservative that if only he had been raised in Nazi Germany he would probably have belonged to the Hitler Youth, and he will answer that he is well aware of this elementary fact, and ask what your point is. No one I know of supposes that the undoubted fact that one's adherence to a system of political thought and action is conditioned by one's upbringing is a reason for doubting that the political system one favors is—if not the uniquely "correct" one—clearly and markedly superior to its available rivals. And yet any argument to show that the Church's belief in her own uniqueness was arrogant would apply a fortiori to this almost universally held belief about politics. The members of the Church can, as I have remarked, take no pride in her unique relation to God, for that relation is His doing and not theirs. But the superiority of one's own political party to all others must be due to the superiority of the knowledge, intelligence, wisdom, courage, and goodness of one and one's colleagues to the knowledge, intelligence, wisdom, courage, and goodness collectively embodied in any other political party.

While we are on the topic of arrogance, I must say that if I am to be charged with arrogance, it had better not be by the authors of the picture of the world religions that I outlined at the beginning of this essay. Any of *them* that flings a charge of arrogance at me is going to find himself surrounded by a lot of broken domestic glass. I may believe that everything that the Muslim believes that is inconsistent with what I believe is false. But then so does everyone who accepts the law of the excluded middle or the principle of noncontradiction. What I do *not* do is to inform the Muslim that every tenet of Islam that is inconsistent with Buddhism is not really essential to Islam. (Nor do I believe in my heart of hearts that every tenet of Islam that is inconsistent with the beliefs of late-twentieth-century middle-class Anglo-American professors is not really essential to Islam.) Despite the fact that I reserve the right to believe things that are not believed by Muslims, I leave it to the Muslims to decide what is and what is not essential to Islam.

"But why should membership in the unique instrument of God's salvation depend upon accidents of birth? Isn't that rather unfair to those born at the wrong time and place to belong to it? Wouldn't God's unique instrument of salvation, if there were one, be universally available?"

This is a serious question. Before I answer it, let me remove a red herring. It is not necessary for Christians to believe that there is no salvation outside the *visible* Church. I do not know how widespread this belief has been in the past, but it is certainly not widespread today. (In my own lifetime, a notorious Roman Catholic priest—remember Father Feeney?—was excommunicated for obstinately teaching this doctrine.) Nor do very many Christians believe that those who died before the creation of the Church are denied salvation. (There would certainly be biblical difficulties with this idea, since the salvation of the

Good Thief in St. Luke is explicitly stated, despite the fact that his death occurred not only before the creation of the Church on the day of Pentecost, but before Christ was raised into the new life that is transmitted to us through the Church.)[16] The medieval legend of the Harrowing of Hell may be without any actual basis in the Apostles' Creed, but it testifies to the popularity of the belief that Christ's salvation is offered to those who died before His Incarnation.

So much for the red herring. Now for the serious question. This question would be unanswerable if Christians believed that salvation came through a religion called "Christianity" rather than through the Church. But I take the only sure condition of damnation in which Christian belief is involved to be the following: Anyone who has accepted Christian belief and rejects it and rejects it still at the moment of his death—and rejects it with a clear mind, and not when maddened by pain or grief or terror—is damned. ("Which Faith, except everyone do *keep* whole and undefiled, without doubt he shall perish everlastingly"; "which except a man believe *faithfully,* he cannot be saved.") What provision God makes for those who have never heard the Christian message, or who have heard it only in some distorted and falsifying form, I do not know. That is God's business and not ours. Our business is to see that as many as possible do hear the Christian message, and do not hear it in a distorted and falsifying form. (But I do know that one of the things that may keep a person from hearing the Good News in its right form is the presuppositions of his native culture and religion. A Christian of our culture may know the words that a missionary has spoken to, say, a Buddhist who thereafter remains a Buddhist; he will not necessarily know what the Buddhist has heard. I do not know, but I suspect, that many people in our own culture who are, formally, apostate Christians may never have heard the Christian message in its right form. I certainly hope so, and the statements that many apostate Christians make about the content of the Christian message encourage me in this hope.)

The way for a Christian to look at the saving power of the Church is, I believe, like this: The Church is like an invading army that, having established a bridgehead in occupied territory, moves on into the interior, consolidating its gains as it goes. All those who do not consciously and deliberately cast in their lot with the retreating enemy and flee with

16. The salvation of Enoch, Abraham, Moses, and Elijah seems to be clearly implied in various passages of the Old and New Testaments—and, indeed, the salvation of a great cloud of pre-Christian witnesses.

him to his final refuge will be liberated—even those who, misled by enemy propaganda, fear and mistrust the advancing army of liberation.

If an army establishes a bridgehead, it must establish it at some particular place. "And why in Palestine?" Because that's where Israel was. "And why did God choose to locate His people there rather than in India or China?" Well, it would have to be *somewhere*. Why *not* there? The question borders on the absurd, although it has been pointed out that Palestine is approximately at the center of the great Euro-Afro-Asian supercontinent. Why did the Allied armies land in Normandy? No doubt Eisenhower and Montgomery had their reasons. But if a skeptical Norman farmer or Resistance fighter had heard rumors of the Allied landing, and had asked "Why *here?*" you wouldn't have to know the reasons the Allied commanders had for choosing the Normandy beaches to answer him. It would suffice to point out that the same question could be raised about any reported landing site by those who happened to be in its vicinity, and that the question therefore raised no doubts about the veracity of the rumor.

"But why should our salvation be accomplished by the institution of something that can be compared to an invading army?" I have no idea, although I am glad that God has chosen a method that allows some of His servants the inestimable (and entirely unearned) honor of being His co-workers in bringing salvation to others. Perhaps there was no other way. Perhaps there were lots of other ways, but this one recommended itself to the divine wisdom for reasons that surpass human understanding. Or perhaps the reasons are ones we could understand but that it would not, at present, be profitable for us to know ("What is that to thee? Follow thou Me."). But I am sure of one thing. Anyone who believes in God, in a being of literally infinite knowledge and power and wisdom, and who believes that human beings require salvation, and who thinks he can see that God would not have used such a method to procure our salvation, has a very high opinion of his own powers of a priori reason.

If we are Christians we must believe that salvation has not come to humanity through Confucius or Gautama or Mohammed. We must believe that the salvation of humanity began with events that were quite unrelated to the lives and teachings of these men. We must believe that it began when some women standing outside a tomb were told, "He is not here." Perhaps there is some authority who has discovered good reasons for thinking that these central Christian beliefs are false. If so, it is not John Hick.

PART III

Trinity and Incarnation

Introduction

CHRISTIANS believe that the Father, the Son, and the Holy Spirit are three distinct persons—three distinct *somethings,* at any rate—and that each of them is God, and that there is only one God. Christians believe that Jesus Christ is God (and thus eternal and omnipresent) and that He is also a human being (and thus came into existence at a certain time in the past and has been at any time in a particular place). These beliefs are described as "mysteries," a theological term of art whose main sense is that they cannot be demonstrated to be true by the use of human reason, and (more importantly for our present purposes) *seem* to be impossible and cannot be seen even to be possible by the use of human reason. Like all Christians, I believe that these apparently impossible beliefs are true and are therefore possible. My own view is that in relation to the Christian mysteries (there are other mysteries than the doctrines of the Trinity and the Incarnation) we Christians are like people who have never seen a mirror, or even a reflection in a pond, trying to grasp the nature of a mirror from listening to one of their fellows who has been shown a looking-glass by a traveler. Perhaps the closest analogy the observer of the mirror can find is provided by pictures scratched in the sand: "A 'mirror' is a kind of flat plate that shows pictures like the ones we scratch in the sand, but they're three-dimensional—looking at a mirror is almost like looking through a window, even though the mirror has hardly any thickness and you just see an ordinary surface if you turn it around and look at the back—and they're in color, and they're absolutely perfect pictures (except that they're backward), and they change and move just the way real things do, and the mirror always shows pictures of the things right in front of it." One can easily imagine the conceptual havoc a skeptical philosopher among these people could wreak on this attempt at description. I could myself, as a sort of mechanical philosophical exercise, construct a very plausible argument—it would be plausible to someone who had never seen a mirror—for the conclusion that the description ascribes logically incompatible properties to "mirrors." Nevertheless, considering the situation of the speaker and the speaker's audience, it's a good, practical description of a mirror. (It would, for example, almost certainly enable people who had never seen a reflection to recognize a mirror on their first encounter with one.) In my view, creedal descriptions of the Trinity and the Incarnation are good, practical descriptions of real things, descriptions that will do till we no longer see through a glass darkly. I am confident that they are at least as good as descriptions of curved space or the wave-particle duality in works of popular science. (It is easy enough, as a sort of mechanical philosophical exercise, to construct very plausible arguments—they would be plausible to someone who was unaware that these concepts played a central role in modern physics—for the conclusion that the idea of curved space and the idea of the wave-particle duality are self-contradictory: "Space is what things that are curved are curved *in*"; "A wave is a disturbance in some medium. A wave 'moves' only in the inverted-commas sense in which the locus of disturbance in a row of falling dominoes moves. A particle is a *thing*. Particles really, literally, move about in space.")

In the two essays in this section, I have not tried to *penetrate* either of the mysteries they address. One might say that someone who knew nothing about the general theory of relativity or quantum field theory, but who took a physicist's word for it that the sentences 'Space can have non-o curvature' and 'An electron is both a wave and a particle' can be given a sense in which they do not express impossible propositions, was in a position analogous to someone who took the Church's word for it that the sentences 'God is three persons in one being' and 'Jesus Christ is fully divine and fully human' can be given a sense in which they do not express impossible propositions. It can, however, be at least plausibly argued that there really are human beings who actually grasp the possible propositions expressed by the former pair of sentences; but no one even claims to grasp, in any adequate way, the supposedly possible propositions expressed by the latter pair. I have not in these two essays tried to provide nonmysterious paraphrases of the sentences of Trinitarian or Incarnational theology that have traditionally been held to express mysteries. If that could be done, it would have been done long ago. Attempts to do so have invariably led to that radical and serious distortion of doctrine that the Church calls "heresy." (Considered on a purely intellectual level, these heresies can be compared to deciding that, since space can be curved, space must be like invisible rubber. But the Church does not bother to call theological mistakes heresies if they have no consequences outside the world of the speculative intellect. The doctrines of the Trinity and the Incarnation play important roles in the lives of Christians; mistaken beliefs on doctrinal matters are called heresies only if they subvert these roles.) What I have tried to do is to show that these doctrines can be formulated in a way that allows no formal contradiction to be deduced from them. "Can be formulated": I do not claim that these formulations are correct or even that they are not heretical. Christians disagree about who has the authority to decide whether the sort of thing I have put forward in these two essays is a permissible statement of doctrine. I need not enter into that question here, except to note that I am quite certain that *I* do not have this authority.

8

And Yet
They Are Not Three Gods
but One God

I

CHRISTIANS believe that the love of one person for another is an essential part of the internal life of God. This is consonant with the Christian belief that all good things in creation are, in some way or other, copies or images of the uncreated. God Himself, Christian theology teaches, could not invent the idea of a good that was not prefigured in His own nature, for in the radiant plenitude of that nature, all possible goods are comprehended. And this holds for the supreme good, love. All forms of human love are (we believe) copies of the love that is internal to God. The natural affections of the family, friendship, sexual love (insofar as it is uncorrupted), the charity that will endure when faith has been swallowed up in sight and hope in fulfillment—all of these are creaturely images of the love that already existed, full and perfect and complete, when Adam still slept in his causes.

Like Christians, Jews and Muslims believe that power and goodness and wisdom and glory are from everlasting to everlasting. But only Christians believe this of love, for the eternality of love is a fruit of the uniquely Christian doctrine of the Holy Trinity. The doctrine of the Trinity is no arid theological speculation. It is not a thing that Chris-

Selection is taken from *Philosophy and the Christian Faith*, edited by Thomas V. Morris © 1988 by the University of Notre Dame Press, 1988. Used by permission.

tians can ignore when they are not thinking about philosophy or systematic theology. The doctrine of the Trinity ought to have as central a place in Christian worship and religious feeling as the doctrines of the Crucifixion and Resurrection.

Let me give one example of how the doctrine of the Trinity touches the deepest concerns of Christians. When we think of our hope of salvation, we tend to think of something individual. If you had asked me a year ago what I thought salvation consisted in, I think I should have said something like this: Each of us bears within him an image of God that has been distorted by sin, and his salvation will be accomplished when—if—that image has been restored in Christ. I do not mean to imply that I now think that this answer is wrong; but I do now think that it is incomplete. The Christian hope is not merely a hope about what will happen to us as individuals. The Beatific Vision is not something that each of the saints will enjoy separately and individually, alone with God. *Vita venturi saeculi* is a corporate life, the life of the Church Triumphant. And the establishment of this corporate life will consist in the whole Body of Christ coming to be an undistorted image of God. If you and I are one day members of the Risen Church, then you will indeed be a restored image of God and I shall indeed be a restored image of God. But there is more: The love we have for each other will be a restored image of the love that the Persons of the Trinity have for one another.

But can this really be? If the "eternal life we are by grace called to share, here below in the obscurity of faith and after death in eternal light,"[1] is the life of the Trinity, had we not better worry about the very logical possibility of the Christian hope? For how can the love of one person for another be internal to the life of God, who is, after all, one being? ("Hear, O Israel, the Lord our God is one Lord.") Must not Jew and Muslim and unbeliever join in demanding of us that we disclose the ill-concealed secret of all the Christian ages: that we are mere polytheists? Or if we are not mere polytheists, then are we not something worse: polytheists who are also monotheists, polytheists engaged in a pathetic attempt to remain loyal to the God of Israel through sheer force of reiterated logical contradiction? For do we not say all of the following things? There is one divine Being, but there are three distinct Persons, each of whom is a divine Being; and the one divine

---

1. Paul VI, "Credo of the People of God" (pronounced 30 June 1968), *Acta Apostolicae Sedis* 60 (1968), 9.

Being is a Person, thought not a fourth Person in addition to those three; nor is He any one of the three.[2]

My primary purpose in this essay is to explore one way of replying to the charge that Christians are either simple polytheists or else polytheists and monotheists at the same time. I shall not be terribly unhappy if the reply I propose to explore turns out to be unsatisfactory. The Trinity has always been described as a mystery, as something that surpasses human understanding. If one is unable to answer satisfactorily questions posed by a mystery—well, what should one expect?

Now if the Christian faith were a human invention, a theory devised by human beings to explain certain features of the world, then we should be wrong to be complacent about our inability to answer pointed questions about it. In such a case, if, after lengthy, determined, and serious effort to answer these questions, we should find ourselves still unable to answer them, then we ought to consider replacing our theory with one that does not pose these apparently unanswerable questions. But, as the pope recently had occasion to remind the Roman Church in Holland, the faith is no human invention. It is, quite simply, news.

Have we ever been promised by God that we shall understand everything He tells us well enough to resolve all the intellectual difficulties it raises? God's concern with us—just at present, at any rate—is not the concern of a tutor who fears that we shall fail to grasp some nice point: God fears that we shall lose the end for which we were made. His concern with us is entirely practical. It may well be that if I had the opportunity to ask God to explain His triune nature to me, He would say, "What is that to thee? Follow thou Me." It is, as Thomas

---

2. Keith Yandell has called my attention to the following passage from St. Augustine's *On Christian Doctrine* (I. 5. 5): "Thus there are the Father, the Son, and the Holy Spirit, and each is God and at the same time all are one God; and each of them is a full substance, and at the same time all are one substance. The Father is neither the Son nor the Holy Spirit; the Son is neither the Father nor the Holy Spirit; the Holy Spirit is neither the Father nor the Son. But the Father is the Father uniquely; the Son is the Son uniquely; and the Holy Spirit is the Holy Spirit uniquely." Yandell has also called my attention to the marvelously splenetic Socinian attacks on the doctrine of the Trinity that are cited in Leonard Hodgson's *The Doctrine of the Trinity* (New York: Charles Scribner's Sons, 1940), pp. 219 ff. I wish I had the space to reproduce them all. Here is my favorite, from a work that was (understandably) published anonymously in 1687. It has been ascribed to the notorious Socinian John Biddle. "You may add yet more absurdly, that there are three persons who are *severally and each of them* true God, and yet there is but one true God: this is *an Error* in counting or numbering; which, when stood in, is of all others the most brute and inexcusable, and not to discern it is not to be a Man."

à Kempis observed, better to be pleasing to the Holy Trinity than to be able to reason about the mysteries of the Holy Trinity.[3] It may be that it is important for us to know that God is (somehow) three Persons in one Being and not at all important for us to have any inkling of how this could be—or even to be able to answer alleged demonstrations that it is self-contradictory. It may be that we *cannot* understand how God can be three Persons in one Being. It may be that an intellectual grasp of the Trinity is forever beyond us. And why not, really? It is not terribly daring to suppose that reality may contain things whose natures we cannot understand. And if there were such natures, it would not be so very surprising if the highest nature of all were among them. As to alleged demonstrations of contradiction—well, our faith is: There is some way to answer these demonstrations, whether or not *we* can understand it.

The world, of course, has a handy word for this sort of thing: "obscurantism." I would remind the world of certain cases that have arisen in twentieth-century physics. An electron, we are told, is both a wave and a particle. One can ask pointed questions about *this* thesis. A wave is a spreading, periodic disturbance; a particle is lump of stuff; How can something be both? I think that there are two equally respectable answers to this question: (1) No one knows; (2) Quantum field theory explains how something can be both a wave and a particle.[4] Let us suppose that the second of these answers is correct, and that some people, those who are at home in quantum field theory, know how something can be both a wave and a particle. Still, there was an interval during which physicists went about saying that electrons were both waves and particles, and had no satisfactory reply to the childishly

3. Thomas à Kempis, *The Imitation of Christ*, I, 1.
4. The idea of drawing an analogy between a Christian mystery and the wave-particle duality is due to John Polkinghorne (formerly Professor of Mathematical Physics in Cambridge University and now an Anglican parish priest). See his book of Christian apologetic *The Way the World Is* (Grand Rapids, Mich.: Eerdman's, 1983). Fr. Polking-horne's position on the wave-particle duality is that quantum field theory *shows* how an electron can be both a wave and a particle (i.e., can be both diffracted on its way to a detector and give up its energy to the detector in a particle-like manner). My impression from reading popular works on quantum mechanics is that not all physicists and philosophers of physics are willing to say this. If there is indeed real disagreement on this point, I expect it is philosophical disagreement: disagreement about what counts as *really* having "shown how something can be." One man's "showing how something can be both *X* and *Y*" is another man's "constructing a formalism that allows you to treat something as both *X* and *Y* without getting into trouble." Fr. Polkinghorne, by the way, has written an excellent popular book on quantum mechanics, *The Quantum World* (New York: Longman, 1984).

simple question, "How can something be both a disturbance and a lump of stuff?" (I do not think anyone would say that there was a good answer to this question before Dirac formulated quantum field theory. I am willing to be corrected on this point, however.) And I do not think that anyone should blame the physicists for this. I do not think that anyone should have blamed them even if quantum field theory had somehow never been discovered. There were certain undeniable but absolutely astounding experimental data (a "revelation" from nature, as it were); there was a theory that explained those data (a human invention, to be sure, and an extraordinarily brilliant one at that, but not a human invention in the way a motet or an abstract painting is—the theory purported to represent physical reality); and that theory implied that an electron had both a mass and a wavelength.

Might it not be that the Christian who accepts the doctrine of the Trinity, even though he is unable to answer certain pointed questions about it, is in a position analogous to that of quantum physicists before the advent of quantum field theory? The world, of course, will reply that the Christian "revelation" is a fantasy, while the revelation disclosed by nature in the double-slit experiment or in the phenomenon of electron diffraction comprises hard facts of observation. But may we not ask the world to consider the question hypothetically? Suppose the Christian revelation were *not* a fantasy. If the Holy Spirit really existed and had led the mind of the Church to the doctrine of the Trinity,[5] *then* might not the Trinitarian be in a position analogous to that of the physicist to whom nature had revealed the doctrine of the Duality? The world may abuse us for believing in God and revelation if it will, but I think the world should admit that once we have accepted something as a revelation, it is reasonable for us to retain it even if we cannot answer all the intellectual difficulties it raises; or at least the world should admit this if the subject matter of the putative revelation is one that it is plausible a priori to suppose we should find it very difficult to understand.

While I accept all this as a Christian, I could not help being disappointed as a philosopher if there were no good, humanly accessible replies to the pointed questions raised by the doctrine of the Trinity. These questions are, after all, questions about number, identity, discernibility, personhood, and being. That is to say, they are logical and metaphysical questions, and therefore questions that I am profession-

5. Some might prefer to say: to an explicit and systematic statement of that which is present implicitly and in an unsystematic form in Scripture.

ally interested in. In this essay, my main purpose is to explore one way of responding to these questions. I should say, first, that I do not endorse the way of looking at the Trinity I shall ask you to consider, but I do think it is worth considering. It is worth asking whether the theses I shall put forward for your consideration are coherent and whether such light as they cast on the doctrine of the Trinity is orthodox and catholic (in the nondenominational senses of those words). I should say, secondly, that I do not propose to *penetrate* the mystery of the Trinity. I propose to state the doctrine of the Trinity (or part of it: the part that raises all those pointed logical and metaphysical questions) in such a way that it is demonstrable that no formal contradiction can be derived from the thesis that God is three persons and, at the same time, one being.

I do not propose to *explain* how God can be three persons and one being. Here is an analogy. I believe (and I hope that you do, too) that God exists necessarily—that, like a number or a proposition, He exists in all possible worlds; and I also believe (as I am sure you do, too) that, unlike numbers or propositions, He is a concrete being possessing causal powers. I have no idea how something could both exist necessarily and possess causal powers. And I think that no other human being does. How there could be something with both these features is a mystery. But I do not see any reason to suppose that a contradiction might be derivable from the thesis that God is both necessary and concrete, or from this thesis taken together with any plausible logical or metaphysical assumptions. It is in more or less this condition that I should like to leave the doctrine of the Trinity. But, as I have said, I shall not achieve even this modest goal in the present essay. I wish only to propose a way of stating that doctrine that can be shown to be free from formal inconsistency. Whether the doctrine, so stated, actually is the catholic faith (which I mean to keep whole and undefiled) will be a matter for further discussion.

The device I shall exploit for this purpose is the notion of relative identity, familiar to us from the work of Professor Geach. Professor Geach has discussed the abstract notion of relative identity in some detail, and has made some helpful and suggestive remarks about relative identity and the Trinity.[6] What I shall try to do is to expand these

6. I have paid special attention to "Identity" and "Identity—A Reply" in *Logic Matters* (Oxford: Basil Blackwell, 1972), pp. 238–249, and to "Ontological Relativity and Relative Identity" in *Logic and Ontology,* ed. Milton K. Munitz (New York: New York University Press, 1973). On the matter of relative identity and the Trinity, my main sources are *The Virtues* (Cambridge: Cambridge University Press, 1977), pp. 72–81, and

suggestive remarks in such a way as to enable us to see what a systematic and thoroughgoing attempt to express the propositions of Trinitarian theology in terms of relative identity would look like.[7] While the entire impetus of the thoughts of this essay is thus due to Professor Geach, we should not suppose that the idea of applying the notion of relative identity to the problems about identity and counting posed by the doctrine of the Trinity is an idiosyncratic whim of one twentieth-century Roman Catholic logician. Professor Geach, when alluding to the historical antecedents of his views—and rarely if ever does he do more than allude—usually manages to mention Thomas Aquinas. But the following (rather scattered) quotation from the *Quicunque Vult*— a document that was certainly in more or less its present form by about A.D. 500—speaks for itself:

> The Catholic Faith is this: That we worship one God in Trinity, and Trinity in Unity, neither confounding the Persons, nor dividing the Substance.
> For there is one Person of the Father, another of the Son, and another of the Holy Ghost . . .
> The Father eternal, the Son eternal, and the Holy Ghost eternal.
> And yet they are not three eternals, but one eternal . . .
> So likewise the Father is Almighty, the Son Almighty, and the Holy Ghost Almighty.
> And yet they are not three Almighties, but one Almighty.
> So the Father is God, the Son is God, and the Holy Ghost is God.
> And yet they are not three Gods, but one God.
> So likewise the Father is Lord, the Son Lord, and the Holy Ghost Lord.
> And yet not three Lords, but one Lord.
> For like as we are compelled by the Christian verity to acknowledge every Person by himself to be both God and Lord,

---

Peter Geach and G. E. M. Anscombe, *Three Philosophers* (Oxford: Basil Blackwell, 1963), pp. 118–120. I do not claim that Geach would agree with everything I say about relative identity in this essay, either in the abstract or in relation to the Trinity.

7. This has been attempted at least once before, by A. P. Martinich. See his papers, "Identity and Trinity," *Journal of Religion* 58 (April 1978), 169–181, and "God, Emperor, and Relative Identity," *Franciscan Studies* 39 (1979), 180–191. The relative-identity treatment of Trinitarian doctrine of the present essay was devised when I was unaware of these papers; the two treatments are thus independent developments of Geach's work. My treatment differs from Martinich's principally in devoting a good deal of attention to the problem of translating English sentences containing the singular terms—at least they have the syntax of singular terms—'God', 'the Father', 'the Son', and 'the Holy Spirit' into the language of relative identity. I do not accept any of Martinich's supposed examples of nontheological "cases of relative identity."

So we are forbidden by the Catholic Religion, to say, There be three Gods, or three Lords.[8]

Before turning to a detailed treatment of relative identity and the Trinity, I shall make some remarks on the meaning of the word *person* in Trinitarian theology.

II

Anyone who undertakes to give an account of the Trinity will find it hard to avoid falling into some heresy that is summarized in a helpful little article in the *Oxford Dictionary of the Christian Church*. Roughly speaking, these heresies are bounded on the one side by Modalism and on the other by Tritheism. Modalism, in its crudest form, holds that the Father, the Son, and the Holy Spirit are the same person and the same being, this one being or person being conceived, on various occasions, under each of these names in relation to an office, function, or "mode" appropriate to that name. (I say "in its crudest form" because Modalism may be variously disguised.) Thus, 'the Father' is simply a name of God, one we use when we are thinking of Him as our creator and judge, rather than as (say) our redeemer or our comforter. Modalism is associated historically with Sabellius (it is sometimes called Sabellianism) and with Peter Damian. Tritheism is, of course, the thesis

---

8. The translation is that of *The Book of Common Prayer* (According to the Use of the Episcopal Church, New York: Seabury Press, 1979), p. 864 f. In the Prayer Book of 1662, the *Quicunque Vult* is printed following the Order for Evening Prayer. The Latin text I have used (on the advice of Eleonore Stump) is that of J. N. D. Kelly, *The Athanasian Creed* (London: Adam & Charles Black, 1964), pp. 17–20. The Prayer Book translation is accurate enough (allowing for changes in English since 1549), although it sometimes departs from the literal sense of the Latin in aid of liturgical euphony. (For example, the title of the present essay, literally translated, would be "And yet [they are] not three Gods, but there is one God.") I do not know what Latin text Cranmer—or whoever—used, but it does not seem to have been significantly different from the text in Kelly's book. We may note that in several places the Creed makes use of a grammatical device that English idiom resists: the use of adjective as substantive: "And yet not three eternals *[aeterni]* but one eternal *[aeternus]*." "Three eternal *whats*?" the English speaker wants to ask. (After all, they *are* three eternal *personae*.) I take '*tres aeterni*' to be equivalent to '*tres substantiae aeternae*'; I would defend this reading on the basis of the earlier warning about "dividing the substance." It is possible that the earliest users of the Creed—and the Scholastics as well—would dispute my contention that there are, after all, three eternal *personae*, on the ground that this implies that the *aeternitas* of the three *personae* is "divided." I am not sure what that means, however. *I* mean only that there are three *personae* and that it is true of each that *He* is eternal. The eternity ascribed to each Person can be "the same," though I am not sure what that is supposed to imply. I certainly want to say that the word 'eternal' is applied to each Person in the same *sense*, if that helps.

that there are three Gods. Of these two heresies, Tritheism would seem to be the more serious. If Modalism subverts the doctrine of the Incarnation of the Word by flatly contradicting either our Lord's divinity or else His consistent representation of Himself and His Father as distinct persons, Tritheism strikes, by definition, at the very root of monotheism.

Nevertheless, it is Tritheism that I shall risk. I have two reasons. First, the language of the Creeds is as safe from a modalistic interpretation as any language could be. If a philosopher or theologian is guided by the Creeds, he will be directed resolutely away from Modalism, and I propose to be guided by the Creeds. Secondly, I think that Modalism is a far easier heresy than Tritheism to fall into in our time, and is, therefore, a doctrine that a Christian thinker ought to stay as far away from as possible. I have recently heard a priest of my own communion, guided, I suppose, by a desire to avoid saying anything that implied that God had a sex, bless the people at the end of Mass not with the prescribed words, " . . . the blessing of God Almighty, the Father, the Son, and the Holy Ghost," but rather with the words " . . . God our Creator, God our Redeemer, and God our Sanctifier." Note that what are enumerated in this formula are not persons but functions, offices, or modes, and that this formula has been used in place of a customary and familiar formula in which the divine Persons are enumerated. The "new" formula is no more a Trinitarian formula than is 'the God of Abraham, the God of Isaac, and the God of Jacob.' You may tell me that the three offices enumerated have been, in liturgy and tradition, associated respectively with the Father, the Son, and the Holy Spirit. I will reply that that is true but does not affect my point. (Moreover, the nature of that "association" or "appropriation" is a nice theological problem. Whatever it means, it does not mean that, e.g., only the Father was involved in the Creation. The Nicene Creed says of the Son: "by whom *(per quem)* all things were made," and in this it echoes Colossians 1:15–17 and the opening words of John's Gospel.) My priest, of course, was not a Modalist and did not intend to preach Modalism. But note how easy it is for one whose purposes are remote from questions of Trinitarian theology inadvertently to use words that are, in context, Modalistic in tendency.

It is my intention in this essay to avoid Modalism by adhering rigorously to the doctrine that there are three distinct divine Persons. Two comments are in order.

(1) I shall ignore all problems related to the predication of wisdom, goodness, knowledge—and personality itself—and other attributes

predicable of created persons to the divine Persons. Such predication is, I think, as much a difficulty for the Unitarian (i.e., the Jew or Muslim) as for the Trinitarian, and I think it is the *same* difficulty for the Unitarian and the Trinitarian. In any case, I cannot attend to all the problems of philosophical theology at once.

(2) It is sometimes contended that 'person' in Trinitarian theology does not mean what it means in everyday life or in the philosophy of mind or even in non-Trinitarian applications of this word to God. Professor Geach has answered this contention with his usual vigor, and I am of his party:

> Some will protest that I am equivocating between the normal use of the term 'person' and its technical theological use. I reject the protest. The concept of a person, which we find so familiar in its application to human beings, cannot be clearly and sharply expressed by any word in the vocabulary of Plato and Aristotle; it was wrought with the hammer and anvil of theological disputes about the Trinity and the Person of Christ.[9]

He goes on to say, "The familiar concept of a person finds linguistic expression not only in the use of a noun for 'person' but also in the use of the personal pronouns." In addition to the uses of personal pronouns in connection with the divine Persons that Geach proceeds to cite, we may call attention to the English translation of the *Quicunque Vult* quoted above ("to acknowledge every Person by himself to be both God and Lord"), and the closing words of Proper 27 of the Episcopal Church: "where with thee, O Father, and thee, O Holy Ghost, he liveth and reigneth ever, one God, world without end."[10]

III

In this section, I shall outline a system of formal logic I shall call Relative-Identity Logic, or RI-logic for short.[11] I shall also attempt to

9. *The Virtues*, p. 75.
10. Geach cites Ps. 89:26, Ps. 2:7 (it is, of course, rather a controversial reading of these verses to regard them as describing exchanges between two Persons of the Trinity!), and John 17:5. My two citations represent not "intra-Trinitarian" discourse, but unreflective and incidential creedal and liturgical recognition of the personhood (in the ordinary sense) of the Father, the Son, and the Holy Spirit. The sources I cite are not supposed to be authoritative (the personal aspect of "by himself" has no basis in the Latin Creed, which says only "acknowledge each Person *singillatim* to be") but merely typical.
11. I have learned something from all of the following papers and books: John Perry, "The Same F," *Philosophical Review* 79 (1970); Eddy M. Zemach, "In Defense of Relative Identity," *Philosophical Studies* 26 (1974); Nicholas Griffin, *Relative Identity* (Oxford: Clarendon Press, 1977); John Perry, "Relative Identity and Number," *Canadian Journal of Philosophy* 8 (1978); Harold W. Noonan, *Objects and Identity* (The Hague:

answer the question, On what assumptions is a logic of relative identity of philosophical interest?

A formal logic comprises a vocabulary and a set of formation rules, a set of rules of inference, and, sometimes, a set of axioms. We shall require no axioms.

The vocabulary of RI-logic will consist of certain predicates of English (including 0-place predicates: closed sentences), the usual sentential connectives, variables, the universal and existential quantifiers, and suitable punctuation marks.[12] It will *not* include the identity sign, the description operator, or any terms other than variables.

We shall assume that our vocabulary contains all English predicates that conform to the following three constraints.

Martinus Nijhoff, 1980); David Wiggins, *Sameness and Substance* (Cambridge: Harvard University Press, 1980); William P. Alston and Jonathan Bennett, "Identity and Cardinality: Geach and Frege," *Philosophical Review* 93 (1984). But the first drafts of Sections III and IV of the present essay were written before I had read any of these papers and books, and I have found no reason to revise anything I have said in the light of their content. I do not, of course, mean to imply that what is said in this essay supersedes all previous work on the subject; I mean only that what I say here about the concept of relative identity and its logic does not seem to me to require any revisions in the light of what I have read in the authors cited above.

12. "To avoid accusations of provincialism, we should mention that the preferred status of English is a matter only of the authors' convenience; the subsequent treatment would apply as well to French, German, or Coptic" (Donald Kalish and Richard Montague, *Logic: Techniques of Formal Reasoning* [New York: Harcourt, Brace & World, 1964], p. 5).

The somewhat unusual employment of English predicates as items in the vocabulary of a formal logic will make our exposition more compact. Thereby we generate "directly" as theorems what Kalish and Montague (p. 9) call "literal English translations of theorems," and it is these that we shall be primarily interested in. The description of the content of our stock of English predicates that follows in the text is of no formal significance. As long as we restrict our attention to purely formal matters—the statement of formation-rules and rules of inference—we need assume nothing more definite than that we have gone through the class of English predicates and have picked out (somehow) a certain set of them to be our vocabulary items. We must also assume, of course, that each of the chosen predicates has a clear and definite number of "places." And we must assume that our two-place predicates have (somehow) been partitioned into two classes, the "ordinary two-place predicates" and the "relative-identity" predicates (vide infra). Exactly how these things are to be done is irrelevant to our statement of the formation- and inference-rules of RI-logic, which presupposes only that we have a stock of predicates and a partition of the two-place predicates.

In the text that follows, there are examples and illustrations that presuppose that particular English predicates (e.g., 'is green') belong to the vocabulary of RI-logic. The specially scrupulous may wish to replace illustrative statements of the type '"x is green → x is green" is a theorem of RI-logic' with the corresponding statements of the type 'On the assumption that "is green" belongs to the vocabulary of RI-logic, "x is green → x is green" is a theorem of RI-logic'.

(1) Our stock of English predicates will not include any that contain the informal analogues of the things we have pointedly excluded from our formal apparatus: identity, descriptions, demonstratives, and names. Thus we exclude 'α is identical with some Albanian', 'The tallest man is rich', 'That is a dog', and 'α is Jack's father'. It would cause no *formal* difficulties to include such predicates in the language of RI-logic, since a formal logic does not "interact" with the semantic content (if there is any) of the items it manipulates formally, but to do so would be confusing and contrary to the motivating spirit of RI-logic.

(2) With the exception of a special class of predicates noted in (3) below, our stock of English predicates will include no predicates containing count-nouns. (A count-noun is a noun which has a plural form and which can be modified by the indefinite article.) Thus we exclude: 'α is an apple', 'α owns three horses', and 'α has more children than β'. Some acceptable predicates are: 'α is heavy', 'α is made of gold', 'α is spherical' and 'α is taller than β'. We shall not, however, be really fanatical about excluding count-nouns. We shall be liberal enough to admit count-nouns that are mere grammatical conveniences. For example, we shall admit 'α has six sides' because one might just as well express what is expressed by this predicate by writing 'α is six-sided'. The rough rule is: A count-noun is "all right" if its use does not commit its user to there being things it counts. If one says, "The box weighs four pounds," one does not lay oneself open to the following sort of ontological interrogation: "Just what is a 'pound'? What properties do these 'pounds' have? You say the box weighs four of them; but how many of them are there (in all, I mean)?"

(3) Consider phrases of the form 'α is the same N as β', where 'N' represents the place of a count-noun. Sometimes predicates of this form are used in such a way as to imply that α and β are Ns and sometimes they are not. If I say, "Tully is the same man as Cicero," I imply that Tully and Cicero are men. If I say, "The Taj Mahal is the same color as the Washington Monument," I do not imply that these two edifices are colors. Let us call a predicate of the form 'is the same N as' a *relative-identity predicate* (or "RI-predicate") if it is satisfied only by Ns. A predicate that is not an RI-predicate we call an *ordinary* predicate. Thus, 'is the same man as' is an RI-predicate, and 'is the same color as' is an ordinary predicate—as are 'is green', 'is round', and 'is taller than'. (Actually, we should not say that predicates of the form 'is the same N as' are or are not RI-predicates *in themselves*, for a

predicate of this form may be used sometimes as an RI-predicate and sometimes as an ordinary predicate. Consider, for example, 'Magenta is the same color as bluish-red'. In this sentence, 'is the same color as' functions as an RI-predicate. In the sequel, I shall ignore this complication.) Count-nouns—seriously meant count-nouns like 'apple', 'horse', and 'child'—may turn up in our stock of English predicates in just one way: as components of RI-predicates. Thus we admit 'α is the same apple as β', 'α is the same horse as β', and so on.

Having introduced RI-predicates, we may introduce ordinary predicates of the form 'α is a(n) N' (e.g., 'α is an apple'; 'α is a child') by abbreviation: 'α is an apple' abbreviates '$\exists \beta$ α is the same apple as β', and so on. To be an apple, in other words, is to be the same apple as something.

The formation rules of RI-logic are the obvious ones.

The rules of inference of RI-logic are simply the rules of ordinary quantifier logic—developed as a system of natural deduction—supplemented by two rules for manipulating RI-predicates. Since RI-predicates are closely connected with the idea of identity, we should expect these rules to be in at least some ways analogous to the inference-rules governing classical identity. This is indeed the case. The two rules are:

Symmetry From $I\alpha\beta$, infer $I\beta\alpha$

Transitivity From $I\alpha\beta$ and $I\beta\gamma$, infer $I\alpha\gamma$.

Here, of course, 'I' represents any RI-predicate and the Greek letters represent any variables. Using these two rules, we may prove something that will be a minor convenience to us, the general fact of which the following statement is an instance: '$\exists y$ x is the same apple as y' is equivalent to 'x is the same apple as x'.[13] "Right-to-left" is simply an instance of Existential Generalization. We proceed from left to right as follows: We have 'x is the same apple as z' by Existential Instantiation; from this we infer 'z is the same apple as x' by Symmetry; from these two sentences, 'x is the same apple as x' follows by Transitivity.

This result is a convenience because it allows us to regard, for example, 'x is an apple' as an abbreviation for 'x is the same apple as x' instead of for '$\exists y$ x is the same apple as y', which will simplify the

13. Two sentences are equivalent in RI-logic if their biconditional is a theorem of RI-logic. In the present section, I shall assume that the reader is familiar with the usual conventions for omitting universal quantifiers.

no rule corresponding to the reflexivity rule of classical identity logic. A reflexivity rule for RI-predicates would look like this: From any premises, infer $I\alpha\alpha$. But if we had this rule, we could prove, for example, that everything is the same apple as itself—that is to say, we could prove that everything is an apple.

Do we need further rules for manipulating RI-predicates? It might be argued that we must have such rules if RI-logic is to be at all interesting. Developments of the classical logic of identity always include some rule or axiom motivated by the intuitive idea that if x is identical with y, then x and y satisfy all the same predicates. In fact, all the classical principles of identity can be derived from a reflexivity rule ('From any premises, infer $\alpha = \alpha$') and an "indiscernibility" rule: 'From any premises, infer

$$\alpha = \beta \rightarrow (F \ldots \alpha \ldots \leftrightarrow F \ldots \beta \ldots)'.$$

Here $F \ldots \alpha \ldots$ represents a sentence in which β does not occur, and $F \ldots \beta \ldots$ represents the result of replacing any (or all) free occurrences of α in $F \ldots \alpha \ldots$ with β. for example:

$$x = y \rightarrow (\exists w \; z \text{ is between } x \text{ and } w. \leftrightarrow \exists w \; z \text{ is between } y \text{ and } w).$$

If RI-logic is to be interesting (it might be argued), it must be supplied with some analogue of this rule. What would this analogue be? It will certainly *not* do to have the following rule (call it 'The Proposed Rule'): 'Where I is any RI-predicate, from any premises infer

$$I\alpha\beta \rightarrow (F \ldots \alpha \ldots \leftrightarrow F \ldots \beta \ldots)'.$$

For example:

$$x \text{ is the same man as } y \rightarrow (z \text{ is west of } x \leftrightarrow z \text{ is west of } y).$$

If we added the Proposed Rule to RI-logic, we should get a logic that treated RI-predicates as if they were all of the form 'x is an N & $x = y$', where N is a count-noun and ' $=$ ' represents classical, absolute identity.[14] For example, the resulting logic would treat 'x is the same apple as y' as if it had the logical properties ascribed to 'x is an apple & $x = y$' by the classical logic of identity.

We may put this point more precisely as follows. Call a sentence like 'x is the same apple as y' that is formed from an RI-predicate and

---

14. I shall not pretend to be careful about use and mention in the remainder of this essay. The content of general statements about words and symbols will be conveyed impressionistically.

like 'x is the same apple as y' that is formed from an RI-predicate and two occurrences of variables, an *RI-expression*. Call the sentence 'x is an apple & $x = y$' the *classical image* of the RI-expression 'x is the same apple as y'. Similarly 'z is a horse & $z = w$' is the classical image of 'z is the same horse as w'; the definition is obvious. More generally, the classical image of a *sentence* of the language of RI-logic is got by replacing each occurrence of an RI-expression in that sentence with its classical image.

Adding the Proposed Rule to RI-logic has this consequence:

> A sentence is a theorem of RI-logic if and only if its classical image is an instance of a theorem of the classical logic of identity.

By an instance of a theorem of the classical logic of identity, I mean a sentence that results from such a theorem by substituting English predicates (consistently) for all of its predicate-letters. (Of course, most instances of theorems of the classical logic of identity are not classical images of any sentence of RI-logic; '$x = y$ & x is green. → y is green', for example, is not.) The following three sentences are instances of theorems of the classical logic of identity:

x is an apple & $x = y$. → .y is an apple & $y = x$

x is an apple & $x = y$ & y is an apple & $y = z$. → .x is an apple & $x = z$

w is an apple & $w = y$. → (w is green ↔ y is green).

Therefore (if the above thesis about adding the Proposed Rule to RI-logic is correct), the sentences of which these are the classical images are theorems of RI-logic supplemented by the Proposed Rule. (Hereinafter, 'RI-logic+'.) For example, the sentence

w is the same apple as y → (w is green ↔ y is green).

is a theorem of RI-logic+. And it is, I think, intuitively obvious that a sentence is a theorem of RI-logic+ if and only if its classical image is an instance of a theorem of the classical logic of identity. It does not seem to be overstating the case to say that RI-logic+ treats 'α as the same N as β' as a stylistic variant on 'α is an N & $\alpha = \beta$'. If RI-logic+ is the correct logic for reasoning about relative identities, then there is no point in having a special logic for reasoning about relative identities. The correct principles for reasoning about relative identities follow from the correct principles for reasoning about absolute identities. One need do no more than put a check mark beside each instance of a theorem of the logic of classical identity that is a classical image of some sentence in the language of RI-logic and say, "These are the formal truths about so-called relative identities. You may pronounce, e.g., 'z is an apple & $z = y$' as 'z is the same apple as y' if you care to."

A logic of relative identity will be interesting only if there are instances of theorems of the classical logic of identity that are the classical images of *nontheorems* of that logic of relative identity. A philosophically interesting logic of relative identity must be (in that sense) "weaker" than the classical logic of identity. (As with paraconsistent logic, "intuitionist" logic, quantum logic, and David Lewis's counterfactual logic, a good deal of the philosophical interest of the topic arises from the fact that certain sentences that one might expect to be theorems are not theorems.) I propose to achieve this end as follows: to resist the temptation to supply RI-logic with any special rules of inference beyond Symmetry and Transitivity. This, of course, will not ensure that RI-logic is of any philosophical interest. It is certainly of no formal interest. Considered formally, it is simply the quantifier calculus with its two-place predicates partitioned into two classes, within one of which Symmetry and Transitivity apply. What interest it has must come from two sources: first, from the thesis that this rather weak logic does indeed embody all the formal principles of inference that one should have when one reasons about relative identities, and, secondly, from such applications as it may have. The main philosophical interest of "intuitionist" logic lies in the claim that it embodies all the principles of formal reasoning the mathematician can legitimately employ. Quantum logic has no philosophical interest apart from its intended application.

The effect of having no special rules of RI-logic beyond Symmetry and Transitivity (and that comes down to having neither the Proposed Rule nor any restricted version of it) is exemplified by the following case:

x is the same apple as y → (x is green ↔ y is green)

will not be a theorem of RI-logic, despite the fact that its classical image

x is an apple & $x = y$. → (x is green ↔ y is green)

is an instance of a theorem of the classical logic of identity. More generally, RI-logic differs from RI-logic+ in the following way. Call sentences of the following form *dominance* sentences:

$$I\alpha\beta \rightarrow (F\ldots\alpha\ldots \leftrightarrow F\ldots\beta\ldots),$$

where $F \ldots \alpha \ldots$ is a sentence in which β does not occur, and $F \ldots \beta$ $\ldots$ is like $F \ldots \alpha \ldots$ except for having free occurrences of β at some or all places at which $F \ldots \alpha \ldots$ has free occurrences of α. All dominance sentences are theorems of RI-logic +. In general, dominance sentences are not theorems of RI-logic—unless they are instances of theorems of the sentential calculus, or are of the type 'x is the same apple as $y \rightarrow$ (x is the same apple as $z \leftrightarrow y$ is the same apple as z)'.

In refusing to add the Proposed Rule (or any restricted version of it) to RI-logic, we are in effect saying that each dominance sentence embodies a substantive metaphysical thesis—or perhaps in some cases a trivial metaphysical thesis, but at any rate a *metaphysical* thesis, one that ought not to be underwritten by the formal logic of relative identity. If there were a formal criterion by which we could separate the trivial metaphysical theses from the substantive ones, then we might consider adopting a restricted version of the Proposed Rule, one that yielded only the trivial theses. But there could not be such a formal criterion: If some dominance sentences are substantive and some trivial, the distinction lies in the English meanings of the predicates they contain.

In refusing to adopt the Proposed Rule, we are (in effect) saying to whoever proposes to construct a derivation containing RI-predicates: "If you think that a dominance sentence like 'x is the same apple as $y \rightarrow$ (x is green $\leftrightarrow y$ is green)' is *true,* you are perfectly free to introduce it into your derivation *as a premise.* But then defending it is your responsibility. Formal logic alone does not endorse it." If someone does regard the dominance sentence 'x is the same apple as $y \rightarrow$ (x is green $\leftrightarrow y$ is green)' as true, let us say that he regards the RI-predicate 'is the same apple as' as *dominating* the predicate 'is green'. (If he believed that x and y might be the same apple and nevertheless be of different colors, then he would deny that sameness among apples "dominated" color.) Informally, for I to dominate F is for I to "force indiscernibility" in respect of F. Formally, an RI-predicate I dominates a predicate F (F may be of any polyadicity and be either ordinary or RI) if all sentences of the form '$I\alpha\beta \rightarrow (F \ldots \alpha \ldots \leftrightarrow F \ldots \beta \ldots)$' are true. We say that an RI-predicate that dominates every predicate is *dominant.* It seems a reasonable conjecture that most of us would regard, for example, 'is the same apple as' and 'is the same horse as' as dominant.

The question now arises, *are* there any RI-predicates that are not dominant? Are there any false dominance sentences? If all dominance sentences are true (if all RI-predicates are dominant), then the Proposed Rule can never lead from truth to falsity. And if the Proposed Rule can never lead from truth to falsity, then the project of constructing a logic of relative identity is of no interest. It can be accomplished by stipulating that a sentence is a "theorem of the logic of relative identity" if and only if its classical image is an instance of a theorem of the classical logic of identity. There is, after all, no point in refusing to include the Proposed Rule among the rules of inference of a logic of relative identity if that rule can never lead from truth to falsity. And the Proposed Rule can lead from truth to falsity only if some RI-predicates are not dominant.

A trick of Professor Geach's shows that some RI-predicates are not dominant.[15] Let us introduce an RI-predicate 'is the same surman as' by the following definition:

α is the same surman as β = df α is a man and β is a man and
$\quad\quad\quad\quad\quad\quad\quad\quad\quad\quad$ α and β have the same surname.

Thus, John Locke is the same surman as Don Locke. It is evident that 'same surman' fails to dominate a great variety of predicates: 'is alive in the twentieth century', 'has never heard of Kant', 'is the same man as', and so on. Or, at least, 'same surman' fails to dominate these predicates if it really is an RI-predicate. But it would seem to be: 'surman' is a count-noun ("John Locke is a surman"; "Geach and Locke are two surmen") and if x is the same surman as y, then x and y are both surmen (i.e., each is the same surman as himself).

But this trick, it seems to me, does not show that the project of constructing a logic of relative identity is of interest. It is true that 'is the same surman as' is nondominant. But it is also easily eliminable from our discourse. Anything we can say using 'is the same surman as' we can say without it; we need only use the (presumably dominant) RI-predicate 'is the same man as' and the ordinary predicate 'has the same surname as'. Let us say that if a nondominant RI-predicate has these features, it is *redundant*. More explicitly: a nondominant RI-predicate is redundant if everything we can say by making use of it we can say using only dominant RI-predicates and ordinary predicates. If the *only* nondominant RI-predicates are in this sense redundant, then there is no real point in having a special logic of relative identity. If the only nondominant RI-predicates are redundant, then—at least when we are engaged in constructing formal derivations—why not just translate all of our premises into sentences containing only dominant RI-predicates and ordinary predicates? Having done that, we may replace

15. See the article "Identity" cited in note 6.

each premise that contains RI-predicates with its classical image and employ the classical logic of identity. If it pleases us, we may replace all occurrences in our conclusion of, for example, 'x is a man & y is a man & x and y have the same surname' with 'x is the same surman as y'. In short, the "surman" trick provides us with no motivation for constructing a logic of relative identity. A logic of relative identity will be of interest only if there are *nonredundant* RI-predicates that are not dominant.

Are there nonredundant RI-predicates that are not dominant? Is there a nonredundant RI-predicate that fails to dominate some predicate? It is tempting to think that if there is such a relation as classical, absolute identity, the answer must be No. (If that is right, the project of constructing a logic of relative identity is interesting only on the assumption that classical, absolute identity does not exist.) Consider, say, 'is the same apple as'—which we shall suppose for the sake of the example not to be redundant—and 'is green'. Suppose that there is such a relation as classical identity. Obviously (one is tempted to say), if x is the same apple as y, then $x = y$. We have as an instance of a theorem of the logic of classical identity: $x = y \rightarrow (x$ is green $\leftrightarrow y$ is green). Hence, if x is the same apple as y, then x is green if and only if y is green. That is, 'is the same apple as' dominates 'is green'. Essentially the same argument could be constructed for the general case: to show that for any nonredundant RI-predicate I and any predicate F, I dominates F.

The tricky step in the argument for the general case will be the premise that, for just any nonredundant RI-predicate I, if Ixy then $x = y$. (A redundant RI-predicate R may, of course, be such that Rxy & $\sim x = y$. The two Lockes are the same surman but not absolutely identical.) Is this true? Does every nonredundant RI-predicate dominate classical identity, assuming there to be such a relation as classical identity? Put the question this way. Call a predicate *subdominant* if it is dominated by every RI-predicate other than those that, like 'same surman', are redundant; Is it a part of the *concept* of classical identity (whether or not any relation in fact falls under that concept) that it be subdominant?

If the answer to this question is Yes, then RI-logic is an interesting topic only if classical identity does not exist. (And it seems to be the consensus among the friends of relative identity that classical identity does not exist.)

I am unsure what to say about the subdominance of classical identity. I know of only three relevant arguments, and they are inconclusive.

First, one might argue that if there is such a relation as classical identity, then, for any nonredundant RI-predicate 'is the same N as', the following equivalence should hold:

x is the same N as $y \leftrightarrow .x$ is an N & $x = y$.

And it obviously follows from this that every nonredundant RI-predicate dominates classical identity. I think that those friends of relative identity who assume that their position is incompatible with the existence of classical identity have something like this in mind. (But why exactly should one accept this equivalence? Call a count-noun *proper* if, unlike 'surman', it does not form a redundant RI-predicate. Why is it incoherent to suppose that, where N is a proper count-noun, x is an N, y is an N, x and y are the same N, and x and y are not absolutely identical?)

Secondly, one might argue ad hominem that the philosopher who believes that RI-logic is an interesting topic should not mind denying that classical identity is subdominant. After all, he must hold that *some* predicate is not subdominant. Now the really puzzling thing—one might argue—is that *any* predicate should fail to be subdominant. Once someone has admitted *that,* he should have no scruples about saying of any *given* predicate—classical identity, for example—that *it* is not subdominant.

Thirdly, one might point out that all the theorems of the logic of classical identity follow from '$x = x$' and '$x = y \rightarrow (F \ldots x \ldots \leftrightarrow F \ldots y \ldots)$' by quantifier logic. This fact suggests that only two properties are constitutive of the *idea* of classical identity: identity is *universally reflexive* and it *forces absolute indiscernibility.* And it is hard to see how these two properties might entail subdominance.

As I have said, I regard these arguments as inconclusive. In the sequel, therefore, I shall assume neither that classical identity exists nor that it does not exist.

We may note in this connection that it is possible for one to employ in certain contexts a symbol that behaves like the classical identity-sign without thereby committing oneself to the existence of classical identity. The contexts in which one may do this can be described as follows. Let G be a one-place predicate. Let us say that an RI-predicate I *G-dominates* a predicate F if all sentences of the form

$$G\alpha \ \& \ G\beta. \rightarrow [I\alpha\beta \rightarrow (F \ldots \alpha \ldots \leftrightarrow F \ldots \beta \ldots)]$$

are true. Suppose that, for the duration of a certain project, one is willing to restrict the scope of one's generalizations to objects that satisfy G. And suppose that one believes (1) that all the RI-predicates one is employing in this project G-dominate all the predicates one is employing, and (2) that, for any x, if Gx, then for some RI-predicate I that one is employing, Ixx. Then one may introduce a predicate ' $=$ ' as the disjunction of all the RI-predicates that one is employing and one may regard this predicate as governed by the two rules that define the logical behavior of the classical identity-sign. (That is, Reflexivity and the Indiscernibility of Identicals; see above.)

A philosopher who denies the existence of classical, absolute identity may find materials in the procedure I have outlined for an explanation of the fact that most philosophers and logicians have assumed that there is such a relation as classical identity. Might it not be that all commonly used RI-predicates G-dominate all commonly used predicates, where G is some predicate that comprehends all the objects that philosophers typically think of as central or paradigm cases of "objects"? If this were so, it would go a long way toward explaining how a belief in absolute identity could be pervasive but incorrect. (One might compare an explanation of this sort with the usual explanations of how a belief in absolute, Euclidean space could be pervasive but incorrect. Each sort of explanation postulates a natural but unwarranted inference from "local" features of the world to the features of the world as a whole.)

Now whether or not there is such a relation as classical identity, RI-logic is of interest only if there is an RI-predicate I (from now on, when making generalizations about RI-predicates, I shall regard the qualification 'nonredundant' as "understood") and a predicate F such that I does not dominate F. We should have such an I and F if there were some count-noun of English N (from now on, when making generalizations about count-nouns, I shall regard the qualification 'proper' as "understood") such that, for some x and y, x is green and y is not green and x is the same N as y. (In this case 'is the same N as' fails to dominate 'green'.) Or we should have such an I and F if there were two count-nouns of English, M and N, such that, for some x and y, x is an M and x is an N and y is an M and y is an N and x is the same N as y and x is not the same M as y. (In this second case, 'is the same N as' fails to dominate 'is the same M as'. This second case has been said to be a necessary and sufficient condition for RI-logic being of interest; but it is not necessary, as the first case shows.)

How plausible is it to suppose that there is some RI-predicate that fails to dominate some predicate? (In the present section I shall examine the question whether there are such predicates insofar as this question touches on objects belonging to the natural world. Theological speculations are reserved for Section IV.) The literature on relative identity suggests several candidates for this position, several of which are worthy of careful examination. I pick one as representative. It is sometimes said that there are such things as "quantities of clay" (and of other stuffs, of course). A clay vase is a quantity of clay, a clay statue is a quantity of clay, and an unformed lump of clay that no potter or sculptor has touched is a quantity of clay. ('Quantity' does not here mean *amount;* 'quantity' is like 'lump', only even less demanding: a lump has to be in one piece—one would suppose—while a quantity may be scattered to the four corners of the earth.) It is sometimes suggested that the RI-predicate 'is the same quantity of clay as' does not dominate, for example, 'is less than one hour old'. It is suggested that it may be that there is a vase and there is a lump of clay (currently vase-shaped and coincident with the vase) such that the former is the same quantity of clay as the latter, despite the fact that the vase is less than one hour old and the lump more than one hour old. (For no vase could ever have been of a radically different shape—spherical, say— while a lump of clay might be vase-shaped now and have been spherical yesterday.) A philosopher who doubts the philosophical utility of the concept of relative identity will not be moved by these suggestions, however. He will contend that there is no need to suppose that 'is the same quantity of clay as' fails to dominate 'is less than one hour old'. He will suggest that it is simpler to suppose (a) that there is such a relation as absolute identity, (b) that 'x is the same quantity of clay as y' is equivalent to 'x is a quantity of clay & $x = y$', and (c) that it *can* be true of a vase that *it* was once spherical; he will suggest that a clay vase *is* (absolutely) just a quantity of clay; one that was once (say) spherical and is now vase-shaped. In other words, this philosopher will suggest that "being a vase" is a *status* that a quantity of clay may temporarily acquire, much as "being a president" is a status that Ronald Reagan has temporarily acquired: Just as the President existed before he was a president, so the vase existed before it was a vase. I have not the space to consider all the cases that have been devised by philosophers in the attempt to show that there are nondominant RI-predicates (ones having only natural objects in their extensions), but I think that the enemies of relative identity will be able to produce replies to them as effective as the reply I have suggested for the case of the clay vase. I can find nothing in the natural world to suggest that there are any nondominant RI-predicates. As far as I am able to tell, RI-logic has no utility outside Christian theology. (This need not raise doubts about the coherency of Christian doctrine. Like quantum mechanics and the more rarefied parts of pure mathematics, the doctrine of the Trinity treats of objects extraordinarily different from the objects of ordinary experience, ones that are perhaps sui generis. If it could be shown that a certain exotic nonclassical logic had an application—if anywhere—in quantum physics or in the study of the nonconstructive infinite, this result would not necessarily raise doubts about the coherency of quantum physics or the nonconstructive infinite. Of course, someone who already believed that one of these things was incoherent might regard this result as providing indirect confirmation for his belief: if, e.g., quantum mechanics is hospitable to a logic in which conjunction fails to distribute over disjunction—he might say—that's one more strike against quantum mechanics.)

Let us close our discussion of RI-logic with a brief look at the topic of singular reference. The language of RI-logic contains no singular terms. Given our decision to be noncommittal about the existence of classical, absolute identity, this is no accident. The philosopher who eschews classical, absolute identity must also eschew singular terms, for the idea of a singular term is—at least in currently orthodox semantical theory—inseparably bound to the classical semantical notion of reference or denotation; and this notion, in its turn, is inseparably bound to the idea of classical identity. It is a part of the orthodox semantical concept of reference that reference is a many-one relation. And it is a part of the idea of a many-one relation—or of a one-one relation, for that matter—that if x bears such a relation to y and bears it to z, then y and z are absolutely identical. (That's what it says on the label.) For example, if 'the tallest man' denotes y and denotes z, then y and z are absolutely identical. (This point "works" better in respect of descriptions than in respect of proper names. The friends of singular terms must concede that, e.g., 'John Frederick Harris' might, and in fact does, name numerically distinct objects. Let us ignore this awkward fact, which can be dealt with in various ways, and remarkably messy and ad hoc ways they are, too.)

If the RI-logician has no singular terms at his disposal, how shall he accomplish singular reference? Must he be content with general statements? In a sense, the answers are: He shan't accomplish it, and he must be content with them. In *what* sense does he face these unpleasant consequences? In any sense of "singular reference" in which the idea of singularity is infected with the idea of classical, absolute identity. This is pretty evident when you think about it. Nevertheless, the RI-logician is not without resources. He has the resources to accomplish *relative* singular reference, a sort of singularity of reference that stands to classical, absolute singularity of reference—the sort that is supposedly accomplished by singular terms—as relative identity stands to classical, absolute identity. Relative singular reference can be accomplished by a device suggested by Russell's theory of descriptions. It is illustrated by the following examples of translations of English sentences containing (what are traditionally called) definite descriptions into the language of RI-logic.

The king is bald

$\exists x$ (x is a king & $\forall y$ (y is a king → y is the same king as x) & x is bald).

The queen is the monarch

$\exists x$ (x is a queen & x is a monarch &
$\forall y$ (y is a queen → y is the same queen as x) &
$\forall y$ (y is a monarch → y the same monarch as x)).

Or, at any rate, this is one way to translate these two English sentences into the language of RI-logic; this is the way to do it without making any suppositions about dominance. But if we assume, for example, that 'is the same man as' dominates 'is the same king as', it might be more natural and useful to translate 'The king is bald' as

$\exists x$ (x is a king & $\forall y$ (y is a king → y is the same man as x) & x is bald).

IV

In the present section, I shall show how to translate certain central theses of Trinitarian theology into the language of RI-logic. The vocabulary we shall employ would hardly do for devotional purposes, but (I hope) we can use it to express certain of the *propositions* that are expressed in devotional discourse about the Trinity. It will not be difficult to show that what we want to say about the Trinity in this vocabulary is free from formal contradiction.

We have, to start with, two undefined RI-predicates:

is the same being as[16]

is the same person as.

---

16. Or 'is the same substance as' or 'is the same *ousia* as'. Geach employs the predicate 'is the same God as' to do essentially the task that I assign to 'is the same being as', as does Martinich, in the articles cited in note 7.

We shall not assume that either of these predicates dominates the other. And, of course, we shall not assume that either of them is eliminable in favor of dominant RI-predicates and ordinary predicates. It is of particular importance that we not assume that 'same being' dominates 'same person', for that would entail that if x is the same being as y and x is a person, then x is the same person as y. (In at least one other context—the theology of the Incarnation—it would be important not to assume that 'same person' dominates 'same being'.)

I do not refrain from defining these predicates because I think that there is any particular difficulty about what it is to be a being or a person. Something is a being (is the same being as something) if it has causal powers. A being is a person (something that is the same being as something is also the same person as something) if it is self-aware and has beliefs and plans and acts on the basis of those beliefs to execute those plans. (As Boethius says, a person is an individual substance of a rational nature.) But to say this much is not to give a general account of '*same* being' or '*same* person'. If we regard a definition of a sentence in the austere fashion of logicians as a recipe for eliminating that sentence *salva extensione* in favor of another sentence containing the same variables free, then the account I have given of 'person' and 'being' provides us with definitions of 'x is the same being as x' (or, equivalently, of 'x is the same being as something') and 'x is the same person as x,' but not of 'x is the same being as y' or 'x is the same person as y.'[17] (It allows us, for example, to define 'x is the same being as x' as 'x has causal powers'.)

---

17. I can imagine here someone making the following remarks: "Say that a being that is self-aware, etc., is *rational*. You have said, in essence, that 'person' means 'rational being'. But, then, by what we may call 'the principle of intensional substitution',

x is the same person as y ↔ x is the same rational being as y.

But, evidently,

x is the same rational being as y ↔ x is the same being as y & x is rational & y is rational.

It is obvious that 'same being' dominates 'rational':

x is the same being as y → (x is rational ↔ y is rational).

But from these three sentences there follows by RI-logic:

x is the same being as y → (x is the same person as z ↔ y is the same person as z).

That is, 'same being' dominates 'same person'."

But I have not said that 'person' means 'rational being'; not if that entails that 'person' and 'rational being' can replace each other in any context *salva extensione*. I have said only that 'x is the same person as x' and 'x is the same being as x & x is rational' can replace each other in any context *salva extensione*.

If we believed that there were such a relation as classical, absolute identity, and if we believed that this relation was subdominant, then we *could* extract from our account of 'person' and 'being' definitions of 'same person' and 'same being'. For example:

x is the same being as y = $_{df} x$ has causal powers & $x = y$.

The reason that the existence and subdominance of classical identity would enable us so to turn a definition of 'x is the same being as x' into a definition of 'x is the same being as y' is that the subdominance of classical identity (its domination by all RI-predicates) entails the conditional

x is the same being as $y \to x = y$;

and from this conditional one may infer (by the rules of the classical logic of identity) the biconditional

x is the same being as $y \leftrightarrow .x$ is the same being as x & $x = y$.

But if the above definition of 'is the same being as' were correct, it would follow that if a person x and a person y are the same being, then x and y are the *same* person.[18] The Trinitarian must, therefore, assume either that classical, absolute identity does not exist or that, if it does exist, it is not dominated by 'is the same being as'. (Or, at least, he must make one or the other of these assumptions if his thinking about the Trinity is to be based on a logic of relative identity. This result is essentially an application to the case of a relative-identity treatment of the Trinity of a point made in Section III about relative-identity treatments of anything: If there is such a relation as classical, absolute identity, and if it is subdominant, then all RI-predicates are dominant.) Nothing, of course, prevents him from introducing by the device out-

---

18. The subdominance of classical identity entails 'x is the same being as $y \to (x = x \leftrightarrow x = y)$', since '$x = x$' does not contain '$y$' and '$x = y$' is like '$x = x$' except for containing a free occurrence of 'y' where '$x = x$' contains a free occurrence of 'x'. '$x = x$' is a theorem of the logic of classical identity. From these two sentences the conditional in the text follows. The biconditional is proved as follows. *Left-to-right:* assume the antecedent; '$x = y$' follows from the antecedent and the just-proved conditional; the other conjunct of the consequent, 'x is the same being as x', follows from '$x = y$' and the antecedent by Substitution of Identicals. *Right-to-left:* assume the antecedent; the consequent follows by Substitution of Identicals.

Suppose 'x is the same being as y' means 'x has causal powers & $x = y$'. If x is the same person as x (i.e., if x is a person), and if x is the same being as y, then it follows by Substitution of Identicals (since '$x = y$' follows from the definition of 'x is the same being as y') that x is the same person as y.

lined in section III a predicate that behaves within a certain restricted area of his discourse—say, the part that does not have to do with the Trinity—in the way the classical identity-predicate is supposed to behave throughout all discourse.

We shall have several ordinary predicates, which will be introduced as we need them. The first is 'is divine'. A definiens for 'x is divine' might look something like this:

> x is necessarily existent; essentially almighty, all-knowing, and perfect in love and wisdom; essentially such that nothing contingent would exist unless x willed it.

But you may have your own ideas about how to define this predicate. Since any reasonable list of the attributes constitutive of divinity must include attributes implying power and knowledge, the following would seem to be a conceptual truth, and I shall assume it to be such:

CT1 $\forall x$ (x is divine $\rightarrow$ .x is a being & x is a person).

Indeed, the first conjunct of the consequent is, strictly speaking, redundant, since any person is, necessarily, a being:

CT2 $\forall x$ (x is a person $\rightarrow$ x is a being).

It follows from CT1 that something is a divine Person if and only if it is a divine Being:

CT3 $\forall x$ (x is a person & x is divine. $\leftrightarrow$ .x is a being & x is divine).[19]

We shall assume that 'is the same being as' dominates 'is divine'; that is, we shall assume.

CT4 $\forall x \forall y$ (x is the same being as $y \rightarrow$ (x is divine $\leftrightarrow$ y is divine)).

The most important consequence of CT4 is that if a being is divine, then any being who is the same being as that being is divine. (We shall not assume that 'same person' dominates 'divine'. We shall not need this assumption, and it might cause difficulties for the theology of the Incarnation, since, on the obvious interpretation of the doctrine of the Incarnation, there is an x such that x is divine and there is a y such that y is not divine and x is the same person as y. Owing to similar considerations, we should not want to assume that 'same person' dominated such predicates as 'is a man and was born in the world'.) It

---

19. "But doesn't CT3 entail that the number of divine Persons is the same as the number of divine Beings?" No. This apparent paradox will be cleared up in a moment.

follows from CT1 and CT4 that if x is a divine Person and y is the same being as x, then y is *a* person. It does not, of course, follow that y is the *same* person as x.

Let us now introduce abbreviations for 'same being', 'same person', and 'divine:'

$\underline{B}\alpha\beta$ α is the same being as β
$\underline{P}\alpha\beta$ α is the same person as β
$D\alpha$ α is divine.

(In virtue of CT1, 'Dx' may be read, 'x is a divine Person' or 'x is a divine Being'. If 'a God' is equivalent to 'a divine Being'—as I suppose it to be—'Dx' may also be read 'x is a God'.) We underline 'B' and 'P' to remind us that they abbreviate RI-predicates. We shall further abbreviate, for example, '$\underline{B}xx$' as '$\underline{B}x$'.

We may express using only these three predicates three central propositions of Trinitarian theology:

(1) There is (exactly) one God
$\exists x\ (Dx\ \&\ \forall y(Dy \to \underline{B}yx))$

(2) There are (exactly) three divine Persons
$\exists x \exists y \exists z\ (Dx\ \&\ Dy\ \&\ Dz\ \&\ \sim \underline{P}xy\ \&\ \sim \underline{P}xz\ \&\ \sim \underline{P}yz\ \&$
$\forall w(Dw \to .\underline{P}wx\ \text{v}\ \underline{P}wy\ \text{v}\ \underline{P}wz))$

(3) There are three divine Persons in one divine Being
[There are three divine Persons] $\&\ \forall x \forall y(Dx\ \&\ Dy. \to \underline{B}xy)$.

It is easy to see that (1) through (3) and CT1 through CT4 together compose a set of sentences from which no contradiction can be derived in RI-logic.

To show this, let us consider the following reinterpretation of our three predicates. (Admittedly, it is rather unedifying; it has been chosen for its mnemonic virtues.)

$\underline{B}\alpha\beta$ α is the same breed as β
$\underline{P}\alpha\beta$ α is the same price as β
$D\alpha$ α is a dog.

Now assume that there are exactly three dogs and that nothing besides these dogs has either a breed or a price. Assume that these dogs are for sale at different prices and that each is a purebred dachshund. Given these assumptions, it is easy to verify by inspection that the sentences (1) through (3) and CT1 through CT4 are true on the proposed reinterpretation of '$\underline{B}$', '$\underline{P}$', and 'D'.

This reinterpretation of our predicates shows that no formal contradiction can be deduced from (1) through (3) and CT1 through CT4 by standard quantifier logic, since (by a well-known property of quantifier logic) no formal contradiction can be deduced in that logic from a set of sentences that are true on some interpretation. The only rules of RI-logic other than those of quantifier logic are Symmetry and Transitivity. Since '*x* is the same breed as *y*' and '*x* is the same price as *y*' express symmetrical and transitive relations, it follows that no formal contradiction can be deduced from (1) through (3) and CT1 through CT4 by the rules of RI-logic. (Nothing I have said should be taken to imply that 'is the same breed as' and 'is the same price as' are relative-identity predicates. In fact, these predicates are *not* RI-predicates, at least as we are using them. On this point, see our discussion of 'is the same color as' on pp. 233–234.)

Our consistency result shows that 'Something is a divine Person if and only if it is a divine Being' [CT3] is formally consistent with 'There are three divine Persons' [(2)] and 'There is one divine Being' [(1)]. This formal result can be understood philosophically as follows. Without classical identity, there is no absolute counting: there is only counting by Ns. For example, if propositions (1) and (2) are true: Counting divine Beings by beings, there is one; counting divine Persons by beings, there is one; counting divine Beings by persons, there are three; counting divine Persons by persons, there are three. But if someone asks us how many divine Beings there are, it is presumably a "conversational implicature" of his question that he wishes us to count divine Beings by beings—that is, by the count-noun *he* used. And the same goes for, "How many divine Persons are there?" That is why 'There is one divine Being' is a natural English translation of the symbolic sentence (1) and 'There are three divine Persons' is a natural English translation of the symbolic sentence (2). If, on the other hand, there is such a thing as absolute identity, there is such a thing as absolute counting. For example, if absolute identity exists, it follows from (2) and CT3 that there are three divine Beings and three divine Persons, counting absolutely. If absolute identity not only exists but is subdominant, an absolute count of Ns will force the same count on all relative counts of Ns. (In that case, of course, CT3, (1), and (2) could not all be true.) If absolute identity exists but is not subdominant—if, in particular, it is not dominated by 'same being'—then it may be true that there is one divine Being counting by beings and, at the same time, true that there are three divine Beings counting absolutely.

Let us now turn to the problem of singular reference.

We must find some way, using only the resources of RI-logic, to do the work of the English singular terms 'God', 'the Father', 'the Son', and 'the Holy Spirit'.[20] We have seen how to supply a relative-identity surrogate for classical definite descriptions. The singular term 'God' should obviously be thought of as an abbreviation for 'the divine Being' or (like the Arabic 'Allah') 'the God'. Thus, using our relative-identity surrogate for classical definite descriptions, we may translate the English sentence 'God made us' into the language of our RI-logic as

$$\exists x \ (Dx \ \& \ \forall y (Dy \rightarrow \underline{B}yx) \ \& \ x \text{ made us}).$$

It will be convenient to abbreviate '$Dx \ \& \ \forall y \ (Dy \rightarrow \underline{B}yx)$' as '$Gx$' (and similarly for other variables). 'Gx' may be read 'x is one God' (cf. Deut. 6:4) or 'x is the only God' or 'x is the divine Being'. The word 'God' in English is sometimes a common noun ('There is one God') and sometimes a proper noun ('In the beginning, God created the heavens and the earth'). When 'God' is a common noun in English, it is a count-noun. In the special vocabulary of the present section of this essay, the work done by the English count-noun 'God' is done by the predicate 'is divine': 'There is a God' is read 'Something is divine'. The work done by the English proper noun 'God' is also done by 'is divine': to say what is said by an English sentence of the form 'God is ø', we say 'The only God (the one God, the divine Being) is ø'. Or, making use of the above abbreviation, '$\exists x(Gx \ \& \ øx)$'.

But how shall we translate English sentences containing the terms 'the Father', 'the Son', and 'the Holy Spirit'?[21] It is a commonplace of Trinitarian theology that the Persons of the Trinity are individuated by the relations they bear to one another. Two relations, the Creeds tell us, individuate the Persons; we may express them by these predicates:

α begets β

α proceeds from β through γ.

20. I call these phrases 'singular terms' because they have the syntax of singular terms: they are noun-phrases that require a singular verb. But I do not mean to imply that they have the *semantic* features which orthodox philosophical semantics ascribes to what it calls "singular terms" (and which orthodox semantics, for all I know, takes to be part of the meaning of 'singular term'). In particular, I do not mean to imply that there is a relation—call it 'reference' or what you will—such that if, e.g., 'God' bears this relation to x and to y, then x is absolutely identical with y. I do not know of a phrase that has the syntactical but not the semantical implications of 'singular term'.

21. And what of the phrase 'the Holy Trinity' itself? I take these words to be short for 'the Father, the Son, and the Holy Spirit', much as 'the Holy Family' is short for 'Jesus, Mary, and Joseph'. One might say, "In this painting, the Holy Trinity *is* represented as

(I hope that the wording of the second of these is acceptable to both the Eastern and the Western Churches.)[22] These two relations hold only within the Godhead:

CT5 $\forall x \forall y (x$ begets $y \rightarrow .Dx$ & $Dy)$

CT6 $\forall x \forall y \forall z (x$ proceeds from y through $z \rightarrow .Dx$ & Dy & $Dz)$.

Every divine Person enters into the "procession" relation:

CT7 $\forall x (Dx \rightarrow .(\exists y \exists z$ x proceeds from y through $z)v$
$(\exists y \exists z$ y proceeds from x through $z)v$
$(\exists y \exists z$ y proceeds from z through $x))$.

If x, y, and z enter into the "procession" relation with one another, then x, y, and z are distinct Persons:

CT8 $\forall x \forall y \forall z (x$ proceeds from y through $z \rightarrow. \sim \underline{P}xy$ & $\sim \underline{P}xz$ & $\sim \underline{P}yz)$.[23]

If x, y, and z enter into the "procession" relation with one another, then no other Persons do (nor do x, y, and z enter into it in more than one way):

CT9 $\forall x \forall y \forall z \forall t \forall u \forall v$ (x proceeds from y through z & t proceeds from u through $v. \rightarrow .\underline{P}xt$ & $\underline{P}yu$ & $\underline{P}zv)$.

The two relations, procession and begetting, are not independent:

---

present in the Eucharist." But then one might say, "In this painting, the Holy Family *is* shown entering Jerusalem."

22. I allude, of course, to the *filioque* controversy. As I understand the present state of this controversy, the concern of the Eastern Chuch is to say nothing that could be taken as a denial of the doctrine that the Father alone is the *fons et origo* of Deity, while the concern of the Western Church (i.e., Rome) is to do justice to Jesus' statements about His relation to the Paraclete, especially John 16:14–15. It is my understanding that many theologians, both Roman Catholic and Orthodox, believe that the formula 'the Holy Spirit proceeds from the Father through the Son' does justice to both of these concerns. But I speak under correction.

23. It is perhaps tendentious to call CT7 and CT8 "conceptual truths," since they together entail that if there are any divine Persons, there are at least three (a thesis shared by Catholic Christians and atheists, but rejected by Arians, Jews, Muslims, and, probably, most agnostics). What I mean by calling CT5–13 "conceptual truths" is this. Trinitarians *allege* that certain relations hold within the Godhead—that is, among the various divine Persons. CT5–13 display certain properties that Trinitarians *say* are essential to these relations. Arians, Jews, and Muslims can agree that CT5–13 display properties that are essential to the Trinitarian concepts of "procession" and "begetting" (just as they can agree that *being square* is an essential component of the concept of a round square), and go on to comment that these concepts are like the concept of a round square in that nothing could possibly fall under them.

CT10 $\forall x \forall y \forall z (x$ proceeds from y through $z \rightarrow y$ begets $z)$

CT11 $\forall x \forall y \, \exists z (x$ begets $y \rightarrow z$ proceeds from x through $y).$[24]

Begetting has features analogous to the features ascribed to procession in CT8 and CT9:

CT12 $\forall x \forall y (x$ begets $y \rightarrow \sim\underline{P}xy)$

CT13 $\forall x \forall y \forall z \forall w (x$ begets $y \, \& \, z$ begets $w. \rightarrow .\underline{P}xz \, \& \, \underline{P}yw).$[25]

It will be convenient to introduce three one-place predicates by definition:

α begets $\qquad = {}_{df} \exists\beta \; \alpha$ begets β

α is begotten $\; = {}_{df} \exists\beta \; \beta$ begets α

α proceeds $\qquad = {}_{df} \exists\beta\exists\gamma \; \alpha$ proceeds from β through γ.

Propositions CT5–13 entail that each of these predicates is satisfied (if at all) by a divine Person; that if x and y satisfy any given one of them, then $\underline{P}xy$; and that if x satisfies one of them and y another, then $\sim\underline{P}xy$. We may therefore treat 'the Father', 'the Son', and 'the Holy Spirit' as equivalent to, respectively, 'the Person who begets', 'the Person who is begotten', and 'the Person who proceeds'. More exactly, we shall read, for example, 'The Father made us' as

$\exists x (x$ begets $\& \, \forall y (y$ begets $\rightarrow \underline{P}yx) \, \& \, x$ made us$)$.

Let us abbreviate 'x begets $\& \, \forall y (y$ begets $\rightarrow \underline{P}yx)$' as '$Fx$' ("$x$ is the Father"). Let us abbreviate 'x is begotten $\& \, \forall y (y$ begotten $\rightarrow \underline{P}yx)$' as '$Sx$' ("$x$ is the Son"). Let us abbreviate 'x proceeds $\& \, \forall y (y$ proceeds $\rightarrow \underline{P}yx)$' as '$Hx$' ("$x$ is the Holy Spirit"). (And similarly for other variables.)

I now present a list of Trinitarian sentences of English and some proposed translations into our formal vocabulary. All of the translations are provable from (1) through (3) and CT1 through CT13. Note, by the way, that (2) and (3) are provable from (1) and the CTs.

---

24. Since 'x begets $y \leftrightarrow \exists z$ (z proceeds from x through y)' is a logical consequence of CT10 and CT11, it is formally possible to define 'begets' in terms of 'proceeds'. But I doubt whether such a definition would be seen as a fruitful "move" by Christologists or by Trinitarian theologians whose concerns are wider than the logical issues addressed in the present essay.

25. CT12 and 13 are redundant; they can be deduced from CT8–11.

(4) God is the same being as the Father
$\exists x\ \exists y(Gx\ \&\ Fy\ \&\ \underline{B}xy)$.

(5) God is a person[26]
$\exists x(Gx\ \&\ \underline{P}x)$.

(6) God is the same person as the Father
$\exists x\ \exists y(Gx\ \&\ Fy\ \&\ \underline{P}xy)$.

(7) God is the same person as the Son
$\exists x\ \exists y(Gx\ \&\ Sy\ \&\ \underline{P}xy)$.

(8) The Son is not the same person as the Father
$\sim\exists x\ \exists y(Fx\ \&\ Sy\ \&\ \underline{P}xy)$.[27]

Or we might write (giving 'not' "narrow scope"),

$\exists x\ \exists y(Fx\ \&\ Sy\ \&\ \sim\underline{P}xy)$.[28]

We should note that (6), (7), and both versions of (8) are—formally, at least—consistent. More generally: let S be the set of sentences containing (1) through (8) and CT1 through CT13; we can show that no formal contradiction is deducible from S in RI-logic.[29] We can show this by an extension of the "three dogs" reinterpretation of '$\underline{B}$', '$\underline{P}$', and 'D' that we employed earlier. Reinterpret our "Trinitarian" predicates as follows:

α begets β   α barks at β

α proceeds from β through γ   α prances from β to γ

Now let our three dogs be *A, B,* and *C.* Suppose that *C* prances from *A* to *B* and does no other prancing and that nothing besides *C* prances. Suppose that *A* is barking at *B* and at nothing else and that nothing

26. That is, God is an "individual substance of a rational nature"; (5) is not meant to imply that God is a *prosopon* or a *hypostasis.*

27. The formal translations of the following English sentences are also deducible from (1)–(3) and CT1–13: 'The Father is the same being as the Son'; 'The Father is the same being as the Holy Spirit'; 'The Son is the same being as the Holy Spirit'; 'God is the same person as the Holy Spirit'; 'God is the same being as the Son'; 'God is the same being as the Holy Spirit'; 'The Father is not the same person as the Holy Spirit'; 'The Son is not the same person as the Holy Spirit'.

28. The "wide-scope" version of (8) would be accepted by Catholic Christians, Arians, Jews, Muslims, and atheists. The "narrow-scope" version would be accepted by Catholic Christians alone.

29. S is logically somewhat redundant. Given (1), CT1, CT2, CT4, and CT6–11, one can prove (2), (3), CT3, CT5, CT12, and CT13.

besides *A* barks. Given these assumptions, and our earlier assumptions about prices and breeds, it is easy (if somewhat tedious) to verify by inspection that all the members of S are true on the proposed reinterpretation. Note that the reinterpretation for '*Px*' in (5) should be '*x* is the same price as *x*.' It follows that no formal contradiction is deducible from S in RI-logic.

In order to verify by inspection that all members of S are true, it is necessary to remove the abbreviations in (4)–(8). For example, here is sentence (4) in unabbreviated form:

$$\exists x \exists y (Dx\ \&\ \forall z(Dz \rightarrow \underline{B}zx)\ \&\ \exists w(y \text{ begets } w)\ \&$$
$$\forall z(\exists w\ z \text{ begets } w. \rightarrow \underline{P}zy)\ \&\ \underline{B}xy).$$

The tedium of verifying (4)–(8) on the "three dogs" reinterpretation can be somewhat reduced if we supply appropriate "derived" reinterpretations for the defined predicates '*G*', '*F*', and '*S*:'

*G*α   α is a member of the only breed of dog

*F*α   α barks and any barking dog is the same price as α

*S*α   α is barked at and any dog that is barked at is the same price as α.

It is important to realize that the "three dogs" reinterpretation of our predicates is not intended to provide a model (in any sense) for the Trinity. For one thing, as we have noted, 'is the same price as' and 'is the same breed as' are not even RI-predicates. The only purpose of the reinterpretation is to show that for no sentence is it possible to derive both that sentence and its negation from S by Transitivity, Symmetry, and the rules of quantifier logic. The argument is essentially this: If a contradiction can be formally deduced from S, then the story of our three dogs is inconsistent; but that story is obviously consistent.

Does it seem paradoxical that (6), (7), and (8) are consistent? We must remember that it is an essential part of the position we are exploring that the English sentences (6), (7), and (8) do not wear their real, underlying logical structures on their sleeves: They are not really of the forms '*Pgf*', '*Pgs*', and '~*Pfs*'. According to this position, the underlying logical structures of these sentences are given by their RI-translations; and no sentence in the language of RI-logic could be of these forms, for that language contains no terms but variables. We should note that '~($\underline{P}xy\ \&\ \underline{P}xz\ \&\ {\sim}\underline{P}yz$)' is an easily proved theorem of RI-logic, and is, therefore, by our consistency result, formally consistent with (6), (7), and (8). The tendency to think that the consistency of (6), (7), and (8) is paradoxical is rooted, I think, in our tendency to suppose that 'God', 'the Father', and 'the Son' are singular terms (in the orthodox semantical sense).

Other "paradoxical" groups of sentences can be found. For example:

(9) God is begotten
$\exists x \, (Gx \, \& \, x \text{ is begotten})$

(10) God is unbegotten
$\exists x \, (Gx \, \& \, {\sim}x \text{ is begotten})$.

These two sentences are formally consistent with, and, in fact, provable from, the members of S. Are they theologically acceptable? Well, one sometimes sees references in Christian theological writing (usually in rhetorical opposition) to begotten and unbegotten Deity, so I suppose that they are.

A perhaps more serious problem of the same sort is raised by the Incarnation. It seems plausible to define 'x is incarnate' as '$\exists y(y$ is a human being $\& \, \underline{P}xy)$'. On this reading, however, 'God is unincarnate'—'$\exists x(Gx \, \& \, {\sim}\exists y(y$ is a human being $\& \, \underline{P}xy))$'—will "come out true."[30] I think that the best course for the philosopher who proposes to express the doctrines of the Trinity and the Incarnation in the language of RI-logic is to insist that this sentence is literally true but misleading. He will be able to adduce in his support the demonstrable facts that (if Jesus of Nazareth is the same person as one of the divine Persons), then 'God is incarnate' is true and 'it is not the case that God is incarnate' is false. But I can do no more than allude to the problems raised by the Incarnation.

I have shown how to represent certain Trinitarian sentences of English in our formal vocabulary, and I have shown that no contradiction can be deduced in RI-logic from the formal translations of these sentences. I note in passing that there are interesting sentences expressible in terms of the predicates we have at our disposal that allow us to make distinctions that cannot be made easily in English. Consider this sentence

(11) $\exists x(Gx \, \& \, Fx)$.

---

30. This sentence will "come out true" in the sense that its symbolic translation is deducible from S and the proposition that some divine Person is unincarnate: '$\exists x \, (Dx \, \& \, {\sim}\exists y \, (y$ is a human being $\& \, \underline{P}xy))$'.

This sentence expresses a truth; or at least it is provable in RI-logic from the members of S. How shall we express its content in English? Not, certainly, as 'God is the same being as the Father' or 'God is the same person as the Father', for these are the equivalents, respectively, of the RI-sentences (4) and (6). I would suggest: 'God and the Father are one absolutely'. It might be said that the ideas conjured up by the predicate 'are one absolutely' are contrary to the spirit of RI-logic. Perhaps so; but sentence (11) is a perfectly respectable sentence, and I am at a loss for a better informal expression of its content. We may note that if my suggestion for translating (11) into English is followed out consistently, the English sentence 'God and the Son are one absolutely' will express a truth, and the English sentence 'The Father and the Son are one absolutely' will express a falsehood.[31]

I have said that in this essay I should risk Tritheism. Have I fallen into Tritheism? What can be said with certainty is this. The sentence (1)

$$\exists x(Dx \ \& \ \forall y(Dy \rightarrow \underline{B}yx)),$$

which—it may be argued, at any rate—expresses the thesis of monotheism, does not yield a formal contradiction in RI-logic; nor does the whole set of sentences S that we have "endorsed," and to which (1) belongs, yield a contradiction. Consider, moreover, the sentence

$$\exists x \exists y(Dx \ \& \ Dy \ \& \ \sim \underline{B}xy),$$

which—it may be argued, at any rate—expresses the thesis that there are two or more Gods. The negation of this sentence can be formally deduced from (1). But these results do not protect us from all the dangers of Tritheism. Perhaps the most objectionable—I do not say the only objectionable—feature of polytheism is that if one believes that Zeus and Poseidon are real and are two divine beings and two divine persons, one must admit that one has no guarantee that Zeus and Poseidon will not demand contrary things of one. And there is nothing in the notion of "same being," taken by itself, that entails that two divine Persons who are the same Being will not, despite their being the same Being, demand contrary things of one. It must certainly be a feature of any adequate Trinitarian theology that whatever is demanded of one by any divine Person is demanded by all, and, more generally, that the idea of a clash of divine wills is as impossible as the idea of a round square. I am pointing out only that the impossibility of a clash of wills among the divine Persons is not a simple consequence of their

31. I.e., '$\exists x(Gx \ \& \ Sx)$' and '$\sim\exists x(Fx \ \& \ Sx)$' are deducible from S.

being one Being. (It may be that, owing to their perfect knowledge and wisdom, no two divine Persons could will differently. If so, this has nothing in particular to do with the unity of being of the divine Persons: the same consequence would follow if there were two divine Persons who were also two beings.)

I believe that the (conceptual) danger of a clash of divine wills can be eliminated in a conceptually satisfying (i.e., nonarbitrary) way if we accept what I shall call the Principle of the Uniformity of the Divine Nature. This principle turns on the notion of a non-Trinitarian—or, as I shall say, "normal"—predicate applicable to God. Roughly speaking, a normal predicate is one that someone who believed that there was exactly one divine Person might coherently apply to that Person.[32] For example: 'made the world'; 'is compassionate'; 'spake by the Prophets'. The Principle of the Uniformity of the Divine Nature is simply this: 'is the same being as' dominates all normal predicates. Formally (where 'N' represents any normal predicate), all sentences of the following form are true:

$$\underline{B}\alpha\beta \rightarrow (N \ldots \alpha \ldots \leftrightarrow N \ldots \beta \ldots).$$

(We may note that CT4 is of this form.) Since such predicates as 'commands Moses to return to Egypt' and 'tells Saul to enter Damascus' are normal, the Principle of the Uniformity of the Divine Nature rules out the possibility of a Homeric clash of divine wills. And it rules out a good many other things; it entails, for example, that it is false that the Father made the world and the Son did not. It is a way of saying formally what the *Quicunque Vult* says in the words, "*Qualis Pater, talis Filius, talis et Spiritus Sanctus*"[33]—although the writer of those words was thinking primarily not of the relations God bears to His creation, but rather of His *intrinsic* normal attributes.[34]

I will close by mentioning some important philosophical questions about the Trinity that I have not touched on. Consider, for example, the relations that individuate the Persons. Are the Persons individuated *only* by these relations, as most of the classical Trinitarian theologians seem to have supposed? Or might it be that each of the Persons has certain intrinsic (nonrelational) attributes that are not shared by the others? Put the question this way. The Father begets the Son, and the

---

32. 'Normal' should not be confused with 'ordinary'.

33. As the Father is, so also are the Son and the Holy Spirit.

34. I say "primarily" because the sharing of the predicate 'is Lord' equally by the Persons is asserted in the section of the Creed that is introduced by these words; and this predicate expresses a relational attribute of God.

Holy Spirit proceeds from the Father through the Son. Why do these two relations hold among the three divine Persons in just *this* way? Is it a brute fact, the three Persons being absolutely descriptively identical except for the manner in which they are related? Or does each of the three Persons have a proper nature of His own, in addition to the nature (Divinity) that is common to all three, in which these relations are "grounded"? To say so might threaten the traditional doctrine of the Divine Simplicity. But the doctrine of purely relational individuation seems to imply the (surely repugnant) thesis that it is intrinsically possible that the Person who is in fact the Holy Spirit beget the Person who is in fact the Father.

A second problem we have not considered, but which has bulked large in the speculations of the great Trinitarian theologians, can be stated very succinctly: Why *three* Persons? I could go on at some length about the problems I have not considered, but I will not. I have been concerned in this essay to touch only on those features of Trinitarian theology most closely connected with problems of counting, identity, and predication.

Even in this limited area of investigation, I have left the mystery of the Holy Trinity untouched. It is one thing to suggest that 'is the same being as' does not dominate 'is the same person as'. It is another thing to explain how this could be. I have no explanation of this fact (if it is a fact); nor do I think that we could hope to discover one in this life, in which we see only disordered reflections in a mirror. One day, perhaps, we shall see face to face and know as we are known.[35]

35. A part of this essay was read at the December 1985 meeting of the Society of Christian Philosophers. The commentator was Eleonore Stump. An overlapping part was read at the University of Notre Dame, at the conference on which the volume in which this essay was originally published is based. The commentator was Keith Yandell. The two commentators have had considerable influence on the final form of this essay. Michael Detlefsen made extremely valuable comments on Section III. He is, of course, not responsible for the confusions that remain—all the more so because I have imprudently resisted some of his criticisms.

9

Not by Confusion of Substance, but by Unity of Person

I<small>N</small> this essay, I propose to see whether the methods of "And Yet They Are Not Three Gods but One God" can be applied to the mystery of the Incarnation: more exactly, to the doctrine of the hypostatic union of two natures—divine and human—in the person of Jesus Christ.[1] I shall offer a formulation of a part of that doctrine in terms of relative identity. It is my hope that this formulation will be orthodox—that is, consistent with historical orthodoxy. I say "part of" because I believe that there is no clearly demarcated set of propositions that can be called "the doctrine of the Incarnation," or even "the doctrine of the hypostatic union." The "part" of the doctrine that I shall be most concerned with is that part that raises grave metaphysical and logical problems: those propositions of Incarnational theology that appear to require violations of the principle of the transitivity of identity or of Leibniz's Law. (A violation of the former would be a fortiori a violation of the latter, since Leibniz's Law entails the transitivity of identity.) I

First published in *Reason and the Christian Religion*, edited by Alan Padgett, (Oxford: Clarendon Press, 1994).

1. The original version of this essay contained a section on the logic of relative identity (RI-logic), which reproduced material in the previous essay ("And Yet They Are Not Three Gods but One God"). In the present version, this section has been omitted (and a few paragraphs in other parts of the essay have been omitted or condensed) in order to save space. In consequence, the essay is not self-contained; it must be read in conjunction with the previous essay.

shall not claim to have penetrated the mystery of the Incarnation, but at most to have shown that that doctrine can be stated without formal contradiction.

I

The data of the doctrine of the Incarnation (other than the biblical data)[2] are, in my view, contained almost entirely in the following two statements. The first is from the *Quicunque Vult* and the second from the Definition of Chalcedon. I know enough Latin to have satisfied myself that the Latin of the former is unproblematic, except in the matter of the meaning of individual theological terms. I therefore reproduce here the (reasonably accurate) translation of *The Book of Common Prayer*, which, better than anything else in English, captures the sensation of "the great, roaring machine of Latin rhetoric" running at full throttle. But the meaning of the Greek of the Definition is a more delicate matter, and since I know almost no Greek, I use a more scholarly translation.[3]

2. The most important biblical data are, in my view, the opening passages of the Fourth Gospel, of the Letter to the Colossians, and of the Letter to the Hebrews. (Philippians 2:5–11 has, I believe, less to tell us about the nature of the Incarnation than many have supposed.) The theologian, as I see matters, should regard the Bible as the physical scientist regards sense experience. Physical theories cannot be "read off" sense experience, but they are in the last analysis responsible to sense experience and must make sense of sense experience. Theological "theories"—that is, formulations of doctrine in abstract, theoretical terms, and even more abstract theoretical reflection on the allowable interpretations of doctrine and on the nature and methods of the interpretation of doctrine—cannot be "read off" the words of Scripture, but they are in the last analysis responsible to the words of Scripture and must make sense of the words of Scripture. Chesterton says somewhere that the New Testament is a riddle and the Church is the answer. I would say that the biblical passages cited above are a riddle and that the Nicene Creed is the answer. (The Nicene Creed is in its turn a riddle, and the *Quicunque Vult* is the answer. The *Quicunque Vult*—largely a series of quotations from St. Augustine— is a further riddle, to which the speculations of the Medieval Trinitarian theologians are attempted answers. Perhaps riddles come to an end only in the mind of God: there alone is Wittgenstein right: the *riddle* does not exist.)

3. I do not believe that either the Apostles' Creed or the Nicene Creed adds anything of importance to what is contained in the *Quicunque Vult*. But the Nicene Creed (more properly the Niceno-Constantinopolitan Creed) should perhaps be quoted, since, unlike the Q.V., it contains the famous word *'homoousios'*: "And [I believe] in one Lord Jesus Christ, the only-begotten Son of God, begotten of the Father before all ages, God of God, light of light, true God of true God, begotten not made, through whom all things were made, *consubstantial with* the Father. Who, for us human beings and for our salvation, came down from heaven, and was incarnate by the Holy Spirit of the Virgin Mary, and was made man: crucified also for us under Pontius Pilate, he suffered and was buried: and on the third day he rose again in accordance with the Scriptures and ascended into heaven, sits on the right hand of the Father, and will come again with

Furthermore, it is necessary to everlasting salvation that [one] also believe rightly the Incarnation of our Lord Jesus Christ. For the right Faith is, that we believe and confess, that our Lord Jesus Christ, the Son of God, is God and Man; God of the Substance of the Father, begotten before the worlds; and Man, of the substance of his Mother, born in the world; Perfect God and perfect Man, of a reasonable soul and human flesh subsisting; Equal to the Father, as touching his Godhead; and inferior to the Father, as touching his Manhood. Who although he be God and Man, yet he is not two, but one Christ; One, not by conversion of the Godhead into flesh, but by taking of the Manhood into God; One altogether; not by confusion of Substance, but by unity of Person. For as the reasonable soul and flesh is one man, so God and Man is one Christ; Who suffered for our salvation. . . .

In agreement, therefore, with the holy fathers, we all unanimously teach that we should confess that our Lord Jesus Christ is one and the same Son, the same perfect in Godhead and the same perfect in manhood, truly God and truly man, the same of a rational soul and body, consubstantial with the Father in Godhead, and the same consubstantial with us in manhood, like us in all things except sin; begotten from the Father before the ages as regards his Godhead, and in the last days, the same, because of us and because of our salvation begotten from the Virgin Mary, the *Theotokos* [God-bearer], as regards his manhood; one and the same Christ, Son, Lord, only-begotten, made known in two natures without confusion, without change, without division, without separation, the difference of the natures being by no means removed because of the union, but the property of each nature being preserved and coalescing in one *prosopon* [person] and one *hypostasis* [subsistence], not parted or divided into two *prosopa*, but one and the same Son, only-begotten, divine Word, the Lord Jesus Christ, as the prophets of old and Jesus Christ himself have taught us about him and the creed of our fathers has handed down.[4]

---

glory to judge the living and the dead; whose kingdom shall be without end." This section of the "Nicene Creed" is a slightly expanded version of the section of the creed actually issued by the Council of Nicaea. The earlier creed, unlike the later, contained a gloss on the phrase '*homoousios* with the Father': *ek tes ousias tou Patros,* which would seem to be the source—perhaps some scholar will correct me on this point—of the phrase '*ex substantia Patris*' ('of the Substance of the Father' in the Prayer Book translation) in the Q.V.

4. Trans. J. N. D. Kelly, *Early Christian Doctrines,* 2d ed. (London: A.&C. Black, 1960), p. 339 f. I have added the words in square brackets; Kelly's translation has only the transliterated Greek words. The word '*prosopon*', incidentally, like the Latin '*persona*', originally meant 'mask' or 'face'.

Our job is to attempt to show how to translate the central statements of the theology of the Incarnation into the language of relative identity, and to show that the whole set of these statements is free from logical contradiction—at least in the sense that no contradiction can be derived from them by the rules of RI-logic. We adopt the following criterion of adequacy: the translations (and the whole set of their logical consequences) must be in accord with the biblical and creedal data. (And what is the criterion of *that*? Who is to say whether our translations are true to the letter and the spirit of the Bible and the Creeds? We must leave that a subjective matter. Those who are interested in such things must judge for themselves. Obviously we are not going to convince everyone. There are certainly plenty of theologians who think that the Creeds themselves are inconsistent with the biblical data; these people will therefore say a priori that we have set ourselves an impossible task: our translations will, of necessity, be untrue to the Bible or untrue to the Creeds—or, of course, untrue to both.)

We shall retain the following vocabulary from "And Yet They Are Not Three Gods but One God": 'x is the same being (substance, *ousia*) as y'; 'x is the same person as y'; 'x is a being'; 'x is a person'; 'x is divine'; 'x begets y'; 'x proceeds from y through z'.

Before turning to the doctrine of the Incarnation, I wish to add something to what I said about the term 'person' in "And Yet They Are Not Three Gods but One God." As I said in that essay, 'person' in the predicate 'is the same person as' means just what it means in ordinary speech. (But a little caution is needed here. One ordinary meaning of 'person' is, apparently, "human being." I have often talked at cross-purposes with philosophy students who have been puzzled by my speaking of intelligent nonhuman extraterrestrials as 'persons'. C. S. Lewis somewhere records the statement of an uneducated man who said that he did not believe in a "personal devil"; it transpired that he meant only that he regarded the devil as a spiritual being, and not as the horned and tailed biped of popular iconography. Let us say that if we are using 'person' in such a way that the devil and Wells's Martians are "persons," then we are using the word in its "inclusive" sense. My thesis is that 'person' in the Creeds ought to be understood as meaning no less and no more than it does in everyday speech, provided that we understand the everyday word in its inclusive sense.) This position of mine has met with the following criticism:

"[Van Inwagen's] doctrinal formulations seem almost naive: while he has heard that 'person' in Trinitarian theology does not mean what it means in everyday English (as indeed it does not), he is content to brush this aside with a remarkably ahistorical quotation from Geach."[5] I will leave it to Geach to defend himself against the charge of having written something remarkably ahistorical, if that charge in fact means anything and is not simply a hostile noise. As to what *I* have been charged with—"seeming near doctrinal naiveté," we might call it—my first reaction to reading these words was to wonder what their author would produce if he were asked to give an account of what 'person' does mean in everyday English. One is not in a position to write words like those of the above quotation unless one can give some sort of account of what 'person' means in everyday English. And this point applies to everyone, no matter how learned he or she may be about the history of the doctrinal employment of terms like 'hypostasis' and 'prosopon'. (The following objection to what I have just said misses the point: "Since I am a native speaker of English, I have a perfect understanding of the ordinary sense of 'person'." This objection misses the point because one can have all sorts of false *beliefs* about the meanings of words one understands perfectly: witness the famous case of 'by accident' and 'by mistake'.)

The doctrinal meaning of 'person' can be specified "functionally" as follows: persons are what there are three of in the Trinity.[6] The ordinary sense of 'person' is best explained by means of pronouns. Persons are those things to which personal pronouns are applicable: a person can use the word 'I' and be addressed as 'thou' (we can address a skylark or an urn or a flower or a city or an abstraction like "learning" or "fame" as 'thou'—"Thou still unravished bride of quietness"— but this is the rule-proving exception, for we call it personification). A person, if he is male or female or if we are willing to regard him as male or female for certain purposes, is called 'he' or 'she', as opposed to 'it'.[7] (Many languages, of course, do not face the unfortunate gender

5. James Wm. McClendon, Jr., review of *Philosophy and the Christian Faith*, ed. Thomas V. Morris, in *Faith and Philosophy* 9 (1992), 109–116. The quoted passage occurs on p. 113.

6. Or, to employ a syntactical device that is used with great subtlety and flexibility by six-year-olds, persons are what the Father, the Son, and the Holy Spirit are three ones of.

7. I say 'as opposed to' and not 'and not'. The pronoun 'it' can be used in generalizations which are supposed to include persons but which apply to other things as well. We may say of Alice that whenever she admires something, she wants to write a poem about it. This implies that if Alice admires Jack, then she wants to write a poem about him. Ordinary usage is very complicated in the matter of 'he' and 'she'. We use these pronouns when we talk about our pets, and we may use them when talking about very primitive animals in contexts in which their sexes are particularly relevant. But note: we

difficulty raised by the third-person singular pronouns of English.) And it is not only personal pronouns and the closely related possessive and reflexive pronouns that mark a distinction between persons and non-persons. Consider the indefinite pronoun 'one', which is used in generalizations applying only to persons. Consider the contrasting pairs, 'which' ('that')/'who', 'something'/'someone', and 'everything'/'everyone'. We could easily introduce a count-noun 'someone' by means of the definition 'x is a someone' $=_{df}$ 'x is someone'. And this count-noun, I maintain, would mean exactly what the count-noun 'person' (understood in its "inclusive" sense) means, for there is a person—"a someone"—having the feature F if and only if someone has the feature F. (If the devil tempted Sally, then someone tempted Sally. If a Martian can prove Goldbach's Conjecture, then someone can prove Goldbach's Conjecture.) It is evident that the Persons of the Trinity *are* in this sense "persons," *are* "someones": if the Father loves us, then someone loves us, and if the Son was incarnate by the Holy Ghost of the Virgin Mary, then someone was incarnate by the Holy Ghost of the Virgin Mary. But this does not prove that 'person' in Trinitarian theology means "person" in the ordinary (inclusive) sense. After all, all three Persons are *invisibilia,* but this does not entail that 'person' in Trinitarian theology means '*invisibile*'. The real question is whether "persons" in the ordinary sense are "what there are three of" in the Trinity.

In order to investigate this question from the perspective provided by an appeal to relative identity, we must remind ourselves that in our relative-identity language, count-nouns appear only in relative-identity predicates. (We should also remind ourselves that from a relative-identity perspective, there is no such thing as absolute counting, a fact that has the consequence that, from a relative-identity perspective, the phrase 'what there are three of' has to be approached very carefully.) What we need to do is to explain what the relative-identity predicate 'x is the same person as y' means, using the pronominal resources of ordinary English. (A solution to this problem that exploited the pronominal resources of Latin or Greek would differ only in irrelevant detail.) The clearest, most idiomatic pronominal phrase of English that can be used to express propositions concerning the identities of persons is, to my mind, the negative phrase 'someone else'. Accordingly, I offer the definition:

---

can say, "It's hurt" or "Don't go near it" when speaking of a dog of unknown sex; we cannot use these words of a human being of unknown sex.

> x is the same person as y = $_{df}$ x is someone and y is someone but not someone else.

(Another possibility would be, ' . . . but not someone other than x'.) Having this predicate at our disposal, we are able to count by persons— by "someones." To say, for example, that exactly two persons sinned in Eden is to say:

> Someone x sinned in Eden and someone y sinned in Eden and y was someone other than x and anyone who sinned in Eden was either not someone other than x or not someone other than y.

And is it not true that when we count Persons of the Trinity we are counting "someones"? The Father is someone. The Son is also someone. And, surely, He, the Son, is someone *else*? If He were not someone else, could he not say truly, using the *personal* pronoun 'I', "I am the Father"? In general, if someone can say truly, "I am F," then anyone who is *not someone else* can say truly "I am F." And if there is one undeniable datum in Trinitarian theology it is this: the Son (though he can say, "I and the Father are one") cannot say "I am the Father." And, of course, the Father cannot say, "I am the Spirit," nor the Spirit, "I am the Son." Each of the Father, the Son, and the Spirit is "thou," not "I," to the other two. That is to say, each of the Father, the Son, and the Spirit bears the following relation to the other two: *being someone else*. (And it is in fact this very relation that we are counting by when we use the phrase 'the other two'.)

I do not wish to maintain that a technical term of Trinitarian theology like 'hypostasis' is an exact equivalent of 'person' (understood in its inclusive sense). 'Hypostasis', as it is used by many theological writers, no doubt carries a lot of metaphysical baggage that is not carried by the ordinary 'person'. And it may well be that many other writers use it as simply a convenient general term to cover the Father, the Son, and the Spirit and do not trouble themselves too much about its content. What I do maintain is that any theologian of whatever period who says, for example, that the Father and the Son are distinct hypostases says something that entails that the Father and the Son are distinct persons (in the ordinary, inclusive sense) or is at any rate consistent with their being distinct persons in that sense or is simply heretical. (As to the second possibility: it *may* be that the theologian is simply using 'hypostasis' as a place-holder, its use sanctified by tradition, with very little content, no more than this: (a) by definition, the Father, the Son, and the Spirit are distinct "hypostases"; (b) whatever its meaning, 'distinct hypostases' does not entail 'not consubstantial'.) And here is a pair of far more important theses: any theological treatise on the Trinity whose propositions do not entail that the Persons are three distinct persons in the ordinary sense is gravely incomplete; any treatise whose propositions entail that they are *not* three distinct persons is simply heretical. And I am willing to argue that anyone who denies these two theses is philosophically confused, probably about the everyday meaning of the word 'person'. I suspect that anyone who denies these two theses thinks that 'person' in ordinary English means something more or other than it does.[8] (Of course, my being willing to argue for

8. Theologians do not seem to me to speak with one voice on these matters. Here are two quotations, the first from Van A. Harvey's *A Handbook of Theological Terms* (New York: Macmillan, 1964) and the second from Edmund Hill's *The Mystery of the Trinity* (London: Geoffrey Chapman, 1985).

"It is important to note that no important Christian theologian has argued that there are three self-conscious beings in the godhead. On the contrary, Augustine's favorite analogy for the triune God was one self-consciousness with its three distinctions of intellect, will, and the bond between them." (p. 246, article "Trinity")

"Now in God [according to Thomas] what are distinctly subsistent are the mutually opposed and corresponding relationships. So the words 'person' and 'hypostasis' can properly be used in talking of God to refer to these relationships, even though in themselves they do not signify any kind of relationship. Thomas adds that since 'person' means that which is most perfect in the whole of nature, namely what subsists in rational (or intelligent) nature, it is particularly apt for use in talking about God. . . . But Aquinas adds a most important proviso . . . 'But the word cannot be used in the same way of God as of creatures, but in a superlative way. . . '.

"What this superlative . . . way actually means is that . . . to call the Father, the Son, and the Holy Spirit three persons [adds] nothing to what we already know from calling them the Father, the Son, and the Holy Spirit, apart from being our way of saying that they are really distinct from each other. . . . And this is really the point that Augustine is making when he concludes that these words are no more than just labels . . . so that we might just as well, in answer to the question 'Three what?', reply 'Three *X*s', or more elegantly 'Three someones'." (p. 101 f.)

I take the second quotation more or less to support my position, with the following important qualification: Hill seems not to be aware that, or, to choose my words more judiciously, does not accept my thesis that, the meaning of the ordinary word 'person' is just 'a someone'. My difference with Thomas, as Hill represents him, would be just this: I think that the word 'person' *can* be predicated univocally of God and creatures. (Note that the "superlative sense" point would apply if we spoke of God without using Trinitarian language at all; if Thomas is right, then when, say, Alvin Plantinga defines atheism as the thesis that there is no such person as God, the word 'person' in this thesis cannot have the same sense as the sense it has in the thesis that there was no such person as King Arthur—or in the thesis that there is no such person as Satan. This I would deny, for reasons having nothing to do with Trinitarian theology.)

As to the first quotation, I probably do subscribe to various theses that, in the view of its author, no important Christian theologian has held. It is true that I would deny that there are three self-conscious beings in the Godhead, since I would deny that there are three beings of any description in the Godhead. But I would say that the Father is

this implies a willingness to listen to arguments for the conclusion that I ought to change my mind.)

II

I now turn to the theology of the Incarnation. Our first problem is the problem of how to use the sparse referential capacities of our language (supplemented by whatever ordinary predicates may be useful) to refer to particular human beings. How, for example, restricted as we are, shall we talk about Abraham Lincoln? The question is in a way ill-formed, for, if we are really restricted to our "referentially sparse" language, we cannot ask it. But we can observe that there are various sets of ordinary predicates (like 'ended slavery' and 'saved the Union' and 'once practiced law') such that, or so we believe, there is one and only one human being who satisfies all of them. Let 'L' be the conjunction of the members of some suitably comprehensive one among these sets. (Perhaps 'L' is the predicate that, according to the description theory of names, expresses the meaning of 'Abraham Lincoln' in the usage of some reasonably knowledgeable person—if there is such a predicate.) If we take 'being' in the phrase "human being" seriously, it would seem plausible that a sentence of the form 'Lincoln is F' would best be represented in our referentially sparse language by the corresponding sentence of the form

$$\exists x(Lx \ \& \ \forall y(Ly \rightarrow \underline{B}xy) \ \& \ x \text{ is } F).$$

(In this formula, the underlined 'B' abbreviates 'is the same being as'.) Now it is no doubt true that all of us would accept the thesis that if x and y are human beings, then x and y are the same being if and only if x and y are the same person. Accordingly, we would accept a sentence

---

self-conscious (He knows of Himself that He is the Father, and that would seem to be sufficient for self-consciousness) and the Son is self-conscious and the Son is not the Father but rather someone else. And I *think* that Harvey would deny that any important Christian theologian has held this. Whether or not he is right about this, the appeal to Augustine's psychological analogy is not to the point. The relations between intellect and will pertain, in Augustine's analogy, to the nature of the relations in which (as which?) the Father and the Son subsist. The Father and the Son are, for Augustine, *subsistent* relationships, and the mutual relations of intellect and will in human beings, by which we can reach a dim analogical understanding of them, are *not* subsistent relationships. Because the latter are not subsistent, any question about their consciousness makes no more sense than a question about the consciousness of a number or a quality. If there could be subsistent relationships, however, there would be no logical or metaphysical barrier to their being self-conscious. In my view, what Augustine says about the three subsistent relationships in the Godhead commits him to the thesis that each of them is a someone.

of the above form if and only if we were willing to accept the corresponding sentence of the form

$$\exists x(Lx \ \& \ \forall y(Ly \rightarrow \underline{P}xy) \ \& \ x \text{ is } F).$$

(In this sentence, of course, the underlined '*P*' abbreviates 'is the same person as'.) And we should no doubt therefore regard the sentence of the second form as an equally good representation of the corresponding sentence of the form 'Lincoln is *F*'. It is, however, sentences of the first form that I shall be primarily interested in. The reason for this will transpire if it is not already evident.

In order to represent the propositions of Incarnational theology using the apparatus of relative identity, we require only two predicates (both of them ordinary) in addition to the five that figured in our representation of the propositions of Trinitarian theology. The first is '**J**', which we shall use for a predicate that stands to the historical figure Jesus of Nazareth as '*L*' stands to the historical figure Abraham Lincoln. (The exact list of predicates of which '**J**' is a conjunction is of no great interest—but the list is restricted to predicates that neither imply divinity nor involve any of the concepts of Incarnational theology. The list might include 'was born of a virgin', 'was crucified', and 'was raised from the dead'. But it may not include 'is God', 'is the Son of God', or 'is possessed of a human nature that enters into a hypostatic union with the Godhead'. I leave the question of the list of predicates that define '**J**' unresolved because the facts of Jesus' biography are controversial and because even a controversial list would be very long. I assume, however, that everyone who believes that there was a historical Jesus at all will be able to devise a list of predicates he believes applies to Jesus and to no other historical figure.) Having introduced '**J**', we allow it immediately to disappear into an abbreviation:

$$Jx =_{df} \mathbf{J}x \ \& \ \forall y(\mathbf{J}y \rightarrow \underline{B}xy).$$

'*Jx*' may be read '*x* is Jesus (of Nazareth)'. Any sentence of ordinary English of the form 'Jesus is *F*' may be represented in our vocabulary as the corresponding sentence of the form '$\exists x \ (Jx \ \& \ x \text{ is } F)$'.

The only other predicate that we shall need to add to our list of predicates is 'is human'; we shall abbreviate '*x* is human' as '*Mx*'. We abbreviate '*x* is divine' as '*Dx*'. And (as in the preceding essay) we introduce the abbreviations (read, respectively, 'is God', 'is the Father', 'is the Son', and 'is the Holy Spirit'):

$$Gx =_{df} Dx \ \& \ \forall y(Dy \rightarrow \underline{B}xy)$$

$Fx =_{df} x$ begets & $\forall y(y$ begets $\to \underline{P}xy)$

$Sx =_{df} x$ is begotten & $\forall y(y$ is begotten $\to \underline{P}xy)$

$Hx =_{df} x$ proceeds & $\forall y(y$ proceeds $\to \underline{P}xy)$.

The preceding essay listed a set a theological assertions and "conceptual truths" that were held to comprise that part of Trinitarian theology that concerns counting, identity, and predication. The theological assertions were the formal equivalents of 'There is exactly one God' and 'There are exactly three divine Persons'. The "conceptual truths" included some more or less trivial assertions ('Anything that is divine is both a being and a person'; 'All persons are beings') and some more substantive ones. The latter comprehend the assertion that sameness of being dominates divinity (formally: $\underline{B}xy \to .Dx \leftrightarrow Dy$) and various assertions whose collective import is that the relations of begetting and procession hold only among divinities and that these relations uniquely specify the three divine Persons and that nothing besides the three divine Persons enters into these relations. We must now expand this set of statements. We begin with four conceptual truths (the numbers are continuations of the numbering in the preceding essay).[9]

CT14 $Mx \to \sim Dx$

CT15 $Jx \to Mx$

CT16 $Mx \to .\underline{P}x$ & $\underline{B}x$

CT17 $\underline{B}xy \to .Mx \leftrightarrow My$.

Thus, humanity is like divinity in that it entails both personhood and being and in that it is dominated by "ontic identity" or sameness of being. In the preceding essay, I explicitly and pointedly refrained from assuming that personal identity dominated divinity. I now explicitly and pointedly refrain from making the corresponding assumption as regards personal identity and humanity. In the preceding essay, I explicitly and pointedly refrained from assuming that ontic identity domi-

9. No doubt there are other conceptual truths involving the concepts that are represented formally in our language. One candidate for such a truth would be a proposition that has already been mentioned: that sameness of person and sameness of being coincide on human beings. For all we can show, therefore, it may turn out that even though (as we shall see) the truths of Incarnational theology, as they are specified here, are formally consistent, there are plausible candidates for conceptual truths that, if added to our set of truths, would yield a formal inconsistency. But the same might be said of any formal system that is intended to capture the relations that hold among the members of some set of concepts.

nated personal identity. I now explicitly and pointedly refrain from assuming that personal identity dominates ontic identity.

We require two theological assertions. The first is (as I shall call it) the Dogma of the Incarnation:

$$\exists x \; \exists y \; (Sx \; \& \; Jy \; \& \; \underline{P}xy).^{10}$$

That is to say, God the Son and Jesus of Nazareth are one and the same person. And this in the ordinary sense of the words 'same person': the Son is someone and Jesus is someone, but not someone else; the Son can say 'I am Jesus whom thou persecutest' and Jesus can say 'I am *(ego eimi)* God the Son'. (Perhaps, as many have contended, Jesus did not, during His earthly ministry, possess the concept that theologians were later to express by the words 'God the Son'; if not, I expect He does now.) More exactly, these two sentences are ambiguous. The word 'am' that occurs in each *could* be taken to express an ontic identity between the human being from whose lips the word issues and God the Son; if it is taken in that sense, then what is expressed by the two sentences does not follow from the Dogma of the Incarnation (and is, of course, heretical). But if the copula expresses personal identity (much the more natural interpretation, to my mind, owing to the fact that its subject is a personal pronoun), then what is expressed by these sentences—leaving aside the part about persecution—does follow from the Dogma of the Incarnation.

The second theological assertion that we shall require is the thesis that no more than one divine person is incarnate:

$$Dx \; \& \; Dy \; \& \; \exists z \; (Mz \; \& \; \underline{P}xz) \; \& \; \exists z \; (Mz \; \& \; \underline{P}yz). \rightarrow \underline{P}xy.$$

We shall now consider a fairly comprehensive set of English sentences that pertain to the theology of the Incarnation, sentences that can plausibly be said to be parts of or logical consequences of the doctrine of the Incarnation. We shall show how to translate these sentences into our formal vocabulary, we shall show that they are formal consequences of our conceptual truths and our two theological assertions (taken together with the conceptual truths and the theological assertions that were endorsed in "And Yet They Are Not Three Gods but One God"), and we shall show that no contradiction is a formal consequence of this set of sentences.

The most difficult problems of translation arise in connection with sentences containing the name 'Jesus Christ'. Let us begin by consider-

---

10. In unabbreviated form: $\exists x \; \exists y \; [\exists z \; z$ begets $x. \; \& \; \forall y(\exists z \; z$ begets $y. \rightarrow \underline{P}xy) \; \& \; Jy \; \& \; \forall x(Jx \rightarrow \underline{B}xy) \; \& \; \underline{P}xy]$.

ing sentences that do not involve that name. I follow each sentence with a proposed translation.

—God was incarnate in Jesus of Narareth[11]

$\exists x \exists y \ (Gx \ \& \ Jy \ \& \ \underline{P}xy)$.

Or, in unabbreviated form:

$\exists x \exists y \ (Dx \ \& \ \forall y(Dy \rightarrow \underline{B}xy) \ \& \ Jy \ \& \ \forall z(Jz \rightarrow \underline{B}yz) \ \& \ \underline{P}xy)$.

—God the Son was incarnate in Jesus of Nazareth

$\exists x \exists y(Sx \ \& \ Jy \ \& \ \underline{P}xy)$.

Or, in (almost) unabbreviated form:

$\exists x \exists y \ (x \text{ is begotten } \& \ \forall y(y \text{ is begotten} \rightarrow \underline{P}xy) \ \& \ Jy \ \& \ \forall z(Jz \rightarrow \underline{B}yz) \ \& \ \underline{P}xy)$.

(From now on, I will give only the abbreviated forms of sentences.) The next sentence,

—God the Father is not incarnate,

is ambiguous. It could be read either as a predication of 'is not incarnate' of God the Father or as a denial of the thesis that God the Father is incarnate: as

$\exists x \ (Fx \ \& \ {\sim}\exists y \ (My \ \& \ \underline{P}xy))$

or as

${\sim}\exists x \ (Fx \ \& \ \exists y \ (My \ \& \ \underline{P}xy))$.

Some sentences containing the word 'God' are ambiguous in ways that have led to theological controversy. I give two examples. First,

—God died on the Cross.

This might be represented in either of the following ways:

$\exists x \ (Gx \ \& \ x \text{ died on the Cross})$;

$\exists x \exists y \ (Gx \ \& \ y \text{ died on the Cross} \ \& \ \underline{P}xy)$.

The second of these sentences follows from the sentences we have endorsed (given that Jesus of Nazareth died on the Cross) and, I believe, represents something like the position that those who have looked fa-

---

11. Our formal apparatus does not extend to the representation of tenses.

vorably on language like 'God died on the Cross' were defending. The first does not follow from the sentences we have endorsed. In fact, its denial follows, given the additional premise that anything that dies on a cross is a human being. I would suppose that it represents something like the position that those who opposed language like 'God died on the Cross' were trying to guard against. ('God the Son died on the Cross' can be seen to be ambiguous in almost the same way. But all reasonable representations of the sentences 'God the Father died on the Cross' and 'The Holy Spirit died on the Cross' in our formal language can easily be seen to be "false.")[12]

Our second example of an ambiguous sentence is

—Mary was the God-bearer *(Theotokos)*.

Let us invent a predicate 'Vx' that stands to Mary as 'Lx & $\forall y(Ly \rightarrow \underline{B}xy)$' stands to Lincoln and 'Jx' stands to Jesus. And let us suppose that 'x bears y', whatever precisely it may mean, is satisfied by a pair of objects only if the first is biologically female and the second is a living organism (for dualists: has a body that is a living organism) that develops from a gamete supplied by the first. Our sentence may be represented in either of the two following ways:

$\exists x \exists y$ (Vx & Gy & x bore y)

$\exists x \exists y$ (Vx & Gy & $\exists z$ (x bore z & $\underline{P}zy$)).

Remarks similar to the above remarks about the two representations of 'God died on the Cross' apply to these two sentences.

Let us now turn to sentences containing the name 'Jesus Christ'. How are we to understand this name? Logic and etymology would suggest that 'Jesus Christ' means 'Jesus the Messiah'. If that were so, we should represent sentences of the form 'Jesus Christ is F' in our formal language by the corresponding sentences of the form '$\exists x$ (Jx & x is F & x is the Messiah)'. But in theology, as in all other areas of human discourse, established usage laughs at logic and etymology. It may well be that there is no one meaning that "covers" all theologically legitimate uses of 'Jesus Christ', but it seems to me that the term has a "central" meaning in Christian theology, and that whatever else may be true of this central meaning, it somehow involves the idea of the Incarnation, the union of the divine and human natures in a single

---

12. I will call sentences that follow from the sentences we have endorsed "true" (in scare quotes) and sentences whose denial follows from the sentences we have endorsed "false" (in scare quotes).

Person. (I take it that this is not part of the meaning of 'Messiah:' if it had pleased God so to arrange matters, the Messiah might be or have been a human being in whom He was not incarnate.) It would seem that 'Jesus Christ' does not mean the same as either 'God the Son' or 'Jesus of Nazareth' but something more like 'the person who is both God the Son and Jesus of Nazareth'. I would suggest that we represent sentences of the form 'Jesus Christ is *F*' by the corresponding sentences of the form

$$\exists x \ (\exists y \ (Sy \ \& \ \underline{P}xy) \ \& \ \exists y \ (Jy \ \& \ \underline{P}xy) \ \& \ x \ \text{is} \ F).$$

If this is what we mean by 'Jesus Christ', then the formal representation of the sentence

—Jesus Christ is God and man

is "true." Or, at any rate, it is true if we regard it as the conjunction of the two sentences 'Jesus Christ is God' and 'Jesus Christ is man', and not as predicating of Jesus Christ the impossible property *being-both-God-and-man* (that is, the property expressed by the open sentence '*x* is God and *x* is man'). In other words, we must distinguish between

$$\exists x \ (\exists y \ (Sy \ \& \ \underline{P}xy) \ \& \ \exists y \ (Jy \ \& \ \underline{P}xy) \ \& \ Dx) \ \&$$
$$\exists x \ (\exists y \ (Sy \ \& \ \underline{P}xy) \ \& \ \exists y \ (Jy \ \& \ \underline{P}xy) \ \& \ Mx)$$

and

$$\exists x \ (\exists y \ (Sy \ \& \ \underline{P}xy) \ \& \ \exists y \ (Jy \ \& \ \underline{P}xy) \ \& \ Dx \ \& \ Mx).$$

The former sentence follows from the "endorsed" sentences, and is, I believe, orthodox. The second does not follow from the endorsed sentences; in fact, its denial follows.

One traditional device that is used in discussions of the truth-values of sentences of the form 'Jesus Christ is *F*' is a threefold distinction marked by the use of sentences of the following forms:

Jesus Christ is *simpliciter F* (is *F* without qualification)

Jesus Christ is *secundum divinitatem F* (is *F* "as touching his divinity")

Jesus Christ is *secundum humanitatem F* (is *F* "as touching his humanity").

I shall adopt this distinction. What I have so far discussed is the representation of *"simpliciter"* sentences. The other two types of sentences are represented as follows:

$\exists x\ (\exists y\ (Sy\ \&\ \underline{P}xy)\ \&\ \exists y\ (Jy\ \&\ \underline{P}xy)\ \&\ Dx\ \&\ x\ is\ F)$

$\exists x\ (\exists y\ (Sy\ \&\ \underline{P}xy)\ \&\ \exists y\ (Jy\ \&\ \underline{P}xy)\ \&\ Mx\ \&\ x\ is\ F).$

On this reading, the following theses are true:

Jesus Christ is *simpliciter* human

Jesus Christ is *simpliciter* nonhuman

Jesus Christ is *simpliciter* divine

Jesus Christ is *simpliciter* nondivine

Jesus Christ is *simpliciter* such that there never was a time when He was not

Jesus Christ is *simpliciter* such that in 10 B.C. He did not yet exist.

It is important to realize that there is neither contradiction nor (in my view) unorthodoxy in these theses. Consider, for example, 'Jesus Christ is *simpliciter* nonhuman'. This thesis is not equivalent to (nor does it entail) the thesis

It is not the case that Jesus Christ is *simpliciter* human.

If this equivalence did hold, then some theses in the above list (the second if no other) would be unorthodox and the whole list would be self-contradictory. But the formal representation of 'Jesus Christ is *simpliciter* nonhuman' is

$\exists x\ (\exists y\ (Sy\ \&\ \underline{P}xy)\ \&\ \exists y\ (Jy\ \&\ \underline{P}xy)\ \&\ {\sim}Mx),$

While the formal representation of 'It is not the case that Jesus Christ is *simpliciter* human' is

${\sim}\exists x\ (\exists y\ (Sy\ \&\ \underline{P}xy)\ \&\ \exists y\ (Jy\ \&\ \underline{P}xy)\ \&\ Mx).$

And these two sentences are not equivalent. The first follows from the set of sentences we have endorsed. The second does not follow from those sentences. Is there anything unorthodox about the sentence 'Jesus Christ is *simpliciter* nonhuman'? I should say that there was not. The sentence—or what is meant by it on my reading of it—does not deny the full humanity of Jesus Christ, for it is consistent with 'Jesus Christ is *simpliciter* human'. The truth of what is expressed by 'Jesus Christ is *simpliciter* nonhuman' is simply a consequence of the fact that God the Son, Begotten Divinity, although He is the same person as a certain member of our species, is not (being, as He is, eternal, omnipresent, and so on) "in the strict and philosophical sense" a member of our species. The truth of what is expressed by 'Jesus Christ is *simpliciter* human' is simply a consequence of the fact that Jesus of Nazareth, not begotten of the Father but rather conceived by the Holy Ghost, although He is the same person as a certain Person of the Trinity, is not (being, as He is, temporal, locally present, and so on) "in the strict and philosophical sense" a Person of the Trinity. In the words of the *Quicunque Vult,* Jesus Christ is "One altogether; not by confusion of Substance, but by unity of Person" *(unus omnino non confusione substantiae, sed unitate personae).* As there are in the Holy Trinity three distinct persons who are one by unity of being, so there are in Jesus Christ two distinct beings who are one by unity of person.

It is often confusing to predicate properties of Jesus Christ in the "ontologically promiscuous" manner provided by the form of words 'Jesus Christ is *simpliciter F*'. It is often a more perspicuous procedure to employ an idiom that segregates the properties of Jesus Christ according as they belong to Him in virtue of His divine or His human natures. This is, of course, the function of the other two idioms of predication, predication *"secundum divinitatem"* and predication *"secundum humanitatem."* We may thus say that Jesus Christ is begotten of the Father before all worlds *secundum divinitatem* but is not begotten of the Father before all worlds *secundum humanitatem,* and that Jesus Christ was conceived by the Holy Ghost and born of the Virgin Mary *secundum humanitatem* but was not conceived by the Holy Ghost and born of the Virgin Mary *secundum divinitatem,* and that Jesus Christ is equal to the Father as touching His Godhead and inferior to the Father as touching His manhood. (And so on; there would seem to be no particular difficulty about deciding whether a property that belongs to Jesus Christ according to one or the other nature belongs to Him *secundum divinitatem* or *secundum humanitatem.* There are, of course, many properties that He possesses both *secundum divinitatem* and *secundum humanitatem:* consciousness, free will, and moral perfection, for example. Or at least this is true if these terms can be predicated of God and humanity in the same sense.)

It would seem that a sentence of the form 'I am *F*' spoken by Jesus of Nazareth should express a truth just in the case that the corresponding sentence of the form 'Jesus Christ is *simpliciter F*' is true. Thus, Jesus could say truly both, "I am meek and lowly of heart" (presumably, being meek and lowly of heart belongs to Jesus Christ *secundum humanitatem* and not *secundum divinitatem*) and, "Before Abraham was, I am." This is because 'I' is a personal pronoun and "attaches semantically" to all of the properties of the *person* who utters it; more exactly, if it is uttered by one of two beings who are the same person, that utterance comprehends the properties of both of those beings.[13]

It is time now to show that the whole set of sentences we have endorsed is consistent—that no contradiction can be deduced from its members by RI-logic. It will not be surprising if this is so, for the deductive resources of RI-logic are rather weak, owing to the fact that the inference-rules of RI-logic do not include anything corresponding to Leibniz's Law. (And owing to the further fact that we have not assumed that identity of person dominates either humanity or divinity or identity of being.) Our method is simple. We shall tell a story, a story that is obviously internally consistent, and we shall give each of our formal predicates an interpretation in that story—being careful to interpret both of our RI-predicates as expressing symmetrical and transitive relations. We shall see that all of our endorsed sentences are true on this interpretation. It will follow, by a well-known property of quantifier logic, that if a contradiction follows from our story by quantifier logic, then our story is internally inconsistent—which it is obviously not. Since, moreover, our two RI-predicates are interpreted as expressing symmetrical and transitive relations, our story will be internally inconsistent if a contradiction can be deduced from the endorsed sentences by the rules of quantifier logic plus Symmetry and Transitivity. It follows that no contradiction can be deduced from the endorsed sentences by RI-logic.

The story is an elaboration of the story used for the same purpose in the preceding essay:

Our universe of discourse comprises four animals. There are three dogs of the same breed, *A, B,* and *C* and one cat, a jet-black Manx. None of the dogs is jet-black. Each of the dogs is for sale at a different price,

---

13. There may have been some attempt, either by Jesus or by the Evangelists, to divide His self-ascriptions into those true of Him *simpliciter,* those true of him *secundum divinitatem,* and those true of him *secundum humanitatem.* I have in mind his (or their) use of, respectively, the first-person singular pronoun, 'the Son', and 'the Son of Man'. I do not mean to suggest by this speculation that anyone in the first century was in possession of a fifth-century Christology. I mean, rather, that his, or their, use of these terms may have been a response to the same divine/human reality that was later conceptualized in developed Christologies. (It should not be necessary to make this disclaimer, but one is liable to be accused of just such an anachronism if one says anything that implies that a developed Christology can be of some use in understanding the Gospels.) This speculation faces severe textual difficulties (consider, e.g., Mark 13:32 = Matt. 24:36), but I nevertheless think that it is worthy of careful consideration.

and the cat is for sale at the same price as dog *B*. *A* barks at *B* and at nothing else, and nothing else barks. *C* prances from *A* to *B* and does no other prancing, and nothing else prances.

Here are our interpretations:

$\underline{B}\,xy$	:	x is the same breed as y
$\underline{P}\,xy$	:	x is the same price as y
Dx	:	x is a dog
Mx	:	x is a Manx
$\mathbf{J}x$	:	x is jet-black
x begets y	:	x barks at y
x proceeds from y through z	:	x prances from y to z.

These interpretations of our undefined predicates settle the interpretation of our defined predicates:

$\underline{B}x$	:	x is of some breed
$\underline{P}x$	:	x is for sale at some price
Gx	:	x is a dog of the only breed
Fx	:	x barks and anything that barks is the same price as x
Sx	:	x is barked at, and anything that is barked at is the same price as x
Hx	:	x prances from something to something, and anything that prances is the same price as x
Jx	:	x is jet-black, and anything that is jet-black is the same breed as x.

It is an easy, if a somewhat tedious, exercise to verify that all of our endorsed sentences are true in the story of the four animals, provided that the predicates they contain are interpreted according to this schema.[14] It follows from this fact, and from the fact that "is the same breed as" and "is the same price as" are symmetrical and transitive, that the story of the four animals is internally inconsistent if a contradiction can be derived from the endorsed sentences in RI-logic. But that story is obviously internally consistent. Therefore, no contradiction can be derived from the endorsed sentences in RI-logic.

As I said I should at the beginning of this essay, I have shown how a part of the doctrine of the Incarnation (or of the Hypostatic Union) can be represented in a way that is free from formal contradiction. But, as I said, I have done nothing to make the mystery of the Incarnation any less a mystery. As "And Yet They Are Not Three Gods but One God" left the mystery of the Trinity untouched, so the present essay leaves the mystery of the Incarnation untouched. Indeed, I have done little more than provide a vocabulary in which the mysterious aspect of the doctrine can be stated precisely. But perhaps this vocabulary has the advantage of suggesting a precise description of the relationship between the mystery of the Incarnation and the mystery of the Trinity. The mystery of the Trinity is this: How can it be that ontic identity (which dominates humanity and divinity) fails to dominate personal identity? The mystery of the Incarnation is this: How can it be that personal identity fails to dominate ontic identity—and humanity and divinity as well? These questions raise more general and abstract questions that are no less mysterious: How can *any* relative-identity predicate fail to dominate *all* predicates? (That is to say, how can the whole topic of relative identity be of any interest?—for relative identity is interesting only if some relative-identity predicate is not dominant.) And given that ontic identity and personal identity fail to dominate certain predicates, what is the reason for the fact that they interact differently with humanity and divinity? To none of these questions have I an answer.[15]

---

14. As one would expect, the four dominance assumptions that we have "explicitly and pointedly" refrained from making:

$\underline{P}\,xy \to\,.\,Dx \leftrightarrow Dy$

$\underline{P}\,xy \to\,.\,Mx \leftrightarrow My$

$\underline{B}\,xy \to\,.\,\underline{P}\,xz \leftrightarrow \underline{P}\,yz$

$\underline{P}\,xy \to\,.\,\underline{B}\,xz \leftrightarrow \underline{B}\,yz$

are false on this interpretation.

15. My thinking about the questions addressed in this essay has been stimulated by correspondence with Timothy Bartel.

Index

The entry for a given topic does not in general give page references to essays wholly or largely devoted to that topic. For example, the entry "Ontological argument" gives no page references to Essay 1.